# TRANSMISSION OF AWAKENING

# TRANSMISSION OF AWAKENING

## THE TEACHING OF AZIZ

AZIZ KRISTOF

A New Initiation into the Path of
Self-Realisation

MOTILAL BANARSIDASS PUBLISHERS
PRIVATE LIMITED ● DELHI

*First Edition: Delhi, 1999*

© MOTILAL BANARSIDASS PUBLISHERS PRIVATE LIMITED
All Rights Reserved

ISBN: 81-208-1694-3

*Also available at:*

## MOTILAL BANARSIDASS

41 U.A. Bungalow Road, Jawahar Nagar, Delhi 110 007
8 Mahalaxmi Chamber, Warden Road, Mumbai 400 026
120 Royapettah High Road, Mylapore, Chennai 600 004
Sanas Plaza, 1302, Baji Rao Road, Pune 411 002
16 St. Mark's Road, Bangalore 560 001
8 Camac Street, Calcutta 700 017
Ashok Rajpath, Patna 800 004
Chowk, Varanasi 221 001

PRINTED IN INDIA
BY JAINENDRA PRAKASH JAIN AT SHRI JAINENDRA PRESS,
A-45 NARAINA, PHASE I, NEW DELHI 110 028
AND PUBLISHED BY NARENDRA PRAKASH JAIN FOR
MOTILAL BANARSIDASS PUBLISHERS PRIVATE LIMITED,
BUNGALOW ROAD, DELHI 110 007

Dedicated to My Beloved Soul-Brother:
Houman Emami

# Acknowledgements

*We would like to express deep gratitude to those who helped in the creation of this book.*

*Especially to Beloved Daniel Oz and Anna Gordon for preparing the material from recorded Transmissions; and to Beloved Jamie Graham and Dharanasri for all the corrections regarding the english language.*

# Contents

# Transmission
## from the Dimension of Understanding

I AM is the Light of Creation
the Heart of which
from the Very Beginning
Created ME,
Our Ancient Soul Identity

# Preface

This book that we present has been created out of the teachings given by Aziz during the time of 1998/99. It is not an ordinary spiritual book. This powerful and revolutionary teaching contains the energy of Guidance and Grace. This energy brings us not only to the clarity of Understanding but, most importantly, to inner transformation and Awakening. It is a Transmission from the Plane of Wholeness; a golden bridge through which we can cross over from the darkness of separation to the eternal light of I AM which is the Heart of the Beloved.

# Introduction

"Transmission of Awakening" can be seen as complementary to "Enlightenment Beyond Traditions," written by Aziz and Houman. This time, apart from revealing the deeper layers of Teaching, we also present the more practical examples of Satsang-Transmissions and the Absolute Meditation. In the last part of the book Aziz is answering questions, bringing clarity into the most subtle and complex areas of Spiritual Path. Here all doubts become embraced and dissolved within the holistic and intelligent vision of human Awakening.

Through Aziz's intelligence is being channelled a New multidimensional understanding of the process of Awakening. These teachings are coming from the Dimension of Understanding and Love. His intelligence has to a large degree become one with the Higher Intelligence. Because of his state of complete Self-realisation and the particular quality of his Soul, Aziz has been destined to become a channel for the Understanding relevant to this current stage of the human evolution.

The spiritual and philosophical conclusions created a few thousands years ago by the great Traditions of Enlightenment, no longer seem to match our sensitivity and intelligence. As we are reaching the millennium, the crisis is more and more visible. It is not enough to reform past traditions, for they carry a heavy weight of the already crystallised vision of reality. A New Perception of the spiritual awakening must arise. This new perception includes the full understanding of the complexity of the awakening process as well as the complete inner map of awakening. It includes the understanding of the role of intelligence and the multidimensional reality of Me. It includes the understanding of the emotional evolution in the context of the expansion beyond individuality and, above all, the full understanding of the utmost significance of Grace and the presence of the Other Dimension in our earthly evolution.

Aziz is the creator of the Absolute Meditation. The principles of this Meditation have been discovered in his deep connection with Houman. This meditation is a real gift to the humanity. It is a very simple but powerful tool of transformation. For the first time the inner dynamics of the I Am has been fully grasped. Beyond the simplistic concepts about the State of Meditation, we can see, at last, the richness and the complexity of the internal reality of the Self. Let us begin this journey into the understanding and the realisation of the I Am, the wholeness within.

# About Aziz

An enlightened Master, Aziz, has created a unique and revolutionary teaching beyond Traditions. He transmits the essence of Awakening through group meditations and retreats travelling extensively all over the world.

Aziz's journey to awakening has been as multidimensional and complex; as complex and multidimensional is the "Inner Map of Awakening" which he and Houman have created years later. His yearning for inner completion had to face the fundamental challenges and difficulties of human evolution within the unconscious and insensitive dimension of collective consciousness, where the weight of ignorance is much bigger than the presence of light.

Aziz was born in a small village in Poland. At the age of five in a situation of fear he had his first awakening. From the consciousness of a small child his sense of identity shifted to the dimension of Pure Awareness. During his youth, not having any guidance, he found different ways to tune himself into meditative states. Later he wrote a book about God which was an attempt to translate his still not clear experiences into religious language.

Afterwards Aziz began very intensive studies of different teachings and masters. His interests were mostly evolving around Buddhism and Advaita Vedanta. At that time he connected deeply to the presence and teaching of Nisargadatta Maharaj, a master from Bombay. From him he understood the necessity of stabilisation in the State of Presence which Aziz was already awakened to. In order to deepen his practice, Aziz started a formal Zen practice doing long retreats and studying its philosophy.

One day Aziz took the train going through Russia and China to Korea, where he hoped to complete his training. After doing a long retreat in Korea, he moved to Japan to study Soto and

Rinzai schools of Zen. Staying in the Rinzai monastery, he made the main focus of his practice stabilisation in the State of Presence. This was completed after the very intense and mystical period in Dec. 93. Because his independent and rebellious spirit could not identify itself with Zen teachings, Aziz left Japan and moved to Thailand and finally India.

Going to India was very important for Aziz because of the respect he had for the Advaita-Vedanta tradition. However, the reality was rather disappointing and meeting many well-known Advaita masters brought only frustration. It was at that time that he discovered the co-existence and mutual dependence of the Inner State and the movement of intelligence. He discovered the importance of the Ego and was able to free himself from spiritual conditioning, thus simplifying the understanding of Enlightenment. He thought: "if I am in a state beyond the mind, in the realm of pure Consciousness how is it possible that I still have desires and fears?"

After the stabilisation in the State of Presence, Aziz was convinced of being in the Ultimate State. Even though he knew the teaching of Maharaj about the state beyond Consciousness, he could not accept that there could be something beyond his present experience. In a sense he was conditioned by certain Advaita concepts as well as by J. Krishnamurti, which propagate the view that total insight into the Now should reveal the complete experience of the Self.

Aziz's destiny radically changed when he met his Soul-brother Houman. Because of their passion for the Truth, they immediately became intimate friends. Aziz shared his knowledge and experience of Awareness, whereas, Houman was initiating him into the reality of the Heart as well as into esoteric dimensions. At one stage in their presence they experienced the miraculous manifestation of Grace. The voice from the Other Dimension began to speak to them. Their conscious connection with the Over-soul, the spirit of Guidance, started from this time.

It was the voice from the Beyond that revealed to Aziz that the state he was in, and the one Maharaj was speaking about, were not the same. It was difficult for Aziz to admit that he was not in the Highest State, but he surrendered. It is only when we have the courage to surrender our crystallised belief, when the power of evolution demands that from us, we are truly in alignment with the light of our Soul and her blueprint.

Aziz was given a special practice in order to shift to the Absolute State. He went on a two-month retreat to the South of India, where by his own effort and the power of Grace, the final shift took place. It was beyond anything Aziz could imagine — the Complete Motionless Rest in the Beyond!

Later, Aziz met Houman in America and was further guided to open his heart. The concept of the Soul and the work with the Heart was to a large degree against his conditionings. Particularly having been brought up in a Christian country, where the whole perception of the Soul is rather shallow and naive, on the other hand, being strongly connected to the spirit of Buddhism, which denies the existence of any permanent identity whatsoever, he had developed an aversion to the concept of the Soul. But again, he surrendered to the Guidance. This work culminated in the full Enlightenment to the Heart, which was followed by the Enlightenment to Me, which is the essence of the teaching created by Aziz and Houman.

For Aziz, the spiritual path was not only the path of Self-realisation in terms of reaching the transcendental state, but a path of Understanding as well. His particular intelligence couldn't rest until it reached the complete clarity. This book is a living presentation of this Clarity.

# I

# THE NATURE
# OF
# ENLIGHTENMENT

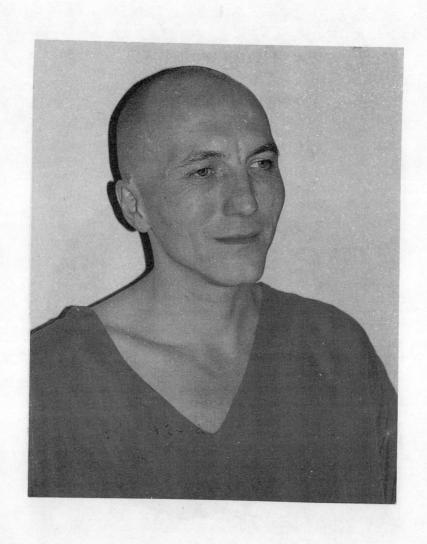

# The Process of Awakening

Awakening is the true goal of the spiritual journey. When reality is experienced only in its phenomenal, shadow-like aspect, one is simply in a dream state, disconnected from the Light of Creation. Therefore, awakening is an urgent necessity. Whose awakening is it? It is an awakening of Me. Me, the foremost expression of the Universal I AM, is itself the goal and the heart of awakening. Me, the mysterious subject behind the multitude of experiences, which we call life, is the essence of Creation. The complex evolution of different forms of life culminates in the sublime awakening of Me to Me.

Life is a movement of Universal Intelligence, which expresses itself in the dimension of time and evolution. Because in our particular dimension, this Intelligence manifests itself initially below conscious level, we call its existence Universal Subconsciousness. Subconsciousness is the presence of an already manifested information-energy existing below the conscious level, that is, not being recognised by any particular Me. It has an inherent wisdom and purpose, which itself is the original instinct of evolution.

Subconsciousness arises from the plane of Universal Unconsciousness, which is the bridge between the Divine Dimension, or the I AM and the subconscious reality. Unconsciousness itself is nothing but the original blueprint, which is the unmanifested wisdom that gives rise to the Creation. We don't wish to speak too much about these details because our purpose is very practical. We intend to explain simply the mechanism of awakening so we can understand it in the context of the evolution of life.

Initially the Creation is non-conscious, that is, not self-conscious. The objectified impersonal subconsciousness is all that is present in the manifestation. In the evolution of subconsciousness gradually the sense of Me develops as a part of reality. We can see it as the primal polarisation, where the objective reality is more and more experienced in the context of a subject. Here the Subconscious Me is born. This impersonal subconsciousness gives birth to the subconscious Me. In the case of subconscious Me, this what occurs in the surroundings (in the particular Here) relates to the sense of a subject or Me behind. This Me does not recognise itself clearly and is not able to take itself out of the context of experiencing. There is an immediate identification with an experience. In the dream state, which represents animal consciousness, what operates is a purely subconscious Me. In a dream we cry, experience fears and joys but these experiences don't pertain to any specific Me — Me is merely an outcome of those experiences.

There are many levels of the subconscious Me. These levels relate to the strength, intensity and depth of the sense of Me within the environment of subconsciousness. For example, if we observe various forms of organic life and further, of animal evolution, we can see how the sense of Me gradually evolves from the very primitive and basic to the complex and highly sophisticated one. These are simply different stages and degrees of growth in the dimension of subconscious Me. For that reason, the human subconscious Me, from the dream state, carries a different flavour and characteristics of Me (as well as the content of course) to that of which a highly evolved animal could possibly experienced.

The evolution continues, but now already within the frame of the subconscious Me. This evolution is no longer purely impersonal, but enriched by the sense of Me, the personal flavour. The flowering of the evolution that runs through the subconscious Me, is the awakening of the Conscious Me. It takes place through the birth of the intuitive intelligence, or ego.

The function of the intuitive intelligence is an ability to sense the Me apart from the movement of subconsciousness. In the case of the subconscious Me, Me is already sensed but as fully identified with the subconscious material. The subconscious Me although having the personal flavour, is an objective not Subjective reality. When the ego faculty develops, in the waking state, a human being is able to sense its Me and to give from this place feedback to the subconsciousness. The self-conscious impulse of Me, from which this feedback arises, doesn't operate though constantly during the waking state. In fact, most of the time, the subconscious, dream like Me is present, and only from time to time the interference of intuitive intelligence takes place.

Although in the case of intuitive intelligence or conscious Me, the subject senses itself as being apart from the subconsciousness, still, the Me is not awakened to itself. It senses itself just enough to be in a observing position, but is not able to experience itself in a solid and tangible way. Further evolution occurs within the conscious Me. Me at this stage is conscious but not self-conscious in a true sense. Ego, therefore, is a passage from the subconscious Me to the self-conscious Me. It is the intuitive intelligence which is responsible for the awakening of Me. When intuitive intelligence doesn't serve the purpose of awakening, it merely participates in the thinking process - operating within subconsciousness. At the moment when intuitive intelligence, instead of referring to the mind, directs its attention toward the subject or sense of Me, the State of Presence is discovered. This is the purpose of the essential question "who am I?" Who is asking this question? It is the intuitive intelligence of Me which asks this question in order to discover its very Me. Intuitive intelligence is not Me itself - it belongs to Me. It is very important to understand it.

When the State of Presence is born, one experiences for the first time one's Me in a solidified way, as being fully apart from the subconsciousness. The subject is awakened. But is it the whole Me? No, it is only the Awareness aspect of it, the centre in the mind. Many think that the question "who am I" points to one thing, but it is incorrect. The reality of Me is multidimensional. Witnessing consciousness or thoughtless Awareness is certainly not the whole of Me.

It is truly amazing to see how Me discovers itself within the environment of subconsciousness. We need to remember that subconsciousness is the physical and psychological environment of Me. Continuing its evolution, Me expands into the deeper layers of itself. The subconscious Me and later the conscious Me evolves in order to awaken its own presence experienced independently from the subconscious reality. When this is done, Me grows within itself. But we shouldn't forget that the intelligence of Me is always operating within the field of impersonal subconsciousness from which it receives information - it is always a mixture of the spontaneous arising of thoughts and conscious feedback. Even when the Me is present to itself, its intuitive intelligence stays at the level of "conscious Me."

The evolution of Me from the State of Presence continues into the dimension of Being and Heart. Dropping into Being, Me becomes for the first time deeply and firmly rooted in Reality. It not only experiences itself in a solidified way - now it is also rooted in the Now, beyond its crystallised self-identity. It is rooted in the Universal I AM, the dimension of Beingness, the Source itself. Me can discover itself fully only in the context of that from where it arises within the Now.

Finally, through the Heart, Me awakens to the essence of itself, which is the Divine. Here the beauty, sensitivity and bliss are added to the reality of Me. Heart is the true centre of Me, for it is in the Heart that it meets the Creator, the Beloved; as it originally got created from this very Heart.

Let us repeat. The evolution of impersonal subconsciousness, which is life itself, gives rise to different levels and variations of personal subconsciousness, where the subconscious information comes back to the sense of Me. Here the subconscious Me is born. The evolution of the subconscious Me brings about the awakening of intuitive intelligence, the conscious Me. Here Me can, in a conscious way, refer to itself in the context of the mind, and gives self-conscious feedback to the information it receives. The evolution of intuitive intelligence results in the recognition of Me itself, which is self-attention, the State of Presence or the centre in the mind. The following evolution deepens the reality of Me by adding the restfulness of Being and the Divine sensitivity-warmth and expansiveness of the Heart. Awareness, Being and Heart are the three centres of Me. When awakened to itself, Me dwells finally beyond subconsciousness in the wholeness of the Universal I AM.

Even though Me is awakened to itself, experiencing itself fully beyond subconsciousness in the complete unity with the Universal I AM, it still functions in the dimension of time. Because it exists in time, it continues to live in the environment of impersonal subconsciousness and subconscious Me; in the process of becoming, it encounters them continuously through its own intuitive intelligence.

# The Absolute Meditation

The principles of the Absolute Meditation are simple but at the same time revolutionary. It is the complete seeing of the mechanism of awakening which makes them revolutionary. One of the most important insights on which the science of this Meditation is based is the clear differentiation between two different qualities which are present within the I AM: Awareness and Being. Next is the clear technology of the awakening of these qualities. Absolute Meditation apart from working with Awareness and Being emphasises the awakening of the Heart. Awakening to the Heart is seen here as an indivisible part of the journey into the holistic experience of our inner reality. In addition to the process of bringing one into the state of the I Am, we clarify the role and importance of Intelligence. How this dynamic intelligence and the presence-energy of the Inner State relate to each other was barely understood by any past tradition.

## Three Pillars of the Absolute Meditation

### 1. *Awakening of Awareness*

The awakening of Awareness is connected with the crystallisation of Attention. Bringing energy and focus into the mind is essential, otherwise the mind is in a state of complete chaos without any centre and continuity of intelligence. To activate attention one needs to choose one of various objects of concentration. One can follow the breath in the belly or watch the mind. We emphasise continuity of attention for it allows the Awareness to shift into the higher state, where its very centre is recognised. The general development of mindfulness is an indirect way. The preparation for the final insight into the essence of the mind. The direct way of awakening Awareness refers to the immediate recognition of the centre in the mind, the State of Presence. To help one to recognise the centre of Awareness we use several techniques.

## Observation of the Mind

One makes a conscious attempt not to be identified with thinking. One tries to be aware of the arising of thoughts. Apart from observing the thoughts with a sense of distance, one is looking for the One who is aware. One tries to "observe the observer," so to speak. This very attempt turns attention back to itself and should give rise to the state of self-attention.

## Repeating a thought

Here, instead of observing the mind, one focuses on one thought, repeating it like mantra in the mind. For example, one can choose a thought: "attention in." One repeats it very slowly in a very contemplative and conscious way. In this exercise one becomes aware of the fact that a thought is merely a mental object on the screen of consciousness. But who is the observer? Who remains behind the observing process? One makes a conscious attempt to recognise the sense of Me in the mind, pure I, Awareness itself which is independent of the thinking process.

## Conscious thinking

Here one is asked to think consciously and to be fully present. One doesn't merely repeat one thought, but chooses any subject and focuses on it. When one thinks consciously, one knows that one is thinking; one feels the sense of Me as participating in the thinking process. But again who is this "I" that is thinking? One tries to distinguish the thinker from the thinking, making a step back in the mind to the sense of Me.

## Direct recognition of the Presence

This is a direct technique where one makes an attempt to recognise the centre in the mind in an instant. First one becomes aware of the space in the mind. Next, seeing how thoughts come and go, one tries to pay attention to this which is immediate, the closest to what we translate as the "I." This instantaneous touch of attention itself is the I, the centre of Awareness.

When the sense of Me is recognised in itself within the field of the mind, behind thoughts, one is asked to retain it as one's own centre. As much as one holds it, one needs to relax it in the head so it reaches more and more natural and effortless condition. Holding and letting go is the art of working with the State of Presence in the integration and stabilisation process.

## 2. Awakening of Being

Being is simply an ability to rest within, in the vertical energy of isness. The combination of expansion and the transmutation of energies in the energetic centre of our being or Hara, and the conscious vertical surrender where Me drops more and more into the depth of the Now, gives rise to the experience of Being. Beingness is the energy linking an individual existence with the ground of Existence or the Source. All beings rest upon the Absolute, but in the case of human beings their sense of identify has shifted into the mind. The energy is too much up, disconnected from the force of gravity. Therefore, first we must free ourselves from the unconscious identification with the mind through the activation and crystallisation of attention; and next we relax, letting go into Being. In Being, attention dissolves into the open space of pure abiding or isness, which is rooted in the unmanifested. Awareness, however, remains an indivisible part of this experience - otherwise it could not be "an experience."

The awakening of Being is directly related to conscious surrender. This surrender is a function of the subtle will, but in order to succeed it must encounter the matured and transformed energy of Beingness within the individual I Am. Even though the dimension of Beingness is universal and transcendental, existing beyond our individual self, still, from the perspective of separation, the reaching of it and the depth of experience depends fully on the maturation of our own energy system.

Prior to the reaching of the Absolute State, in a mysterious way we experience energies of Beingness within our own separate system of consciousness-energy. This all relates to how the energy or vital force, that was given to us, is distributed within our individual existence; whether this force is more on the side of our individuality or whether it drops into the Beyond transcending the frontiers of a separate self.

The work with Being has two sides - the maturation of energy and the element of conscious surrender. The transformation of energy is a foundation. Although conscious surrender already affects the energy system, deepening it. Continuing to breathe into the belly helps enormously. We need to breathe very slowly into the belly and the exhalation should be complete. This practice must become a part of our everyday routine. It is wisdom.

What is conscious surrender? When one's attention is crystallised in the mind we are fully present. Awareness, however, can become a burden if one is not able to surrender it into Being. This surrender is a subtle act of the vertical letting go. This letting go affects the direction of the energy flow. In the state of Non-doing, where one is deeply relaxed and passive in a centralised way, the energy by its very nature gravitates downward. It gravitates towards the centre of gravity, which is located, according to our design, in the Hara. But the experience of Being is not in the physical body. There is a physical representation of the centre of energy in the belly, but the experience of it is situated in the dimension of Beingness, beyond our physical form. How one translates this experience is a feeling of calm and non-abidance, where one feels nowhere and everywhere at the same time. This non-abidance itself is the freedom from the individual self.

When we keep ourselves as close as we can to the Now by being in the centre of attention, the State of Presence, the surrender becomes like an arrow pointing to the Source of time. It reaches the heart of the Now - pure abidance in the plane of Beingness, the Primordial State of Rest.

## 3. Awakening of the Heart

The Heart is simultaneously a dimension of Feeling and Being. Feeling is the dynamic part of the Heart, while Being the static one. It is not possible, however, to experience the Being aspect of it if the Heart is not fully activated; neither is it possible to experience the feeling aspect fully if one is not able to rest within. The Heart is the secret gateway to the Divine dimension, to the Heart of the Creator. The Heart has many layers. On the surface there is the play of personal emotions — the more gross level of the psyche. Further down one reaches the deeper feelings pertaining to the Soul. Here we might experience deep longing, sadness, real joy or love. Going still deeper into the Heart, we discover the Soul herself, the Soul at rest. The Soul at rest is merged with the Creator, with the Divine. The Soul is a pure channel through which the Divine is experienced in the time dimension. She is one and separated from the Beloved. When the Soul feels herself, her flavour of human emotion, she experiences herself as relatively separated from the wholeness. When she merges into the Heart, she experiences unity with the Creation. However, this unity is experienced through her own presence, where the Soul in a inexplicable way is a part of this experience of Oneness.

Awareness and Being create a perfect foundation upon which the full discovery of the sun within, the Heart, can take place. Now, as there is a continuity of intelligence and deep rest, we can go fully into the Heart. The awakening of the Heart occurs on two levels; one is the level of energy and the second is the level of feeling-sensitivity.

The foundation is the energy activation of the Heart centre. The experience of the Heart is primarily an energy phenomenon. When this energy is activated, its very presence completely changes the quality of the I Am. The Heart is a middle point between the inner and the outer, the perfect balance between the Absolute and the Creation. The second aspect of the awakening of the Heart relates to the growth of sensitivity on the feeling-emotion level. One not only experiences the energy of the Heart but feels it as a feeling centre. It is the Soul that is being awakened and touched. It is through this profound sensitivity that the Soul is discovered.

There are some traditions which speak about generating from the Heart feelings of compassion and love toward all beings, but they bypass the discovery of the Soul herself. When the energy of the Heart is used to generate feelings toward the external reality only, one is still not aware of the Soul. The awakening of the Soul takes place when the energy-feeling of the Heart turns inward towards itself. In this intimate encounter, the ultimate sensitivity of the Heart, which is the Soul, is discovered.

So far we have spoken about two layers of awakening within the Heart. First: the energetic activation of the Heart centre; and second: the awakening to the Soul, to the profound essence of the Me in the Heart. There is, however, one more step to be made: the awakening to the Beloved. This takes place when the Soul surrenders herself completely to the depth of the Heart space. In this letting go of herself she merges with the Divine. In the depth of the Heart, in this mysterious place from which our individual heart arises, the Beloved dwells. She awaits the Soul, her child, to return to the state of unity with her. Surrender, the intelligence of the Soul and her utmost sensitivity finally allows the recognition of the Beloved to take place.

How do we work with the Heart? We simply start by paying attention to the Heart. Breathing to the Heart centre, keeping our hands on it, praying, listening to music which channels heart energy. The discovery of the Heart is a long journey, for the reality of the Heart is multidimensional and more complex then the one of Awareness. But when the clear intention arises in us to awaken the Heart, the power of evolution and Grace undoubtedly take us to the goal.

In the I Am we awaken the centre of Awareness, we awaken the Heart and we learn how to reach the condition of pure rest in the dimension of Being. Parallel to this process our intelligence-sensitivity growth, bringing the light of understanding and clarity. The end result is the unity of Understanding and the very presence of the I Am, the state of inner wholeness.

# The Map of Awakening

In the collective consciousness of seekers the term "Enlightenment" represents usually a "one state." We find this misconception highly dangerous. Therefore, we feel the necessity to draw again the inner map out of compassion for those who are on the Path to clarity and completion. Different levels of Enlightenment refer to the depth of the experience and integration with the I Am. For that reason, it is only when we fully understand what the I Am is that we can have the full clarity in this respect.

## The State of Presence

The first level of Enlightenment is the awakening of the centre in the mind, the State of Presence. Here one is able to experience Awareness itself without content, not referring to any object. This Enlightenment is complete only when one is fully established in the State of Presence and all moments of forgetfulness are eliminated. However, for most seekers it is not the absolute stabilisation that is necessary for the Soul's completion, but the ability to be at one's wish and most of the time in this state.

## Being

Further evolution takes place through the Being quality of the I Am. The centre of Awareness surrenders its self-referring tendency into the space of non-reference, which is Being itself. The energy drops into the Hara and one is more and more in the state of Rest. Completion in this respect can be seen as a certain optimum overall integration between Presence and Being.

## The Heart

Enlightenment to the Heart changes radically the quality of the I Am. The peace is transcended within the sensitivity, beauty and inner warmth of the Heart. Enlightenment of the Heart is fundamentally an energy phenomenon. The Heart is our true centre. For someone who is awakened to the Heart, the sense of identity, the energy experience of oneself, is naturally centralised in the Heart Space.

## Absolute State

The realisation of the Absolute is a destiny of very few Souls. For most Souls the experience of the Absolute would be too "extreme" and is not necessary to reach completion (the blue print). The Absolute is realised in the dimension of Beingness. It is like dropping into the other side of the "black hole" beyond this dimension of time. Here, the experience of Being shifts to the unmanifested. One is in a state free from any movement and fluctuation of energy - in Pure Rest.

## Enlightenment to Me

The Me apart being itself the holistic experience of the I Am, is the mysterious experiencer of it. The experiencer of the I Am is the Soul herself, which dwells in the Heart. Only when the Soul is awakened can one truly knows oneself—one has met oneself. The Soul is a child of the Beloved. In her evolution she transcends the subconscious separation and reaches the conscious unity with the Creator. But even becoming one with the Beloved, she remains a part of this experience. In knowing it, the Soul knows herself. In knowing herself, she merges with the One.

# The States of Awakening

## Ignorance: The state of forgetfulness

Before awakening only the subconscious mind operates mixed with the intuitive intelligence or ego. No centre of identity can be found in such a reality.

## The Fourth State: the State of Presence

Using the Hindu model, there are three basic ways of experiencing reality for the unawakened person: the deep sleep state, the dream state and the waking state. The Fourth State arises when awakened. The Fourth State is the State of Presence or Self-awareness, the centre of Me in the mind.

## The Fifth State: the Absolute

In-between the Fourth State and the Fifth there is the reality of the turiyatitta, beyond the Fourth, where the centre of Presence is already experiencing surrender into Being. Here, Awareness loses its crystallised quality and dissolves more and more into the space of Rest.

The Fifth State is the Absolute. It is realised within Being. The shift into the Absolute is the final expansion in the process of surrender into Being. Consciousness is transcended and one reaches a condition which is freed from any movement of elements.

## The Sixth State: Enlightenment to the Heart

Enlightenment to the Heart is called the Sixth State. It is the Heart which adds the fullness and beauty to the Inner State. The energies of sensitivity, warmth, the divine flavour and, finally, the unity with the Beloved, are integrated with the inner silence and motionlessness of the Absolute. When the Heart opens up fully, reaching complete expansion within itself, we call this Enlightenment to the Heart.

## The Seventh State: Enlightenment to Me

The Seventh State is Enlightenment to Me. When the state of inner wholeness is present, the Soul can finally recognise herself fully as the complete Me. Me has several centres. There is Me within the mind, pure Awareness or atman; there is Me absorbed in Being and there is the Feeling centre of Me in the Heart. The Feeling centre is the closest to Me itself, for it is the essence of the Soul which, by the design of the human body, is located in the Heart. When all faculties of the inner life are activated, the Me can finally awaken to itself. Beyond the inner and outer states, the Soul rests in the Heart and becomes fully integrated with Awareness and Being, merging with her eternal light. Here, the Transparent Me is manifested.

## The Eighth State: Beyond Polarities

The Eighth State arises as a result of a certain deepening within the experience of Me. Prior to this, Being and the Heart are in unconditional Samadhi. Presence, which is the centre of Me in intelligence, even though freed from the mental reality, has some tendency to fluctuate, not being fully in a state of surrender. In the shift Beyond Polarities, Awareness reaches the condition of Samadhi. At this stage, Being, Heart and Awareness (the complete Me) are permanently absorbed in the Universal I AM, the Beloved herself.

We might ask the important question: is this the end of evolution? For the human intelligence: yes. But for this very Intelligence, which runs through human consciousness there is no end to its expansion into the mystery of the Universal Light, the I AM or the Supreme Presence of God.

# No-Mind and Subconscious Mind

One of the ideals in the spiritual teachings, similar to Zen, is a concept of action or perception without the centre of ego behind it. One of the definitions of meditation given, for example, by J. Krishnamurti is: "meditation is a state where the observer is not." Here we encounter a very sensitive area, because this statement apart from being a possible way of describing an awakened state, could also apply to the reality of the subconscious Me. In a dream state the "observer is not" and one has got to practice a long time in order to bring an artificial observer (lucid dreaming) into this reality.

It is not elimination of the observer (the intuitive intelligence) which brings one to the Awakened Perception, but the transcendence of it. Elimination of the observer is, in truth, regression from the perspective of evolution. The observer, being able to stand apart from the subconscious mind and the empirical reality, is the only passage to the dimension of Pure Subjectivity. It is only from the reality of Pure Me that the perceived is embraced in a non-conceptual way.

We must be aware that what most seekers translate in their minds as an experience of no-mind, represents in truth a state of subconscious Me or being "spaced out." The subconscious Me has two basic ways of experiencing its reality: one is being lost in the mind; the second is being lost in the empirical, external perception. When the thought process is "spaced out" and one's sense of identity is dissolved into perception, there is a case of a "negative" no-mind. The positive no-mind is rooted in the Self, that is, the experience of it is fully on the side of pure subjectivity. From the space of pure subjectivity the external reality (and the psychological one) is experienced in a non-conceptual way, as the I Am.

There is also a possibility of experiencing the negative no-mind without the context of perception. In this case, one is not having any thoughts as such and there is no perception of any object, but neither is one unconscious. We call it subconscious Me without content. It is a very interesting state. There is an absence of psychological material but the experience of Me occurs still on the side of the Here, that is, within the objectified space of reality. The mystical Me is itself the pure psychological Hereness. From this perspective we can conclude that if the meditative state can be said to be Consciousness without content - so in the case of the mystical state, negative no-mind or being spaced out it is the subconscious Me without (psychological) content.

# Lucid Dreaming and Intuitive Intelligence

Bringing the element of attention into the dream state is artificial. Being aware that one is dreaming and the State of Presence are not the same. Lucid dreaming relates to the artificial interference of intuitive intelligence, or ego, in the dream state. It is quite interesting that no one so far has seen the distinction between the ability of being self-conscious, as an ego, in the dream and being in the State of Presence, where the permanent centre of Awareness is "witnessing" the dream. Similarly many confuse the term "witnessing" with observing. Witnessing is not of the ego - this term refers to the co-existence of the State of Presence and the mind. On the other hand, observing is a function of ego or intuitive intelligence. Intuitive intelligence doesn't have any solid centre of identity. It creates a momentary centre, within the thinking process, which vanishes as fast as it arises.

Even though intuitive intelligence can be artificially introduced into dreaming, it is not natural and it does not pertain to the same Me as from the waking state. When intuitive intelligence (or the State of Presence) operates in the waking state, it belongs to the much more holistic and integrated experience of Me. Here attention, sensations, physical presence, feelings, energy of being, thoughts and the presence of the Heart are more or less interconnected, functioning as one organism. In the dream state all these parts are disconnected. Energy of being, the heart, attention, sensations are falling apart not pertaining to any clear Me. It is a fragmented, subconscious reality. Even superimposing upon it the element of attention cannot change its subconscious character. Therefore, to be "conscious" in the dream state takes place still within the subconscious Me.

In the case of fully Self-realised being, it is not the gross attention which is present in the sleep state, but certain extremely gentle and subtle presence of integrated energies of Being-Awareness-Heart. This reality is below the conscious level, so no-one can in truth say "I experience it." Unfortunately, many masters following their particular traditions felt obliged to bring the artificial attention into the sleep state. In this way the natural reality of the Enlightened State has been mixed up and confused with man-made superimposition.

# Intuitive Intelligence

Who is the one who discovers the centre of Awareness? Who is the one who tries to keep and remember the State of Presence? It is truly surprising but, so far, the answers given by various spiritual traditions with their authority, have come up with incorrect conclusions. That which is performing all seeking and cultivation is nothing but the intuitive intelligence. It triggers the awakening of the State of Presence, and it remembers to bring back the Inner State when its energetic presence gets lost.

Most of the elements which create our life and our psychology take place beyond our control. For example, our physical organism operates spontaneously. One does not need always to be aware of the process of digestion, the flow of the blood or the beat of the heart. This kind of Awareness would be unbearable and neurotic. Almost everything in life happens by itself. Trees grow, birds fly, the sun shines. The impersonal wisdom of life runs through all. Similarly with us, we are born without being first informed by the Existence about this plan. Our body grows, our brain develops and the five senses operate automatically. Most of our life is a spontaneous impersonal flow of events. Suddenly, into this automatic functioning comes the intuitive intelligence which allows us to respond consciously to the flow of life. This response is our responsibility of co-creation with the rest of Existence. Up to this moment, having only the subconscious Me we were not responsible. But even now our responsibility is limited, as the intuitive intelligence is only a small part of the totality which creates our individual existence.

The intuitive intelligence gives a conscious response to the subconscious mind as well as to the challenges of external reality (which are filtered by our particular subconsciousness). Through this conscious response the subconscious mind and its contents are affected. In this way it evolves, changes and transforms according to its higher purpose, which is the optimum of sanity. The intuitive intelligence is this part of the Subconsciousness, which consciously responds to itself, in the light of intelligence and the very presence of Me. The more Me is awakened to itself, the more meaningful is this response. It is always the intuitive intelligence that responds, but the significance of this response depends on how deeply it is rooted in the whole of Me. This response is total and holistic only if behind it we experience the centre of self-awareness, rest in Being and, above all, the presence of our Heart.

We have to emphasise over and over again the right vision of the sane human consciousness. The centre of an awakened human mind is the State of Presence or Awareness beyond thinking. We call it the "self-conscious Me." On the energetic periphery of the mind occurs the arising of spontaneous thoughts, which, when not controlled by intuitive intelligence, create a spontaneous thinking process. We call this the "subconscious Me." And finally, in-between these two, enters the intuitive intelligence or the observer, who gives feedback to the arising of thoughts. We have named this the "conscious Me."

The State of Presence, the pure I of Awareness, has no way to consciously connect to the subconscious Me. It needs the medium of the intuitive intelligence. This intuitive intelligence participates in two realities. Its very energy centre is the State of Presence, but it lives within and through the subconsciousness. When it directs itself towards the mind, it gives feedback to the subconscious arising of thoughts. When it turns back to the State of Presence, it recognises it as "I" and relates to it using the intelligence, which has been accumulated in the subconscious mind. It cannot exist apart from the subconsciousness, nor can it exist in separation from attention.

It is only now, that we can fully understand how one can experience the spontaneous movement of the subconscious Me, while being simultaneously in the clear State of Presence. In this case the intuitive intelligence is at rest and what remains is the subconscious Me co-existing with the State of Presence. Here, there is no medium, no conscious link between the centre of Awareness, pure I, and the spontaneous activity of the mind. The subconscious Me and the State of Presence co-exist as one reality in a non-self-conscious way, until the conscious Me comes back and performs the conscious checking. For that reason it is false to believe that an enlightened being is always aware of the mind. There is no need for such unnatural control. The intuitive intelligence should interfere only from time to time in the activity of the mind. That is the natural situation.

The functioning of the mind, the emotional maturity and the level of intelligence are founded on the past. Past experiences have crystallised, on the subconscious level, patterns of behavior and the perception of reality. It is similar to an uncultivated garden. It grows as it does without cultivation. The weeds and stones are mixed at random with the medicine herbs, until the gardener comes and makes an order. The garden represents the subconscious mind. The gardener represents the intuitive intelligence and the owner: the State of Presence. The challenge of being a particular Me is that one has to face constantly the conditioning of the past subconscious mind, consciously responding to it. This response always takes place Now, through the use of the intuitive intelligence.

Giving feedback to the subconscious reality we are able to affect its content. The spontaneous psychosomatic movement of our being and the interference of the intuitive intelligence operate as one system. The reality of Me is multidimensional. The essence of Me in consciousness is the State of Presence, or Awareness itself. The essence of Me is the feeling centre in the Heart. Apart from this, Me abides and is rooted in Being. The movement of intuitive intelligence is also Me. Different centres and aspects of Me co-exist as one ecological organism of the I Am.

# Who is the "Observer"?

In spiritual teachings about Awareness, the term observer is often used in an inadequate way. Most practitioners are completely confused when asked about the observer. Who is the observer?

The question about the observer is not equivalent to the question "who am I?" The question "who am I?" points, in truth, to the totality of Me and not merely to the aspect of Awareness. The reality of Me is multidimensional and cannot be just limited to consciousness. The observer is placed only in the mind.

The function of observation involves two elements: the presence of Me and the specific direction the intuitive intelligence takes. The observation is done only by the intuitive intelligence. The intuitive intelligence is a movement of self-conscious intelligence. That which makes it self-conscious is the presence of Me, which is a part of thinking process. But because the sense of Me is fully identified with the thinking process, it experiences itself as being neither continuous nor solid. For that reason, the task which some meditators undertake is to be constantly aware and watchful. This ultimately brings only frustration. This is because that which is observing is simply unable to be constant.

The intuitive intelligence is doing the observing. Behind any conscious act of the mind there is the light of attention. In the case of the subconscious Me, attention is also there (for without attention there is no consciousness), but its energy is totally objectified and lost in the environment of perception. When the conscious Me operates, the sense of Me doesn't have continuity. But the presence of attention, apart from being involved in the thinking process or in the act of perception, carries a certain solidity and to some extend refers to itself, that is, to the subject.

The moment we ask, "who is the observer," we no longer emphasise the function of observing but the centre of identity, on which the self-conscious aspect of intelligence is based. The centre of Me is not doing the observing, but it is the very centre of attention which makes the movement of intelligence to become self-conscious possible.

It is paradoxical but the moment we recognise the observer, it ceases to be an observer. To find the observer, the observation must be directed toward its own centre. The centre is not doing anything. The Me in the mind is like a King. The intuitive intelligence is the Minister. The King and the Minister are one but have different roles and identities.

It is necessary to make the distinction between observing and witnessing. Usually these terms are used interchangeably, which is incorrect. Observing is done by the intuitive intelligence and witnessing designates the presence of Me itself, at the background of the mind. Witnessing means that apart from different functions of the mind, such as thinking or observing, there is a simultaneous presence of self-attention or the centre of Awareness. In the awakened state observing is being witnessed! The State of Presence is witnessing the observing by the light of its own presence. But the State of Presence itself can become observed. But even though it is observed by the intuitive intelligence, still its presence is witnessing all.

The function of observing comes from the third eye, which is the centre of wakefulness. When the intuitive intelligence operates, the partially crystallised attention is a part of the thinking process. The purpose of asking, "who is doing the observing" is to distinguish this attention from the movement of the mind. It is not an intellectual question but a teaching device.

The presence of Me in the mind allows the intelligence to be self-conscious. For the first time it has a centre of identity within its movement. Initially, the mind is simply operating on the subconscious level and there is no sense of Me being able to refer to itself in any possible way. When the sense of Me gradually develops, the intelligence is able to refer to itself. Only the intelligence due to this ability at one stage of its evolution, is capable of asking the question, "who is in my centre?" And here, the Atman, the centre of Awareness is recognised.

The terms "observer" and the "thinker" point to the same reality of Me. The function of conscious thinking or observing is done by the intuitive intelligence, and not by the subject behind, which is simply present as the centre of attention. When the "who" is discovered, it abides beyond any activity of the mind.

The purpose of training is not the stabilisation in the observation or watchfulness, which would be the constant ego, but in the presence of the subject, the pure light of attention. That's why, someone established in the State of Presence does not experience self-conscious intelligence all the time. From time to time it rests and only the subconscious, spontaneous intelligence operates. In such situation the State of Presence is vibrating on the energy level, not being self-conscious, as the intelligence is not referring to itself.

The observer is the intuitive intelligence referring to itself through the sense of Me. The Me is the centre of conscious observation and the place from which conscious perception arises. This Me cannot be called, in truth, the observer, for it is not a function but the non-active presence of pure Awareness. Therefore, the question "who is the observer" is not formulated precisely. The more correct question would be for example, "what is the centre of identity behind the observing?"

# Self-control and Spontaneity

Initially spontaneity equals unconsciousness or the subconscious Me. In a dream state, for example, one is certainly spontaneous for the observer does not exist, but this kind of "natural" flow is not at all the desirable way of living. In our repressed society we promote the ideal of spontaneity but we should be aware as well of the unconscious aspect of it. When to control and when to let go is the true art.

The human being, emerging from the unconscious spontaneity of the animal realm, is able to give feedback to the environment, that is, to bring a conscious element of control. There are various kinds of self-controlling mechanism. Generally controlling is directed into two areas: towards the external reality and towards the subject itself. One can either control one's own mind and behavior or the surroundings. The ability to bring an element of control is very challenging. When it is used in an extreme way, the natural way of responding can be completely lost. On the other hand, by the evolutionary level of our consciousness, the function of self-control cannot be avoided. In truth, it is the very presence of our intuitive intelligence, which has an inherent self-controlling quality.

The path of Awakening requires bringing into the functioning of our mind the very important element of self-control. This control is not directed to our actions or the psychological content, but to the freedom from unconsciousness. In order to transcend mechanical and obsessive thinking, which is the way an ordinary person experiences his/her mind, we must bring the powerful energy of attention. To activate this attention we have no choice but to focus intensively the energy in the mind and to strengthen the function of the observer. When we step out of the mind to centralise ourselves in the essence of attention, the State of

Presence, the spontaneity of thinking is radically broken. That is the danger of this process. But do we really have a choice? We have to make this temporary sacrifice to undo the past unconscious spontaneity.

The essence of the awakening process is, in truth, not the control of the mind, although some meditation schools seem to stop at this level. What matters is the recognition of the centre in the mind, the State of Presence, and the relative or complete stabilisation in it. This turning of attention back to itself and the cultivating process of self-remembrance combine the spontaneous Presence with the control of forgetfulness. That which needs to be under control is the tendency to forget oneself, to become lost in the subconscious mind.

The danger of working with attention is that it can become too crystallised and arrogant, as in Zen, or it can be used in an excessive and imbalanced way for observing purposes, as in Vipassana. Attention is just a tool of freedom from the mind. It has the centralizing quality which gives one the sense of the Self, the I Am in the mind. When one is free from forgetfulness evolution into Being, which is the highest spontaneity, begins. Always using this intuitive intelligence brings excessive self-control. It is intuitive intelligence which connects us to the present moment, but it is not its nature to be constant. It recreates itself from moment to moment and if one tries to make it constant, one must use an enormous amount of mental energy, which is not desirable at all.

When attention is directed into any area of experience, it is not only Awareness which is present, but the mental direction from the mind. To be in the State of Presence constantly, where attention is centralised in attention, is completely natural, for the centre of attention simply abides in itself. On the other hand, to be constantly aware of the environment, like drinking tea or the act of walking is simply an indulgence. We can see that the Zen teaching of being aware of the environment applies strictly to the intuitive intelligence, conscious Me and not directly to the State of Presence. This is also true with Vipassana observation.

The difference is that Vipassana is more mental, enforcing constantly into the observation of the body-mind the preconceived interpretation of reality (as being impermanent, painful and empty of substance). We must be clear that when mindfulness is directed towards an object, it is the intuitive intelligence that is activated. This kind of practice, when taken to the extreme, actually results in the birth of a "constant ego."

One of the biggest and the most harmful mistakes in working with Awareness is the aspiration to eliminate completely the spontaneous arising of thoughts as well as by extension, the activity of the subconscious Me (the thinking as such, without the control of the intuitive intelligence, the checker). Firstly, it is impossible to reach such a state. Secondly, even if one comes closer to it by using strong will and arrests the natural flow of thoughts, the result is truly unwanted — a "self-conscious robot."

We need to learn how to use the controlling quality of the intuitive intelligence in a way that it is balanced with natural and spontaneous behavior. At the beginning of the path more self-control is needed, for one must transcend the past habits of the mind, the state of forgetfulness and unconsciousness. As one progresses, the control can relax more, and the natural spontaneity of the body, mind and emotions becomes manifested. The result of this evolution, of this dance between the spontaneity and control, is relaxed control, which transforms into alert spontaneity.

There are two types of spontaneous action. One is unconscious or subconscious action, which in its essence is impersonal, for there is no one consciously co-creating it — the Me is not conscious of itself. The second type of spontaneous action is fully conscious, when Me is one with the I AM. But even though the Me becomes one with the I AM, still, because of living in the Here it needs to use its intuitive intelligence. Naturally, as the intelligence of Me and its sensitivity matures, the intuition replaces the need to control. Resting in the I AM, the transparency of Me, the movement of thoughts and feelings and the response to the challenge of life — all become one.

# Effort and the Effortlessness

Spiritual evolution includes the essential element of effort and discipline. Effort is simply a tool to reach a certain spiritual goal. When to use effort and when to let go depends on the level of realisation we are in and on the kind of spiritual target that we are aming at. There is always a danger that one can either let go of the practice too soon or too early. There is even an extreme type of seeker who wants to start from the very beginning with effortlessness, in the hope that Enlightenment will follow. That is however a mistaken approach.

To live is an effort. The way our energy behaves when manifested in a particular body and mind is one of effort. One is able to be free from effort only when dwelling within the I Am. Awakening to the I Am, however, requires effort and discipline. The more the I Am is present the more one is able to abide in it, letting go of effort. Therefore, the amount of effort that one needs to utilise on the path, can be measured by the depth of Self-realisation, which is the presence of the spiritual goal.

In the process of awakening we use various types of energies or different kinds of effort. To awaken the State of Presence we must use a very masculine and focussed energy. To go beyond the mind and to retain the centre of attention requires enormous concentration and dedication. The evolution into Being involves more feminine energies. One still needs to make an effort but in a very gentle and effort-less way. Here, one surrenders oneself to the open and restful space of Beingness. To let go is a very special kind of effort where we undo the manipulative tendencies of the mind in the act of surrender. Working with the Heart we also use feminine energy but with a different quality. In the case of Being the energy is more passive and submissive. To awaken the Heart we need to use energy which is completely sensitive and empathetic. Here, we perform an effort of feeling, tuning in and being sensitive.

As different centres are opening up and activated, they begin to vibrate of their own accord. Our effort can finally relax becoming replaced by the very presence of the I Am. But because Me still continues to exist, the effort of living cannot end. There is the effort of reaching the Inner States, and there is the effort of living as a spiritual being in the thick dimension of the Here. As long as we are alive we have to use effort to prolong our existence and to create the maximum harmony within the polarities. However, as the Soul matures and gets closer to the realisation of her blueprint, the other effortlessness becomes manifested. At this stage one's centre of identity moves fully from the Here to the Beyond. One becomes consumed by the Now. Not being Here is the ultimate effortlessness, which in truth is the absence of polarities.

# Meditation is not "Not-thinking"

Meditation is beyond thinking and not thinking. Thinking and not-thinking co-exist in the State of Meditation. The thinking co-exists with feeling, Awareness and the energy of Being. The meditative state is made of the energetic field of the I Am. This field itself is composed of pure Awareness, restfulness of Being and the expansiveness and sensitivity of the Heart. On top of this foundation is the presence of Me. Me in its purity is the Soul itself, the most intimate and personal touch of oneself in the Heart. The experience of Me takes place within the I Am and merges into it. But apart from the co-existence of the I Am and the pure Me, in the State of Meditation, the dynamic extension of Me, the psyche is present. The dynamic part of Me is made up of different elements. There is the movement of feelings (the extension of the original feeling in the Heart) and emotions, the intelligence, the thinking process and the physical form. The movement of intelligence can be either subconscious or conscious when the intuitive intelligence is active.

The foundation of meditation is the energetic presence of the I Am. The presence or absence of thoughts occurs on top of the already present meditative state. That must be clear. As long as one is alive a certain movement of consciousness has to be a part of the meditative experience. Trying to eliminate thinking completely is against nature and as such impossible.

Because meditation is a time for inner silence, like a prayer, we intend not to think purposely. It means that we allow certain thoughts to manifest as they do, but without conscious participation. However, we might find that still, from time to time, the subconscious mind is creating a chain of thoughts. In one situation, a thought arises and because we consciously let go of it, it disappears without creating a subsequent thought. In another case, a thought arises and because we neither pay attention to it nor consciously let it go, it creates a subconscious continuity of thoughts - the subconscious Me is thinking.

The tendency to arrest fully the thinking process, not allowing the subconscious Me to act by forcing into the presence of the mind the constant attention of the intuitive intelligence, is absolutely unnatural and harmful. We recommend balanced approach. There is a wisdom behind the interchanging between the subconscious Me and the conscious Me or intuitive intelligence. Sometimes the intuitive intelligence is absorbed fully into the Inner State, and one rests in the non-conceptual condition. Sometimes, the intuitive intelligence is absorbed but simultaneously gently checks the Inner State, recognising it and giving appreciation. Sometimes, the intuitive intelligence participates in the action of thoughts, while the Inner State is present in the background. Sometimes, the intuitive intelligence is resting in the Inner State, while the subconscious Me is operating.

When the intuitive intelligence is resting consciously in the Inner State, the subconscious mind is arrested. But because the constant focus in the Inner State is unnatural, the subconscious Me at one point comes to the surface. The focus in the Inner State means that not only is this very state present, but on top of it the conscious intelligence of Me pays attention to it. Although the Inner State can be constant on the energy level, the conscious recognition of it and conscious knowing of resting in it cannot be continuous. For the very simple reason that the intuitive intelligence is relative and possesses only a limited amount of energy.

# The Role of a Master

There are two extreme views concerning the importance of a spiritual Guide or Master. One speaks about the absolute dependence on the master who is the source of Grace and transformation. The other one criticizes the dependence on any teacher and calls for individual insight and awakening. Both views are extreme and lack the clear understanding of the student-master relationship.

The presence of a Master is essential in the seeker's evolution. Not all masters represent, however, complete Self-realisation. Many are partially Self-realised and in addition conditioned by their particular traditions. Usually the level of a Master reflects in one way or another the capacity, intelligence and sincerity of a student by whom the particular master has been chosen. The Master is a spiritual guide and a channel of Grace. Guidance from a Master relates to his/her own understanding and the ability to transmit it. The role of a Master as a channel of Grace is based on two elements. Firstly, the very presence of the Inner State which has an immense affect on those who are around a Self-realised being. This presence itself has a transforming power. Secondly, the state of the Master, which is a combination of inner silence, complete rest within and the open Heart, makes him/her a perfect channel-instrument for the Beyond. The Divine needs a channel in order to enter strongly into the earth dimension which is quite thick and insensitive. A Self-realised being is an ideal channel for the energy of transformation. The transforming experiences which people have around masters do not always come from the conscious intention of a master. Grace simply enters according to its inherent wisdom and purpose.

The role of a Master is to guide and transmit the energy of the Inner State and of the Divine. The role of a disciple is to follow the teachings and turn them into understanding, practice and inner realisation. The student's attitude towards the master should be one of respect, humility, sincerity and openness. Nevertheless, the intelligence of a disciple should always be critical, in terms of reflecting the transmitted understanding in the purity of his/her own intelligence. In this way one avoids the danger of being dependent on the Master, in an unintelligent way.

If the disciple follows the teachings and practices diligently and sincerely, the results should be obvious. If the results are not present, one must examine critically one's own work and the validity of the teaching that has been received, as well as the competency of the spiritual teacher.

# The Mind of a Seeker:
# Basic Sincerity

Real seekers of the inner Truth are certainly rare. The two essential qualities of a true seeker are: sincerity of the heart and certain capacity of intelligence. If the Soul is not mature, one will never be able to come close to the light of the Self.

We find that the term "Enlightenment" for most people on the path distorts the clear perception of spiritual reality. The ego gets overly excited by the myth of Enlightenment and loses the basic sincerity. This basic sincerity allows one to look for reality and not for the idea of it. The notion of Enlightenment has poisoned the flesh and blood of collective spiritual consciousness. A new, even more dangerous conditioning has been added to the ordinary plane of ignorance.

Most seekers use Satsang as a sort of spiritual club. They are looking for the energy experiences and emotional security in the presence of a Master. They hate the idea of practice not wanting to sit in meditation. This type of seeker loves to hear that there is no need to practice and that the Self is "already here," and that all one needs to do is to realise it. Many Advaita-Vedanta or Krishnamurti followers have been conditioned by these concepts, coming originally from certain idealism of Hindu spirituality.

Unfortunately, these days we can find around the world many pseudo-masters propagating this simplistic vision of spirituality, not understanding themselves the laws and principles of the spiritual evolution and awakening. They over-emphasise the importance of their own presence and the mysterious and miraculous nature of Enlightenment. Practice is however essential. It is the sacrifice which Evolution expects from a seeker. The human mind, heart and energy have been given to us for a reason, and not just to fall asleep. This reason is to manifest our conscious effort in order to co-create our own awakening.

Another interesting type of seeker is the one who gives a lot of effort to the practice, but still, in a mysterious way is not looking for oneself. For many seekers the Dharma refers to something objective, so to speak. This applies particularly to Buddhist practitioners. In Buddhism, because the Path is usually very elaborated, one simply follows it. The seeker is being replaced by the practitioner. The practitioner does not seek so much anything, but rather practices in order to reach the expected results. The search for the Dharma becomes therefore impersonal. In this way one bypasses the intimate encounter with one's own self.

The general tendency of Buddhist seekers is to search not for the I Am but rather for the "I am not." The basic energy of this approach is rooted in certain philosophical preconceptions. The Buddhist philosophy is profound and certainly valid, but we need to see the dangerous sides of it. This impersonal attitude toward the Dharma can prevent one from the amazing and revolutionary awakening to this very Dharma as one's own self, as the I Am. Here, the practitioner doesn't look for a Dharma as an objectified truth, but becomes centralised in it through his/her sense of identity, the heart of which is Me.

So it is not enough to practice hard. Buddhist practitioners practice very hard and diligently doing many retreats and daily meditations. Why is it that most of them do not reach Self-realisation? We might think that the reason is because Self-realisation as such is too difficult to be reached. But although this is true, those who devote so much time to practice should accomplish it. The real reason that so few succeed on the Path is the lack of basic sincerity. One doesn't look in the right direction; the seeker remains on the "objective" level without the direct reference to his/her own self. One misses the I Am, bypassing the true Intimacy.

The true seeker is a Holder of the Path. He/she is a passage between the collective unconsciousness and the flowering of evolution, the I Am. Developing the right qualities of mind and heart is the basic responsibility of everyone who follows the Great

Path. It is only when Enlightenment refers to us and we relate to it fully and directly, that the proper relationship with the Way is created. Here basic sincerity is manifested.

# II

# BEYOND THE
# "NON-DUALITY"

# The Divine Dimension

Reaching God is itself an energy expansion. It is not in the field of perception that one reaches unity with the Creator. Our Being quality must expand beyond the limitation of the personal self in order to merge with the Beyond. Here, the personal Me crosses over the Lila land of apparent separation, to arrive at the pure rest in the Universal I AM.

The Divine is the Supreme Realm within which Absolute Rest, Intelligence and Love create one unified field of pure knowingness, which is the I AM. It is neither created nor is it uncreated; a mysterious realm.

The Beloved in her original form is in a condition of Rest, where the Absolute and the Heart are one and unmanifested. The Divine Dimension itself is a "result" of the primal polarisation, within the Original State, into the Absolute and the Heart - Beingness and Love. This polarisation gives rise to the field of knowingness, which is the Universal Me. That's why the Divine can be experienced in our heart. In deep sleep, when consciousness doesn't operate, what remains is the Beloved in her original state, the unmanifested energy. That's why the Heart is not experienced in this state. Therefore, the Original State can be seen as the unmanifested Heart, the Divine as manifested Love.

Now we can understand, finally, how Consciousness is born. It is created from this original polarisation between the absolute energy of Beingness and the one of Love. Within the space that arises between the Absolute, which is the ground of Existence, and the Heart, which is the manifestation of Love, the field of knowingness is born, which is the manifested Intelligence of God.

In our reality of separation we are able to experience different aspects of the Ultimate, as if taken out of the universal context. For example, we can experience Consciousness without the Heart, and the Heart without the Absolute; or we can be in the Absolute without Consciousness, like in a deep sleep state. This very ability to have an incomplete experience, paradoxically, is the foundation of the evolution in Time. The Ultimate, experienced from the human dimension, is reached through the channel of Me. That's why it is not the absence of Me, as some past traditions claim, that is the presence of the Ultimate, but the awakening to this very Me. When Me is absent, what remains is the Beloved at rest, prior to Consciousness. Indeed, the Existence of Me makes it possible to experience the Divine in the human realm.

The Divine is beyond time - it eternally Is. It is not touched by the movement of becoming. It does not arise in time - it simply Is. The polarisation we spoke about, between the Absolute and the Heart of the Creator, has not been created. It is not an outcome of an event in time - it is present timelessly. But even though the Divine is not in time, its abidance is not one of pure absence, which is the Original State. The field of knowingness, its inherent brilliancy, and the infinite mystery of its transcendental Intelligence, which is Love in truth, indeed, allows us to perceive it as the "Created Reality."

The Divine looked upon from the viewpoint of the Original State, is "created," metaphorically speaking; whereas seen from the perspective of phenomenal reality, it is uncreated: The Supreme Dimension, which is timelessly present in-between the realm of the Creation and the one of the Original State, is itself the Primordial manifestation of the Light of God.

# Prayer

Prayer is nothing but the essential connection of the created being with the Light, Love and Intelligence of the Creation. This connection is found at the point in the middle of the chest by the design of the human body. Prayer is a direct communication of the Soul with her Creator - a communication of love and humility. The created Soul is truly a child of the Divine, completely dependent upon it in all areas of existing. The understanding of it is itself an Awakening.

Prayer fundamentally is the feeling of the Beloved in the Heart, which includes an intention. This intention can be unconditional, where the Soul surrenders herself to the Beloved in the experience of love and unity. Or it can involve a more personal communication in which our desires, fears and longings are expressed.

Prayer is a part of the blueprint of being human. It means that it is expected by the Divine. It is the Beloved's wish to be communicated in this way. Here we can speak about the relationship between the Creator and the Soul. The relative separation allows a wide range of feelings to be experienced in this whole journey of returning home to the state of Unity. Prayer is the essence of this relationship, the expression of the Soul's intelligence, which is Love.

# Where does Me Exist?

The impersonal subconsciousness is a necessary environment within which Me can exist in the realm of time, that is, in duality. Me, as an angle of perception of the I AM, requires Here-ness in order to manifest itself. Me is the consciousness of I AM. It is universal, for it shares the universal qualities and it is particular for it possesses the unique flavour of individual creation.

The Here is an objectivisation of reality - both physical and psychological. The psychological Here is called psyche. Subconsciousness is a designed objectivisation, in which the Me can be reflected. Through this polarisation the subjectivity can become self-conscious. Here-ness is a playground of Me. Through the psyche and physicality Me not only experiences the Here, but also in the relative reality becomes itself a part of it. In this way a particular Me itself can be experienced by different Me's as a part of their Here.

Me is born at the meeting point of the unmanifested energy of the Universal I AM and the field of subconsciousness - the Here-ness. The Now is the Beloved; the Here is life. The experiencer of life, the Me, is born at their meeting place.

The I AM is the unmanifested energy; Me is the manifested. When the I AM manifests itself, it becomes Me. When the Me rests upon the I AM, the I AM becomes a conscious experience for this particular Me. When Me in its evolution becomes conscious of itself, it is the I AM that is conscious of itself as a Me. When Me discovers its origin, the I AM, the I AM becomes conscious of itself through Me. When Me is fully awakened to itself in the context of the I AM, the I AM knows itself as the unity of Me and itself. Here the evolution of Me reaches its very peak and the meaning of our journey has been fully understood.

Me exists in time. What is time? Time is the becoming of Here-ness, the dynamics through which it arises from the Now.

The Here is the shape-form of time, the information of existence to which time refers. Here-ness is the context in which Me can experience itself. In referring to itself it simultaneously refers to the Here. How does Me connect to the Here? Through the senses, physicality, the emotional body and the mind or Awareness. There are many expressions of the Here, not merely the physical one. In the evolution of Me the very concept of Here-ness, in which it lives, becomes transformed into the Ultimate Here, which is one with the Now. The Ultimate Here is the Universal I AM. In this stage the Me, in the supreme dimension beyond oneness and separation, merges with the ultimate Here-ness, transcending it's very Me, through which this experience is known.

The Now itself is the primordial presence of the unmanifested energy of the I AM, the source of Creation. Me arises from the Now into the Here. Through the Here it knows that it exists. The awakening of Me takes place in the exact balance between the Now and the Here. Resting fully in the Now, Me is embraced by the Here. As the evolution into the Transcendence continues, Me becomes more and more absorbed into the Now - it transcends Here-ness. The evolution of Here-ness, therefore culminates in its own transcendence, which takes place in the final Samadhi in the Now. In this Samadhi Me still exists, the Here still exists - but the perception and experience of them have lost any trace of relative character. At this stage the Soul shifts her perception of reality and herself fully into the Beyond, to the other side of the Now, which is free from the relative Here. The Final Transcendence.

# Me Meets the Beloved

The awakening to Me is the final goal of our evolution in time. Enlightenment to Me is the complete experience of the Soul. The Soul apperceives herself as a unity of thoughtless Awareness, absolute rest in Being, pure Intelligence and the infinite depth and sensitivity of the Heart. This total experience takes place beyond the inner and the outer state, giving birth to the Transparent Me. Here, the evolution of human intelligence reaches its highest peak and exhorts itself.

At this stage, the power of Grace enters again to create a new momentum of evolution. The Transparent Me becomes pulled from the cross-section of the Here and Now, where it gave birth to itself, into the vertical depth of the Now. Within this vertical depth of the Now, which is the Beloved herself, Me becomes one with the original Light. When Me meets the Beloved, its will becomes consumed in the ocean of the Divine. One enters the final Samadhi - in the Heart of the Beloved.

# Karma and Grace

Karma means that different elements in Existence are interconnected and mutually dependent. Ultimately the notion of Karma applies to all that exists, for everything has its reason and is directly or indirectly affected by the multitude of events and causes. But in Existence there is also the element of accidentality where events take place at random and the link between them cannot be clearly understood. These events can still be seen in the context of Karma, but Karma understood in a different, broader way.

For example, if someone steals our shoes we may wish to explain this event in terms of the law of Karma. But it doesn't always work in this way. There is a possibility, that the past connection with the individual who has stolen our shoes could be an indirect reason of this happening. Possibly, we ourselves had taken some possessions from this person, in another time and in other circumstances. But there is also a possibility that there is no direct karmic link between the thief and the victim. In such a case the law of Karma still operates but should be explained in a different way. The victim here might not be responsible karmically for being robbed (apart from being careless), but the thief had his own reasons to behave in this way, which means that the karmic cause needs to found on his part alone. The poverty of the thief, the situation in his country and the world in general, the weather (maybe he needed those shoes), the tendencies of the mind, the opportunity to steal and other numberless reasons could explain the simple fact that the shoes were stolen. Therefore, although the things are interconnected, the responsibility is not always shared in a simplistic understanding of this term.

When two people meet and there is a special connection, we

speak about the karmic link between them. This link can be from past lives where these Souls had already shared some significant experiences, or that their particular sensitivity and intelligence has the same quality on the metaphysical level - the same energy and parallel vision of evolution. This is mostly what is understood by the term Karma. Here, two elements (two Souls) are mutually connected. There is a wisdom and purpose, which can be traced and explained on some level. This Karma can be either positive or negative. Some karmic events are nourishing and beneficial and some are painful and unwanted. In both cases there is a possibility of finding some rational explanations of events taking place.

Sometimes, however, we are simply not able to understand and decipher the meaning and purpose of certain events. Particularly, when we are affected in a painful way we try to find some justification for our suffering. And we cannot always do that nor are we always directly or indirectly responsible. We are a part of the Totality. There are many, numberless elements in Existence which create the dance of life. There are certainly some reasons behind all events but these reasons cannot always be clearly seen, and often can only be understood from the higher perspective. Existence does not always operate in terms of "justice." Existence, the creativity of life operating within the imperfection of the particular limited Here, often needs to experiment in order to reach the desired conclusion or blueprint. That's why the element of unpredictability and accidentality is an indivisible part of the movement of life.

We should not perceive the laws of Karma in a too moralistic and dogmatic way. Karma is simply the metaphysical glue keeping all the elements of Existence together. Within the laws of Karma there is always a space for the creativity of Existence, for the unpredictable, for surprise and, most importantly, for Grace. Grace is above Karma, although the Divine certainly always respects the laws of the universe, for it was she who created them.

There is destiny and the freedom of reaching it. There are two kinds of destiny: static destiny and moving (dynamic) destiny.

Static destiny cannot be changed. Certain events in our life and the universe simply must take place. For instance, one is born in a particular family, in a certain country, from a certain mother and there is no freedom to change this. Similarly, there are certain events in our future which must occur and they cannot be changed. Certain people we must meet, certain places we must visit and certain experiences we cannot avoid. This is an example of static destiny.

Between these points which are designed by static destiny, there are many dynamic elements and possibilities which correspond to moving destiny. For example, one may be destined to reach the State of Presence in one particular lifetime. This cannot be avoided, but the question of how and when exactly one would fulfill this task relates to our relative freedom and the creativity of the universe. Another example of moving destiny is when one actually goes beyond what was destined. Let's say that one was destined to reach the State of Presence and due to Grace one attains the Absolute State. Or, one was destined to be in a relationship with a Soul-mate, but other elements could re-arrange this destiny - emotional immaturity, for example, could destroy a profound connection between two people.

The laws of Karma are complex and touch many areas that really cannot be completely seen. Accepting fully the validity of this concept, we recommend treating it in a relaxed way, avoiding the danger of becoming too opinionated or unimaginative. Let us respect the laws of this Universe, which are divine in their essence. Respecting them we naturally become responsible for our life and actions, as we are the co-creators of the Becoming Existence. But simultaneously, let us be aware of the mystery of life and our limited understanding of it. As the laws of this universe are creating constantly the phenomenal expression of it, so the mystery of Grace, the divine creativity, is constantly re-arranging different elements, manifesting the Unpredictable Future and the Unknown Now. For that reason, in truth, the future cannot be predicted. One can only touch upon different possibilities within the Known. That which created Karma is above it and can always change the Predictable.  That's why, in reality, the highest freedom that we have is to pray.  Through the act of prayer, we co-create in the deepest and the most meaningful way with the Beloved, the manifestation of ultimate happiness, the end of the journey in time, which is the Complete Now.

# Higher Intelligence
## and the "New Age"

Higher Intelligence is another name for Grace or Guidance. Higher Intelligence is multidimensional, embracing all possible dimensions of Creation and it mysteriously dwells in the Heart of the Creator. It is inconceivable but its rays are reaching us bestowing Grace and loving care. Guidance is the intelligence of God.

Higher Intelligence is complete and absolute, but its expressions represent different grades of truth, depending on the level of the dimension where it enters. In the "New Age" movement, for instance, the concept of Guides and Guidance is very popular. Various beings transmit through channelling information and wisdom from other dimensions. A lot of this information is valid and valuable but does not always represent the highest understanding. The Buddha Mind, the insight into the Absolute, the inner map of awakening cannot be found in New Age technology. The New Age is not, at all, grounded in Reality, trying to explore the other dimensions and encounter with other beings, because it lacks the fundamental experience of the I Am. Even when we can find in this movement the notion of the I Am, it still remains on the purely conceptual level.

The New Age message is, in truth, awakening to the Soul, but bypassing the basic work with Awareness and the connection with Being. We can understand, however, why the Buddha's insights have been unconsciously ignored by this Movement. For the very simple reason, that in the message of the East, the Soul has been negated. Therefore, the deepest meaning of the meeting between West and East is, in reality, the meeting of the Self with the Soul. The "New Age" is valid but it must include in its vision evolution into Inner States. We can say that the understanding of the New Age is still confined to the horizontal reality. The vertical dimension of the Self, the centre of gravity which is Being and the presence of awakened Awareness are completely lacking.

# The Over-soul

As there is the Soul, so is there  the Over-soul. The Over-soul is that which gives birth to the Soul - it is the Soul's parent. The Guidance, which revealed to us the Supreme Understanding beyond traditions, is nothing but the Over-soul itself. The Over-soul is this particular part of Universal Intelligence, which encompasses the number of Souls having the same blueprint of their completion. When a Soul finishes her journey in time, she becomes a part of the Over-soul. The Over-soul is not "a being," nor does it exist in time or place. Its fundamental quality is Love and Understanding which is immediate. The Over-soul is the link between the Soul and the Beloved.

The Over-soul controls lovingly the Soul's evolution. It creates the right circumstances on the path of life, bringing Grace and multidimensional healing. It cleanses the past of the Soul in order to manifest her Future, the ultimate Completion.

# The Soul's Destiny

We are unable to have a clear vision of the spiritual evolution unless we understand the role of the Soul's blueprint. The blueprint is an inherent vision of the Soul's destiny and her completion. Spiritual traditions tend to superimpose one and unquestionable vision of the ultimate goal for all seekers. We can say that they perceive a global or general blueprint. But, even though there are certain universal elements in the evolution of each Soul, at the same time, each Soul is unique and possesses an unique blueprint or evolutionary plan.

The challenge of each one of us is to discover which elements need to be present in our life in order to manifest the true completion, that is, happiness. Each Soul must find her way to her destination and transcendence. It usually involves an emotional fulfillment, reaching certain essential Inner States, realizing basic desires, adventuring in life, and ending of the Karma, which in truth contains all of the other aspects.

The Soul lives mysteriously between the inner and the outer reality. In herself, she is neither created nor uncreated. She grows in the world, maturing emotionally and developing her intelligence; while from the other side, through the inner expansion, she finally reaches the union with the Beloved, her Source. In order to be complete for the Soul, both the inner and the outer elements must be present.

The blueprint is the Soul's destiny, but how she will reach it is her relative free will. She may accelerate or delay her evolution. Her journey in time is confined to the laws of the Universe. She co-creates her task of reaching the completion with the whole of Reality and the presence of Universal Intelligence and Love.

# Pure Me and the Psyche

Me in its pure form is the Soul herself, in her original state. When Me is awakened in the human dimension, it experiences itself beyond the environment of the subconsciousness and the psychological self. The psyche is this layer of Me which allows one to experience the Here. The psyche, simply speaking, is a mixture of the subconscious mind and the emotional body. It constitutes the "mood" of Me within the Here, that is, in the world. In the case of an unawakened person, what exists is this mood only, the personality alone. When one is awakened, Me experiences itself out of the context of the psyche. However, it is because of the psyche that Me can live in this dimension of time, the psyche still remains as a part of the multidimensional reality of Me.

After the awakening of Me, further evolution aims at the purification of the psyche. The psyche needs to be aligned with the purity of the Soul. It has gathered from the infinite past the dust of negative experiences and ignorance. Now the process of cleansing the subconscious mind and emotional maturation can begin.

How can the psyche be re-aligned with the Soul?  In truth higher technology is needed, which is Grace or the intervention of Higher Intelligence.  It has been an experience of many enlightened beings that even after Self-realisation, the psyche has not changed, but remains as it used to be. Of course, a new level of freedom has been added which is the very presence of the Inner State. For that reason, the idea of disidentification from the mind has been so strong in some traditions. Because one is unable to change the mind, one negates it as "not Me" and chooses to abide in the safety of the Inner State. If the Soul, however, wishes to be truly whole, certain work with the psyche must take place.

As we can see, there have been two main streams in spiritual evolution. One speaks about transcending the personality by reaching the I Am. That is the foundation of all traditions aiming at Enlightenment. The second stream is directed towards the transformation of the personality in order to bring it as close as possible to the Soul's original purity, the principle of harmony and love. Because psychological work has proved to have very little effect in the task of transformation, the "New Age" movement emerged. New Age therapeutic work involves more subtle and esoteric tools of transformation. Various beings, channels and energies from the other dimensions are invited into the healing process. But even here human sorrow, sadness and suffering seem to be fundamentally untouched.

Unfortunately, if a person is disconnected from the real centre of the I Am, the transformation of the psyche is barely possible or basically impossible. The mind of Me can become transformed fully only if this very Me is present. The intelligence must have a centre of identity, which is the presence of self-attentive Awareness; the energies of the Heart have to be activated to allow the process of transformation to begin. It is truly sad or even shocking to realise that almost all human beings are devoid of the conscious existence of Me. There is only the collective mind, which runs through the unaware of herself Soul. This is the reality of most. How sad! How can we speak about transformation, if there is no Me present to be healed in the first place?

Both, the negation of personality, where one chooses to rest in the Inner State, and psychological work without the essential presence of I Am, are incomplete. The psyche must be re-aligned with the pure Me. This is a complex process, for the subconscious mind and the emotional body are not conscious and have been crystallised throughout many lifetimes and numberless experiences. Even from this lifetime we carry so many wounds, blocked energies and unconscious negative patterns, that we can hardly conceive of healing all of them. For this reason, higher technology is needed, an intervention of Grace.

What an individual can do is to awaken to the vertical reality of the I Am, as a foundation, and bring as much Awareness and understanding into the functioning of his/her mind and emotions. Apart from this the clear intention to be healed and transformed is essential. Nevertheless, soon one discovers how helpless one is in the attempt to bring about the radical and full transformation of the way the psyche operates. It is at this stage that one needs to invite consciously the help of the Divine. Only the One who created us can finally transform us. In Rumi's words: "whoever brought me here will have to take me home." The presence of Grace and help from the Beyond is always present. It comes from the Over-soul to the Soul as a response to the direction of the Soul's evolution. But a conscious invitation to Higher Intelligence and Love into our healing process, by law, opens the gates of Grace much wider. One simply receives a bigger dosage of help and healing.

Our evolution is a co-creation. We evolve from the inside and we receive assistance from the Other Dimension. When we see this clearly, the complete understanding arises as to what is happening to us. Through this very understanding the power of co-creation reaches its possible optimum and the destiny of the Soul is manifested quickly. She attains her final future, which is the Complete Now.

# The Awakening of the Soul

The awakening of the Soul is the true purpose of human evolution. The Soul is the pure light of the I AM manifested as the most intimate flavour of Me in the Heart. The Soul is a reflection of the Beloved in her individual creation.

The Soul originally is not aware of herself. She needs first to develop consciousness and the mind in order to become self-conscious. The ego is the mind of the Soul. The Soul is not the mind, but she needs it to be conscious. The Soul needs a certain environment to discover herself. As we need a mirror to see our face, so the Soul needs different elements to become awakened.

The essence of the Soul is in the Heart, but without the support of Awareness the presence of the Heart is unconscious. To discover herself she must first create the environment of the I Am. In truth, the I Am is the all-encompassing presence of the Beloved, the womb within which we incubate and become conscious of our own existence. Therefore, the realisation of the I Am is a foundation upon which we can meet our ancient Soul identity.

The I Am is an impersonal energy. For instance, when we rest in the State of Meditation, we are absorbed in the state of complete peace. That is the ultimate environment where the Soul wishes to abide. The one who experiences the I AM is not the I AM, but the Soul. She lives in the I AM, but she herself remains for ever its innermost expression. The awakening of the Soul is directly interconnected with her dwelling place. The discovery of this Soul's abiding place, makes possible her own awakening.

The awakening to the I AM and the awakening to the Soul are interconnected but not the same. One can fully realise the I AM and not be aware of the Soul. On the other hand, without the realisation of the I AM the awakening to the Soul can be only partial. The complete I Am is like a pure spotless mirror in which the Soul is reflected fully. The Soul is made of the I AM, but simultaneously she constitutes the very individual centre through which the I AM can experience its own existence.

The full awakening to the Soul takes place in the Heart Centre. The Soul encompasses our whole being, but her innermost centre is in the Heart. The manifested centre of the Soul in consciousness is the State of Presence. It is her centre in the mind, the centre of intelligence. When the State of Presence is not awakened, the Soul operates in the mind as the intuitive intelligence or as the subconscious Me. The ego is a shadow of the Soul. When she doesn't recognise herself she lives only as the ego.

When the State of Presence is awakened the Soul has, for the first time, a centre in the mind, the I Am in the mind. The centre of the mind is Me, but not the whole of Me and not the essence of Me. That's why a person whose Awareness is fully activated, still does not necessarily realise the Soul.

Without the ability to rest in Being, the Soul does not have any roots. She is disconnected from the centre of gravity, from the Source. Without Being, the very energy through which the Soul operates is fundamentally restless. She is deprived of depth and of the continuity of Rest. In order to be able to abide in her own presence, the Soul requires the continuity of Awareness and stability in Being.

When all the elements are in the right place, the Soul can discover herself fully in the Heart. It is here that she meets herself face to face. This meeting is itself an expansion. As she meets herself within the space of the I AM, through this encounter with herself, she merges with the essence of the I AM, which is the depth of the Heart, the Beloved herself.

# Incarnation of the Soul

To incarnate is to come from light into the darkness - and back to the light. The Soul forgets her eternal identity and gets lost in the play of phenomenal reality. She is no longer conscious of the light and lives in the dark cave of ignorance among shadows, taking illusions and phantoms as real. She starts to play the role of a manifested being, subject to time. The adventure of apparent separation and the journey in time begins.

Why would a Soul decide to leave her original condition of pure oneness with the Divine, to experience forgetfulness and separation? This decision was not made in a conscious way and there was no one, in the first place, to decide. This decision comes from the impersonal wisdom of the Source itself — it is not made on the personal level. The Universal I AM manifests the conscious Me in order to experience the totality from a certain angle of perception. The sum total of all potential and actual angles of perception constitutes the multidimensional composition of the Creation. The presence of any angle of perception is itself a designed limitation. This limitation is an experience within polarities. The Ultimate is unlimited not only because of being itself beyond polarities, but also because it is able to experience the reality of limitation, through its individual expressions.

We have come from light to darkness so we could experience the grandeur of returning home. Only if one leaves the home, is it possible to be wholly appreciative of its existence. However, it is not only returning to the original light of the I AM, which is the goal of being here. It is also the experience of the Here, which is the created reality, which is a part of our blueprint. If the Soul, for instance, has awakened already to her origin, but has not completed a certain wide range of experiences in the world - she will come back to the Here, she will have to incarnate again.

The concept that one can choose how and when to incarnate, is one of many spiritual superstitions. No one can choose, for the choice is being made by the Higher Intelligence. After the dissolution of the physical body, which is the container of human consciousness, and the only vehicle for it, one dissolves into the state of Rest. The human Soul is unable to exist without the body. There are certainly energies and Presences, which do not need a physical form in order to exist, but they are certainly not human spirits.

Of course, some energy is left after a human being departs from this dimension and this can be felt or experienced. For that reason, the belief in "ghosts," phantoms or conversations with dead, were created. These phenomenon are in truth a combination of human subconscious fears and projections, which are mixed with some residues of energies, that in the past were crystallised as incarnated souls. In this way, the illusion of an objective encounter with the mind or the spirit of a person who passed away appears. But in reality there is nobody there, but a play of subconscious fears, projections and impersonal energies.

After the dissolution of a particular individual human Me, one returns to the deep sleep state, where the information of Existence is not present. There is no need to prepare oneself for the next life or after death challenges. Some traditions, out of fear developed specific practices. For example, their adepts make special visualisations to be able to leave the body in such a way that the negative post-death experiences could be avoided, so that the pure land or heaven could be reached directly. However, there is no reality behind these concepts but simply a false belief system. There are certain areas in life where one simply needs to trust. We didn't decide to come to this life - the higher intelligence decided. Why wouldn't we trust the same Intelligence to direct the destiny of our Soul, according to the principles of love and harmony, also after the dissolution of our human form?

After this dissolution, if the blueprint of a Soul is not complete, soon, when the timing is right, one incarnates again. One finds oneself again in a particular body and in a particular environment to which one has been destined. There are also times when a Soul incarnates into the non-human realm The journey of the Soul's evolution is complex and almost impossible to be grasped by the mind. This information presented here has not been given to explain everything but to create the basic and important understanding of what our purpose Here is. It is essential to remove certain misconceptions and superstitions, which bring confusion and can easily hinder the proper perception of one's evolutionary path.

In the dimension of time, knowing and Not-knowing are mixed and support each other. Our knowledge is ultimately an expression of our essential clarity and intelligence. While Not-knowing, the divine ignorance, represents our humility and child like innocence. Our knowledge is freedom from the false and the Not-knowing, which ultimately is the I AM, is Freedom itself: pure rest within the Heart of the Creator.

# The Realm of Polarities:
# Role of Imperfection

The existence of imperfection is an equivalent of being Here. The reality of imperfection has been designed for a number of Souls who had the wish to experience forgetfulness. Forgetfulness is itself a part of the Soul's blueprint as a temporary experience, but when the Soul gets addicted to it, the Golden Gate to the light shuts down and one becomes completely lost.

The existence of imperfection has a purpose, otherwise it wouldn't become our reality. This purpose can be viewed either from the ultimate or from the relative perspective. The earth, which for some obvious reason is our main concern, is a part of the ecological organism of Totality. Similarly, as a finger is a part of the hand, and the hand is a part of an arm, this earth exists in itself, and simultaneously belongs to the bigger structure of Existence. We tend to give categorical opinions about this reality in terms of good or bad, but do we really see the whole picture? Certainly not. For that reason, in the end, a wise man becomes completely silent transcending any conceptualisation. But even though non-conceptualisation is the highest state, representing the ultimate surrender, it still, in a paradoxical way, must include a certain destined understanding and clarity regarding the meaning of our existence.

The imperfection is equal to the presence of polarities. Some realities are more and some less imperfect. If we imagine, for instance, a planet where beings don't need to eat each other, (unlike on earth), where flowers blossom eternally and everyone is in a state of permanent joy, we might see this as a "perfect place," compared with our planet. But in truth it is the amount and the kind of imperfection that is different there. The very presence of Me involves the existence of imperfection.

Imperfection is the movement of time and perception, which can arise only in duality and relative separation. Evolution, the movement of becoming can only occur when the wholeness of Perfection manifests the presence of limitation within itself; a certain relative absence of the absolute motionless quality of pure isness.

The presence of imperfection constitutes our human reality, and this has to be accepted and respected. These are the laws of the Universe and they were created by the Supreme Intelligence, in front of which we can only bow in humility and silence. It is only due to polarities that we can experience the extraordinary richness of life. Because there is life so there is death; because there is light, so there is darkness; because there is ugliness, so there is beauty. It is the contrast which allows us to appreciate reality. For instance, when we leave the smoggy city, we can recognise blissfulness, the silence of the mountains and the freshness of forests much more deeply. It is due to our loneliness and lack of emotional fulfillment that we can experience the thrilling joy of love and affection. These are the dynamics of living within the polarities.

Our evolution is a divine paradox. We are destined to live within the polarities. At the same time, as our path unfolds, we move more and more into the place beyond polarities, where the I AM alone reigns. On one hand, we evolve within the polarities in the attempt to reach the optimum harmony and maturation in our life and psychology. On the other hand, we are transcending this dimension by becoming one with the unconditional motionlessness of Pure Being, which is the Timeless. Therefore, the Self-realised being is a paradox. He/she dwells in unity with the Divine. Yet he/she still, lives Here, within the imperfection itself, where opposites give birth to each other in the eternal dance of Becoming.

What is the conclusion? It is the presence of imperfection, which creates the initial impulse to move out of the Here and to transcend the state of forgetfulness. One can, indeed, enjoy polarities but one is unable to rest in them, for the Here is restlessness itself. For that reason, the desire to go beyond this reality of limitation arises and one begins the spiritual search, the search for the secret way out of the Here. This is not merely to negate the time-dimension, but to experience it from a higher and deeper perspective — from beyond polarities.

This reality is to be lived. It will never be perfect and that we must see with the utmost clarity. As the Buddha discovered: sickness, old age and death are indivisible from life itself. But life, regardless of our opinions, is to be lived, so our intelligence and sensitivity grow and the primal desire, which originally brought us here, to experience all the richness of life can be realised and fulfilled.

# The End

Do not expect this life to be perfect. Be patient and humble in your meeting with life. Do your best to live in the optimum way which is aligned with your Soul's evolution. In this way you will expand and mature in all areas of your being. In this process you will finally become fulfilled in the outer and the inner reality. And you will let go, let go more and more into the Now, into the Beyond, into the Mystery, into the ultimate surrender, into the Beloved... until you dissolve. And you will dissolve, dissolve into God, into Love, which is the eternal heart of the Now. And at last you will merge into this complete, immediate, supreme understanding that, in truth, nothing has ever happened, nothing has ever existed, only Love. Only Love Is.

KNOW THAT ONLY I AM.

# III

# GUIDANCE
# TO THE
# ABSOLUTE MEDITATION

# Absolute Meditation

## 1st Meditation

Welcome to the Guided Meditation. We would like to present to you the complete Guidance to the Absolute Meditation beyond Traditions.

Absolute Meditation works with different aspects of our wholeness and brings us to the realisation of the complete I Am; to multidimensional Enlightenment. The complete I Am is a unity of awakened Awareness, the State of Presence, awakened Being and the awakened Heart.

The awakened Awareness liberates us from the unconscious mind, creates a centre of consciousness in the mind, the crystallisation of attention, which is the state of self-attention. The State of Presence is a flowering of consciousness, the essence of intelligence, in truth. The aspect of Being, which has its energetic centre in the Hara, refers to that which allows us to rest within the Unmanifested, upon the Source, the Absolute. It brings one to the experience of peace and non-abidance. It frees us from the state of separation and identification with individuality. The awakened Heart is the true goal of our evolution. It is in the Heart that we discover our Soul and our eternal unity with the Divine, with the Beloved.

There is also the fourth aspect of the I Am, which is inherent to it but has a more dynamic quality. It is the Intelligence. The creative movement of the Spirit which evolves eternally into Understanding, more and more Understanding. The intelligence links all other aspects into one unified system. This intelligence is both: conscious and subconscious. The Spirit flows between Awareness, Being and Heart making us alive, letting us know that we are, and allowing us to understand who we are.

Please, take a comfortable seat. Sit in a solid, grounded and relaxed posture and keep your spine straight. The State of Meditation is beyond the physical posture, but at the beginning of practice the body needs to be respected. The motionless and disciplined position of the body is a great help to reach inner stillness.

Take a few deep breaths into your belly. Express an intention in your mind that for the time of this meditation you will let go of all anxieties, desires and concerns revolving around your personal life. Allow yourself to trust and be courageous, so you can experience the time of meditation fully. Relax into the Universal Trust, into the all-embracing wisdom of that which knows you and will take care of your life. In this way, there will be enough space and freedom in you to start the journey Inside.

You start with slow and deep breathing into your belly. Make your exhalation complete until your belly becomes flat and inhale naturally so the belly expands a bit. Breathe deeply and slowly in a relaxed manner. Imagine that your centre is in the lower belly. Be one with breathing...

There is nowhere to go. Stay here in the place of your true home inside. You are in the process of returning home to the place where all is right, absolute harmony and fullness. From the dimension of forgetfulness which is the earth, from the shadow of reality, you are returning to the dimension of remembrance where you know who you are and there are no more doubts.

Continue breathing. Your attention has to flow with the breath. Do not fight with the mind. The purpose of meditation is not to stop thinking but to expand beyond it, to the place which cannot be touched by the mind. If you try to stop thinking, it indicates that you are still identified with it. Do not care whether thoughts are present or absent. In this way, you will be truly independent. Allow the mind to manifest thoughts, as it does, but do not get involved. See the mind as it is and each moment relax into the breath. Ignore the mind. Neither participate nor fight with it. In this way, you are beyond conflict and beyond day-dreaming.

Breathe slowly. You feel how the energy expands into Being,

into the State of Meditation. The State of Meditation is an energy experience where you know that you are, but this knowing is not from the mind. Your experience of yourself is much bigger. The centre of Being is in the Hara. In the Hara, the energy of Beingness is originally centralised. The Hara is the gateway to the Absolute, to the Unborn, to the State of Rest. Simply by breathing in this way, you transform your energy and you regain your fundamental connection with Being. Being means to Be, to rest and to be grounded within. Like a tree, you are growing roots from inside you into the Beyond. You become Connected.

The experience of Being is not given by birth to the human being. You have to give birth to the experience of Being. That is the responsibility of conscious evolution. In this process, you are expanding and surrendering to that which is much bigger than you, to the dimension of Beingness. Only in this surrender can you truly find yourself, peace and happiness. You can discover yourself only within that which makes your existence possible.

Breathing slowly to the belly, we are very alert, very alert and relaxed. The deepening of energy takes place and you are pacifying your emotional body, which is continuously restless. The centres of the emotional body are located in the belly as well. By being alert to the breath, you indirectly develop the continuity of attention in the third eye.

By the simple act of conscious breathing and being attentive, you begin the complex process of transformation. This transformation is your destiny. Your destiny is to reach the State of Light. That is the reason that you are born. You are not born to survive only and to live in fear. Survival is the basic minimum. The ultimate purpose of being alive is to discover oneself and to discover this very light which makes the experience of life possible, the Divine.

We are awakening in you the ancient memory of your true identity and your life's purpose. There is a part of you inside who already knows it; with this you need to create conscious contact. Look deeper and see it. Listen to the call from the Self. The I AM is calling you, so you can discover your original form.

The I AM is pulling you to itself by the gravity of evolution, but you have to co-operate. So look inside and discover who you are, with the divine passion and intelligence.

Deeply relax within your breath, being continuously attentive. Letting go of the mind and relaxing into What Is. You are learning the forgotten language of Being. Just being. You are like a flower that has to open up, so the Sun of the Ultimate can reach your essence, can reach your Heart and can nourish your Soul. Whatever you can do is so little compared with the infinite universe, but you can open up, you can look inside and miracles will happen. You can reach a completely new life that is beyond imagination, where you are still living this human life, but being rooted in the Divine.

Deeply breathing to the belly. Fully alert, letting go of the mind, that is, of fear. Be courageous and surrender into Being. Simply Be. Each moment relax into Being with your intention and with your attention. There is nowhere to go. Where can you go? Remain Here in the dimension of inner silence. Relax into the state of happiness that is already present. Relax into the fullness of Being. The external reality will never satisfy you. Soon all will end, your life will go. Isn't it worth discovering our eternal essence, which is beyond this limited personal and meaningless dream?

Being is wellbeing, a state of contentment inherent to Existence. It is a happy state which is self-fulfilled. Your intelligence must become certain of it so it is fully convinced. When you know it, the surrender into Being will naturally follow. You are here to transcend the fragmented state of ignorance and to reach your wholeness, the I Am, the complete Me. Be like an open sky that cannot be touched by the imperfection of this dimension. Your Heart and your mind must be convinced more and more that what you are looking for is your own light. Relax into it.

Relax into your breath. Relax into yourself... into your existence. Taste yourself. Meet yourself Now. Be. Simply Be. Be who you are. Be present. Meditation is a meeting point of Rest and the presence of Awareness, alertness and calmness, Samadhi and Clarity. Be. Breathe and Be. You are not the mind, you are

Being. Awaken yourself to this truth. Be at ease. Be in peace. Let go of the mind and drop into the Real. Yes...

## 2nd Meditation

As we have mentioned the I Am is made of three aspects: Awareness, Being and Heart. The experience of Being relates to the presence of basic calmness and rootedness within our own existence, but unless we are free from the mind which glues our sense of identity to the unconscious and compulsive thinking, we are not able to drop into Being. How can we experience Being if we are not present in the first place? Therefore, the work with Awareness follows. The crystallisation of attention is an important part of our evolutionary path. Attention liberates. It is the light of consciousness which dissolves all unconscious and subconscious manifestations of the mind. When awakened, it gives us a true centre in the mind, presence free from thinking.

During our work with the breath and deepening of Being, we have been bringing in the element of attention as well. Otherwise, we wouldn't be able to experience the continuity of Being. This attention was operating in two directions: from one side, it was directed to the mind, against habitual thinking and from the other side, attention was directed towards Being, becoming a part of this experience. Attention frees us from the unconscious or semi-conscious state of mind. It frees our very Me, our Soul... so we can experience the other dimensions of Beingness and Existence.

In our second Meditation we are going to work directly with attention. Although attention has already been engaged previously, it was not aware of itself. Attention was operating, but in an objectified way where its very centre was not present to itself. There are two ways of working with attention: direct and indirect. The indirect practice with attention is called mindfulness of the object; the direct practice is called mindfulness of the subject. In the indirect work with attention, attention is not aware of attention but of the object to which one is attentive. The centre of attention is located in the third eye, in the mind. To discover the centre of attention is the same as to discover the witness-presence or the observer.

We begin with focusing on the third eye area to activate it
energetically. We put our attention in the middle of the forehead,
above the eyebrows, not on the surface but more inside the skull.
Our eyes are closed but they are looking upwards to this area.
We imagine that we actually see it and feel it energetically. Soon
you will feel a strong energy moving in your head.

Now you can relax but being still gently focussed in the head.
We do not recommend too much to activate the third eye from
the outside, as we have done a few moments ago. It is helpful
to bring some blood and energy to the mind but the true awakening
of Awareness takes place from the inside. To make this awakening
possible, there has to be a sufficient amount of energy in the mind.
Those seekers who refuse to bring energy into the mind, because
of being conditioned by the no-mind concept, will never be able
to give rise to the State of Presence.

Even though we focus on the mind, please, be all the time, to
some extent, connected gently to the breath in the belly. The
reason is, that when you bring energy up you are less grounded
in Being and, therefore, you can become restless and agitated.

Gently direct your attention to the thinking process, observing
it with a sense of detachment. In observing thoughts, you are
not interested in their content. It is not psychological work. You
see thoughts as thoughts and let them go. There is no substance
in them, they are empty and rootless. They are simply mental
information. If you don't feed them with your interest, they are
unable to last. They vanish into the same void they came from.

To observe the mind is a revolution in the human consciousness.
From the mechanical and semi-conscious state of only thinking,
one is able to make a step back and to create a distance from the
psychological flow. It is in this way that the Me evolves and
gradually emerges from the objectified consciousness into the
light of its own presence. A space in the mind is created. One
becomes an aware being for the first time.

The highest challenge on the spiritual path is to ask the right
type of questions. Most seekers do not make any progress on
the path for the very simple reason, that they are not capable of

asking the right question. When one is able to formulate the right question, only at that stage the right, transforming answer will be presented. The right question already has an inherent answer within itself. An appriopriate and important question to be asked at this moment of our practice is: "who is observing the mind?"

It is not the mind which is aware of thinking. The mind is aware of its own content. That, which is aware of thinking as such, prior to recognition of its content, is the one behind the mind. We call it the witness, the observer, the state of self-attention or the State of Presence. It is the pure I, the subject, that which you are in the mind, your true sense of identity in the mind. Yes, it does refer to You. The observer, thinker, Me, Atman, I...

Observing of the mind is the first step to go beyond the mind. One creates a distance between the mind and the very Me which is doing the observing. Step number two, is to discover the observer itself, where our Me becomes aware of itself. For that purpose attention must turn upon itself in order to discover itself, and non-dual self-awareness is born.

Please, in observing thoughts make a gentle step back to feel the one who observes, which is certainly you. Feel that which never changes, which always has the same flavour of I Am. This Me behind the mind... isn't it so familiar to you? When you were a small child wasn't it the same? All those experiences that you have had during many years have not changed the purity of your Me. This Me is not the ego. It is the pure Me - Awareness itself.

If you wish to be free, you must create the centre of consciousness. Even though to rest in Being is our goal, unless you have a centre in the mind, you will never be able to reach it. The mind is a part of you. For that reason you need to have presence in the mind. If you don't have a clear State of Presence, it is not the mind which is a part of you, but you yourself are only a part of this mind.

At this stage, instead of observing the mind, you will be thinking intentionally. For some reasons, most practitioners are able to recognise the thinker quicker than the observer. The terms, thinker and observer designate the same reality of pure Me, the One behind the mind. Please, choose any subject you like and being fully present, create some coherent chain of thoughts. Think very intensely, one hundred percent, being completely engaged, but in a relaxed manner. Here, it is not merely the mind which is thinking - it is You! You are a part of the thinking process but, at the same time, you are separated from it. Feel it! Your Me is using its will, intention and attention to think. Feel this Me! It is your own presence, behind the movement of the mind. You must separate, within you, the flow of mental objects in your mind from the sense of Me which is in the background. For that, you need a certain amount of concentration in order to freeze the habitual, chaotic fluctuation of the mind energies. Feel the Me, feel the subject...

If you can feel Me, the subject, the direct sense of the naked attention in itself, independently from the thinking process - with the whole force, stay with it. Keep it, hold yourself to the sense of Me as your own centre. Now, you can already let go of thinking and concentrate exclusively on the centre of attention. Your task at this stage is to retain the state of self-attention without losing it. The habitual identification with the mind can take your focus away. That's why you need to focus intensely. Now the object of concentration is the subject. The subject, using the energies of the mind, tries to remember itself. That is the true meaning of Self-remembrance. Before we can talk about Self-remembrance, the Self must be recognised. It is not complex but extremely subtle.

Meditation is the Meditator. The object of Meditation is the subject. We hope that now you understand the meaning of it with full clarity. As you abide in your Me, you keep the important balance of concentration and relaxation. You abide in your own centre. The essence of awakening is the recognition of the State of Presence, for it liberates us from the mind. The next task is stabilisation in it, which is the unbreakable continuity of self-attention, the presence of Me within the mind.

In order to stabilise in the State of Presence, the centre of watchfulness needs to be activated to the point that it operates automatically. When the centre of Awareness is established it vibrates spontaneously whether we are aware of it or not. Before it is stabilised, we have to activate it with our remembrance. The remembrance is itself an energy of attention directed towards its own centre. That which directs this energy is our intelligence. To stabilise in the State of Presence does not mean that we are constantly aware of it. It becomes self-aware on the energy level. It is the flowering of Awareness and conscious evolution.

First, we discover the State of Presence in meditation. We learn how to keep it and not to lose it. We eliminate all the moments of forgetfulness, which are natural in the beginning. Next, we bring the state into activity. We learn how to walk with it, how to eat with it, how to talk with it... etc. We learn to be present to the subject while simultaneously being engaged in external reality.

Please, keep the State of Presence in your mind. This experience is in the head. It is in the middle of the head, but because it sends electricity of Awareness to the whole brain, it can be felt in different areas. It is not to be focussed in any particular place, but to know that this experience is in the head — as if your eyes are looking backwards to the direction of the Seer. The State of Presence has a quality of a centre when you relate to it or consciously keep it, but when you relax with it, when you let go of the self-referral, it opens up and is more felt as a space of Awareness.

Attention is tension. It is this type of tension which liberates from unconsciousness, but when it is already present, we relax it. First, you relax it in the head, as if you let go into Being but only in the head... Letting go of tension into relaxation. You let go of attention but without losing it. It is the art of keeping it and letting go. If you just let go, you will lose the centre. If you only keep the centre, you will become too tense and the energy in the mind will be cooking too much. So keep it and relax. Relax and hold onto it...

The State of Presence and a certain movement of thoughts co-exist. The more grounded and expansive the State of Presence is, the less there is thinking. But, still, the inherent tendency of the mind to manifest some thoughts from time to time cannot be eliminated. That is how it should be. Meditation is beyond thinking and not-thinking; it is a transcendental state containing both polarities. Therefore, an attempt to eliminate thinking completely is a dualistic approach. Such an approach shows that one is not aware of that which contains the polarities. Hence, we fully accept the arising of thoughts, but, ourselves, relax with full attention into the State of Presence.

### 3rd Meditation

At this stage, we let go further of any focus. In an extremely gentle way, we surrender to the state of Non-doing. We allow the energy to gravitate downwards towards Being. No need to do anything, just letting go...letting go. Where are you letting go? You cannot capture it, but know that it is into the direction of the Unborn, the ultimate Source of Gravity - the foundation of Existence. When you stop doing, it pulls you naturally towards itself. That is the law. In order to stop doing, you have to undo the habitual doings of your mind and energy. That's why freedom from the mind and the deepening of your energy system are essential. You are letting go into the softness of pure Being. The energy of Awareness, which you have activated, is a part of this experience. It brings clarity into the calmness.

Now the centre of your identity is no longer experienced in the head only, but all over you - everywhere and nowhere. You become embraced by the holistic experience of the I Am: the unity of Awareness and Being. Being without Awareness is dull and vague. Awareness without Being is too tense and disconnected from the experience of Rest and rootedness in the unmanifested. The state of Shikan-taza, pure meditation, is a unity of Being and Awareness, deep rest and clarity....

Relax into Being in a very clear way, retaining the quality of attention. The I Am is not a static state. It is the movement of silence, movement of consciousness prior to thinking. It is not a psychological movement, but the movement of I Am. The energy within the State of Meditation has a certain dynamic quality. Sometimes you experience more the rest in Being and calmness; and sometimes there is more Awareness and alertness present. Sometimes the energy is more located in the head and at other times, it rests in the Hara. Also, the movement of the I Am is directly related to the quality of a particular Soul. Some practitioners, by nature, are more connected to Being and others have more energy in the mind.

Because the stabilisation in the State of Presence is your relative goal, apart from resting in Being you have, from time to time, to pull attention to the centre in the mind. When it is clear, you again relax into Being.

Finally we are coming to the essence of the I Am — to our Heart. Please, take a few deep breaths to the chest and to the Heart. The spiritual Heart is located in the middle of the chest. Putting your hands on this area, you are feeling your Heart and you are feeling your Soul, which is the most intimate place of your particular Me. Breathing into the chest, feel like the energy of the Heart expands, becoming one with your Being. Your Being is firm like a tree, like a mountain. The Heart brings into it the energy of sensitivity and beauty... a sweet feeling of being touched. That which is touched in the Heart is your Soul. It is touched by the Divine, by the Beloved. When you truly touch your Heart, at this very moment the Beloved is touching You. She abides in the depths of your Heart. The dimension of the Heart is the Divine itself. Your Heart is the temple of the Beloved, the ultimate beauty. It is so sensitive, so vulnerable, that anything can hurt it...and it is only when you can be hurt that you can be loved. Only that which is so sensitive can feel the Creator. When you allow yourself to be vulnerable and sensitive, the Divine is invited to your Heart. For it means that for the first time you have a Soul.

As you feel your Soul and your Heart, let it become one with the State of Meditation. In this way, the fragrance of the Divine, the beauty of the Heart and the inner silence are experienced as one. The vibrant sensitivity of the Heart, the presence of the Soul and deep feeling of prayer enter the inner peace; like music and the fragrance of incense filling the vastness of the empty Temple.

Here, the Path of meditation and the Path of Love finally meet within your own very Self. Here, you have arrived to your eternal home of inner wholeness... the I Am. It is done.

### LOVE PEACE GRACE

# Absolute Meditation: Advanced I

## 1st Meditation

Welcome beloved friends. We would like to invite you to the second stage of the Absolute Meditation, which leads to the realisation of the complete I Am: a unity of Awareness, Being and Heart. The second stage of Absolute Meditation is designed for those who are already awakened to the State of Presence.

The awakening to the State of Presence is a foundation and the true beginning of the journey to inner wholeness. Without the centre of consciousness, the mind cannot be transcended and we have no continuity of intelligence, which is required to reach the deeper experience of Being and Heart.

Sit comfortably with the spine straight and in a disciplined posture. For some time breathe to your belly, calm down and harmonise your energy. Let all thoughts and emotions relating to your personal life relax and dissolve into the Now. Relax. Surrender to the mystery of this moment in which you encounter your own existence. The Now is the point where the dimension of time meets the Timeless, that which is beyond becoming, beyond the movement of relative elements, the underlying source of all, the heart of Reality...

When you feel that your energy has settled down and you experience calmness and relaxation within the very fact of Being, direct your attention to the mind. Bring the State of Presence clearly into focus. The State of Presence is an energy experience in the head. In this place, the pure I is recognised, attention is abiding in its own centre. Here, consciousness recognises itself without the medium of an object. It is the state of pure subjectivity, the essence of the mind, the centre of intelligence.

Keep the State of Presence and relax it simultaneously in the head. In this way the centre of Presence reaches the condition of openness... like a vast sky, a brilliant and serene luminosity of Awareness is manifested. There is no obstruction, no borders and no limits in this place. A new Here has arisen in the place of the old primitive Here of the physical reality.

The purpose of this guided meditation, is to help you reach complete clarity within the experience of the State of Presence, and to establish you in this state. Apart from the fact of being in this state, we want to create in you the Understanding of the internal life of the I Am. How the State of Presence behaves, within the context of Being and the thinking process, has hardly been understood by any past teachings. It is very important to understand the complex and mutual relation between the State of Presence and the movement of intelligence. It is very important to understand how the State of Presence and Being are interconnected and which centres of the I Am are predominant, depending on the situation we are in. If you don't have clarity in these matters you cannot say that you know who you are.

The I Am is a dynamic reality, which has its own laws and principles. The energy of the I Am moves intelligently between the centres: Awareness, Being and Heart. In activity, the State of Presence is experienced more strongly; in meditation, for the very simple reason that we relax, the Being quality is predominant, but that which can be directly brought into life and activity is the State of Presence. We don't speak just about being aware in activity, but about having a solid and stable centre of Awareness. How to bring the State of Meditation into life, has always been the greatest challenge for all meditators. Most meditators cannot find any direct connection or continuity between the periods of sitting meditation and daily activity. In truth, it is the attention aspect of the I Am that can be fully integrated with activity, with the dynamics of life. It has been called Witnessing for it is present to itself at the background of the mind and external events.

You are breathing slowly into your belly and simultaneously holding the State of Presence in the head. You are holding it and relaxing within the head's space. Your relative purpose is stabilisation of the State of Presence. In that way, you will have a permanent centre of identity in the mind. You will be free from the objectivisation of your innermost sense of identity. For that reason, you must try to eliminate all moments of forgetfulness, when the State of Presence is not vibrating and you are simply lost in the peripheries of the subconscious mind; in the movement of thoughts, perceptions and emotions. We want to crystallise the presence of the subject at the background of the psychological self, so it will never leave its own centre. In that way it remains, always, like an inner sun shining the light of Awareness at the centre of the mind.

It is essential to understand that there are two levels of recognition of the State of Presence. The fundamental recognition comes from the presence of the state itself. The very vibration of the State of Presence, which is an energy experience, carries information of its own existence. It knows itself directly without the medium of intelligence. For example, you might be lost in thinking or in some external activity, not paying attention, at all, to the State of Presence, but when you come back to yourself, with the help of a subtle memory, you know clearly that the State of Presence has not been lost but has been vibrating all the time at the background of your apparent forgetfulness. In such a case, the centre of Awareness is present but one is not aware of it. It means that one can be lost in thinking and not necessarily lose the State of Presence. In truth, it is natural, for we do not wish to become overly self-controlling, self-conscious "robots." A certain amount of spontaneous thinking and spontaneous action is indivisible from being alive. We always have to keep a sane balance between self-control and spontaneity.

The second level of recognition of the State of Presence is when you, your intelligence becomes conscious of the Centre. For instance, you are busy driving a car or planning your future, and suddenly, you become aware of the State of Presence. In such a case there are two possibilities: either the State of Presence was there all the time or it was lost and your remembrance brought it back. When you are aware of the State of Presence, the spontaneous vibration of this state is accompanied by the intuitive intelligence looking at it.

In order to have clarity in the cultivation process, it is essential to understand the difference between these two levels of recognition. If you think, for example, that it is You who has to constantly remember the State of Presence, we guarantee you that you will end up in a mental institution. This, that becomes constant is not you remembering the Inner State, but the spontaneous and automatic vibration of that state. However, it is your remembrance which manifests the stabilisation. So what you do in the cultivation period is to remember the State of Presence as much as you can, not blaming yourself when you lose it; and you must become very sensitive to recognising, through subtle memory, the vibration of the State of Presence in those moments when you forget about remembering it!

Who you are is not merely the State of Presence. You are also the creativity of the mind, this very intelligence which brings recognition into all states. Without this intelligence there is no You and there is no evolution. When the State of Presence is not integrated, you have to practice self-remembrance. You make it wake up, you make it vibrate. Otherwise it returns to its dormant condition where it does not vibrate. Remembering the State of Presence is your task. The more the State of Presence is activated and integrated, the less you need to remember it and the more the State remembers itself on the energy level. When the final stabilisation takes place, the need for practice is over.

You are holding the State of Presence and breathing slowly to the belly. In truth, stabilisation of any state happens on the energy level. This has been underestimated by Krishnamurti, for example, or some of Advaita Masters. It is not self-knowledge only, which brings the presence of the complete state. Self-knowledge, which is the very effort of our intelligence to understand who we are, must be supported by the alchemical transmutation of our energy system. Breathing into the belly, which is the energy centre, brings this transformation. It is not only will which can stabilise you. The turning of the key within your energy system does it. Your own effort of remembrance, the breathing and, above all, the power of Grace brings finality to our inner work.

Looking into your mind, please, see that there are several interconnected levels and layers in this mind, creating the whole field of consciousness. In the centre, there is the State of Presence, the host of the mind. That is the nearest to you — the energetic centre in the mind. It is the very presence of Me itself. On the periphery of the mind, is the movement of the subconscious mind with all kinds of thoughts arising, usually carrying information concerning your personal life... and in-between the Centre of the mind and the subconscious arising of thoughts, there is the movement of intuitive intelligence. It is the dynamic, moving centre of Me in the mind or the ego, as opposed to the static centre of Presence. .Intuitive intelligence is the bridge between the subconscious mind and the centre of Awareness.

You are keeping the State of Presence and relaxing it in your head. You are seeing how the mind and the State of Presence co-exist without any obstructions. When the State of Presence relaxes, it reaches its natural condition of openness. In its space, all movements of the mind are embraced, not touching it at all. Allow the State of Presence to be as it is in the natural space of Non-doing, free from any modifications. Let it all be as it is...

## 2nd Meditation

We would like to explore how the State of Presence, Being and the Heart are mutually interconnected and how they relate to each other. You are recognising clearly the centre of Awareness. Feeling it in your head, you relax it into the space-like openness. From that place, breathing gently into your belly, you are dropping into the experience of Being. To experience Being, you do not need to do anything. On the contrary, it is through Non-doing that Being is reached. When you already have freedom from the mind, by the very presence of the centre in the midst of thinking, you can let go... you can let go of effort. To put yourself together and to give rise to a centre in the midst of mental chaos, you need to use strong will and focus; but when the sense of Self is already present and your attention is crystallised, you can let go of will. Letting go of the will is subtle, for you are using will to let go of will. It is similar to the art of falling asleep - one does cooperate.

You are letting go into Being. You have to learn what this means. You have to experience it in yourself and verify it with your own intelligence. You are letting go into non-activity and the energy naturally drops downwards, pulled by the force of gravity. It gravitates into the direction of Hara, the energy centre in the belly. The Hara is the meeting point of the unmanifested energy of the Absolute with the individual I Am. Although we say that energy gravitates toward the belly, in truth, the centre of gravity is beyond our physical form. It cannot be found in the space-time dimension.

Just being. There is no need to do anything. Your attention is not directed anywhere - it rests in Being, in Shikan-taza. You are slowly learning the meaning of non-abidance. Non-abidance is Reality. Because, unconsciously, you are identified with physical reality, the information of non-abidance passes over your head; but if you wish to enter the plane of the Universal I AM, you must reach the complete understanding of Non-abidance.

Being without Presence lacks clarity. Those who experience Being without Presence might go deep into Samadhi, into absorption, but they will never be able to take this experience into life. It is very much the tendency of Hindu spirituality. The Inner State, we are pointing to, is one with life. It contains the dynamics of Existence, the richness and complexity of your Me, the mind and the evolution of feelings.

When you are awakened to the State of Presence and you rest in Being, the presence of Awareness becomes integrated with the depth of inner stillness. The calmness, the energy of rest and the clarity of Awareness create one field of the I Am, the whole experience of the I Am. This is the true meaning of Shikan-taza. To have this total experience of the I Am, all elements need to be awakened and activated. This is Shikan-taza beyond traditions and beyond Zen, for it brings the elements of the Heart and sensitivity into the space of inner stillness. The space of Shikantaza that we transmit to you is soft, delicate and vulnerable...it is a meeting of strength, solidity within and child-like innocence of the Heart. It is the divine paradox.

Because stabilisation in the State of Presence is our priority, from time to time you need to bring attention to the head to activate the State of Presence. The State of Presence must be clear and strong. When you have this experience, next you relax in your head and further let yourself drop into Being, into Nondoing. From time to time you repeat this circular movement. Even when you rest in Being, naturally, at times, Awareness is more activated and you find yourself more in the State of Presence, again you drop into Being.

Sometimes some spontaneous thinking might arise or you simply find yourself thinking about a certain subject...and it is alright as long as you don't lose the energetic presence of your centre. Certainly, thinking is not our intention during meditation, for meditation, like prayer is a time for inner silence and not for mundane affairs; but one cannot fully suppress thinking as long as one is alive. Know it and accept it. When you catch yourself thinking, see it and let go into the I Am.

It is important, from time to time, to check your state. This checking is a function of the intuitive intelligence, which is a combination of a subtle thought, a subtle feeling and the sense of Presence. This checking should not be excessive, but should be done at times to verify the quality of the experience you are in and for the purpose of learning. Simplistic teachings about "no-mind" might give an impression that one should not, at all, use the function of the intuitive intelligence. In that way, one would block the essential process of learning and expansion. As you know, the no-mind state is, in truth, multidimensional and does not merely describe the absence of thinking. To understand what you experience, to appreciate the Inner State and to see if you are making progress, you need to use your intelligence.

Breathing slowly into your belly and relaxing into the pure

experience of Being, into the place where Awareness and the energy of rest meet — the unity of clarity and calmness.

At this stage, you can become aware of your Heart centre. You start with breathing into this area deeply to make it vibrate, to warm it up. The Heart is the ultimate goal c. our practice. Nothing is more important than to awaken our Soul and to meet the Divine...and this takes place only in the Heart. Reaching of the Heart cannot be complete, unless a centre in the mind is created and there is depth of Being. Awareness creates the continuity of intelligence and attention, whereas Being gives us the foundation of rest in Reality. Being and Awareness are like the roots and branches of a tree - without them the flower of the Heart cannot blossom and the fruit of the Soul cannot be born.

Feeling your Heart, please, put your hands on the middle of the chest. Simultaneously, be connected to Being, resting within the Now. The vibration of the Heart changes the quality of Being. It becomes more expansive, more vibrating, warm and sensitive - steeped with the Divine. Yes...

Bring back the clear experience of the State of Presence. During activities you need to remember the State of Presence at all times. Each moment is the moment of practice. While walking, talking, eating, reading — you keep at the back of your mind the State of Presence, until it becomes your permanent abode, your inner refuge. Remember it! It is your best friend. Therefore, do not lose it, do not forsake it.

Keeping the State of Presence and relaxing it in your head. Let it be as it is, in its natural condition without any modifications. Effortlessly, you abide in it. A deep, profound, relaxed space of Awareness that is like a bright sky without limits and boundaries. The Universal Consciousness, the infinite knowingness, pure Awareness free from any object - pure subjectivity... never born but containing all dimensions of time and space: all dreams, containing the infinity of possibilities. That you are...

Breathing gently into your belly, you allow the Presence to drop into Being. Non-abiding - pure consciousness meeting pure rest. That which is prior to consciousness is within Being. Even the infinity of consciousness dwells within it. Just Being, the highest of all arts, where the Soul becomes one with Existence and can finally rest, can be at ease...

What is this Soul? It is in the Heart. It is the essence of your Me in the Heart. Feel it. The ultimate centre of the I Am is the Heart. It is in your Heart that you can meet the Heart of Existence, the Creator, the Beloved herself, your Divine Mother - your true parent.

Feel your Heart. With each inhalation feel the sweet nectar of your Heart and with each exhalation let go, relax, surrender deeper and deeper into the depth of the Heart. Tune into the Other Side of the Heart, which is the Beloved. The Heart is like a palm of a hand: one side is the Soul and the other is the Beloved. The same hand but two sides: Me and the Creator. Who gave birth to your Soul? To discover it is the final Enlightenment, which is not a state but deep understanding of who we really are. It is Enlightenment to the Beloved... beyond meditation, beyond emptiness. At this place we become Love... simply Love.

Your Awareness, Being and Heart melt into one... but the Heart remains your centre, a gateway to the Beyond through which the Beyond has come to pull you to itself, to call you back home into the Light, into Love. You are moved and touched, for you are returning home to the domain of Love. At last you are awakening from the dream of separation. You are returning home...

PEACE LOVE GRACE

# Absolute Meditation:
# Advanced II

Beloved friends, welcome to the second stage of the Absolute Meditation. Absolute Meditation is about our wholeness, about the complete awakening of the I Am: the awakening of Awareness, the awakening of Being and the awakening of the Heart. It aims at a multidimensional awakening and is not simply about awakening to "one thing."

The second stage of the Absolute Meditation is designed for those who clearly recognise the State of Presence, which, in truth, is a foundation and the real beginning of the spiritual path, the path of awakening. The State of Presence represents the awakening of attention, the point where attention recognises attention, where attention becomes aware of attention in an objectless way. That's why we call it pure "I," pure subject, witness, bare-naked Awareness without any object, the centre of the mind, the centre of intelligence, the essence of Consciousness. It is an area of experience where Consciousness recognises itself, frees itself from any object, from any perception, from perceiving the other. It pulls back to itself, turns back to itself and recognises itself as the only reality: as that which does not change, that which is always at the background of becoming, beyond the psychological movement.

When the observer of the mind, the one who is aware of the mind, turns upon itself and sees its own face, the State of Presence is born. That is the awakening. This awakening takes place in the mind. The centre of watchfulness is located in the middle of the brain, in the third eye. It is certainly not the whole of us, but it is our centre in consciousness, the centre of intelligence and its creative movement. We call it the Me in the mind. This Me is not an ego, it is not an outcome of thoughts. It does not change: it simply is...

When you have recognised clearly your own Presence, which is your own light, it is a sign that you have matured, you have grown. You are no longer lost on the spiritual path, you recognise your own centre. Only now can you say: I Am. Here, the goal and its seeker meet. It does not mean that the Path is over, but it is no longer dualistic. The goal is no longer in the future. It unfolds itself as part of the Now. Until your Path is completed, certainly there is an evolution within the Now. You are going deeper and deeper into the Now for, as we know, the Now is multidimensional. The Now is not simply a point between the future and the past. The Now has depth, the depth of Reality. We are delving deeper and deeper within the Now until we reach a point where our individuality merges with Wholeness. Here, human evolution ends but universal evolution continues in a mysterious way and beyond comprehension.

We are now entering a non-dualistic stage of practice, where the Presence is recognised and where awakening refers to the Now. We would like to guide you through the second stage of the Absolute Meditation, because even though you have recognised the State of Presence, you still need to grow and the situation is quite complex. You need to grow into the stabilisation of the State of Presence, and you need to grow in Understanding. You need to understand how the State of Presence and your psyche, your mind, your relative Me relate to each other. Also, you need to grow deeper into your connection with Being and finally you need to evolve into the awakening of the Heart.

Breathing deeply into your belly you relax into Being, relax into the Now, let the energy drop, settle down into the experience of just sitting. If you have any worries about your life, let go of them, have the courage to let go. To let go, you must have the courage, courage which comes from trust and understanding. You are not alone. Intelligence, the wisdom of life is encompassing the whole of you and sees your life, sees your destiny. The less you worry about yourself, the more you are protected, for you trust. — you have matured to trust.

When your energy has settled, please, recognise clearly the

State of Presence in your mind, this crystallisation of attention which is self-attention. The destroyer of the mind, the destroyer of the mechanical mind, your own Presence... It is your own light which replaces the unconscious movement of thoughts. The "I," the subject, the point which is nearest to you. You pull back from being involved in thoughts into the State of Presence. You centralise yourself in that which does not change, does not move, which always has the same taste of I.

We would like to ask you to breathe slowly to your belly throughout the whole meditation, but this time you breathe without special focus, for the focus is on the State of Presence. Fully recognising the State of Presence, let it relax in your head. When you pull back to the State of Presence, there is an element of tension and it is being experienced like a point, a sharp point of Awareness. Now you relax it into the spacious feeling of openness. At this moment of the practice, stabilisation in the State of Presence is our priority. That's why, at all times make sure that you are in this state, that your Presence vibrates in your mind — that there is constantly this point in your mind which is self aware. When you are certain of it, you relax with it into the non-referring space of Being. That is the art of holding and letting go, letting go and holding. If you hold too much, it becomes too tense, when you let go too much, the state can be lost and you become unconscious. This you should not allow.

You are breathing to your belly and somehow relaxing into your Being. You might notice how the energy of Awareness moves into Being and you experience it all-over you. This is what we call, "Shikantaza," just sitting. This state is a unity of Awareness and Being — they meet and merge into one experience. Although the I AM is a unity of Awareness and Being, within this unity, there is a natural movement. When you are calm, when you simply sit down, the Being aspect is experienced more strongly; when you are active, when you become more involved, attention aspect, Awareness is experienced more strongly. We emphasise stabilisation in the State of Presence, for it is this part of the I Am which can be brought fully into life. It can be established as a permanent centre at the background of your psychological self, your relative Me.

Relaxing into Being, the energy drops downwards, according to the law of gravity, and this gravity goes to the belly. The centre of gravity of all Universes is the Absolute, the Unborn, and in our human form the gateway to the Absolute is the Hara. Many seekers are confused because in different teachings we find contradictory information regarding which centre in our body is the most important... but in reality we have, simply, several centres. There is the centre of Being in the belly; the centre of Consciousness in the mind; and there is the centre of our Soul in the Heart. These three centres, in their unity, create the holistic centre of the I AM.

Pull, again, your attention to the mind, to the State of Presence, crystallising the experience of Awareness in the head. From time to time you have to energise the centre of watchfulness in the head by paying attention to it. You are breathing slowly to the belly and keeping your attention in the mind, feeling your State of Presence in a solid way and, at the same time, relaxing it, but in the head not into Being.

If you look at your mind, you will see that the State of Presence and a certain movement of thoughts co-exist. Who you are is not only the State of Presence which is witnessing the impersonal movement of the mind. You are also the intelligence within the movement of the mind. This intelligence is very close to the State of Presence. The State of Presence is being witnessed by the movement of intelligence as well; it is like double witnessing. The State of Presence is witnessing the mind; while, on the other hand, the movement of intelligence is becoming continuously aware of the State of Presence. It is very rich. You, as a State of Presence, you are witnessing the mind; and you, as the mind, relate to the State of Presence. For instance, when you make the intention to become more strongly aware of the State of Presence, you can notice that you change the quality of this state; it becomes intensified. If the State of Presence was only witnessing the mind, it would not change its quality.

Hence, the State of Presence and the mind co-exist. For that reason, the elimination of the mind, the elimination of thoughts is not necessary and, in truth, impossible. When you are connected strongly with the State of Presence, the relationship with the mind changes and there are fewer and fewer thoughts. The thinking process slows down gradually, but thinking should not be completely eliminated for it is part of our wholeness. Those teachers, who speak about not-thinking as the goal, are ignorant.

Apart from the State of Presence in the mind, there is a spontaneous manifestation of thoughts from the sub-conscious mind and, in-between them, we see the creative movement of the intuitive intelligence. The intuitive intelligence is beyond the gross level of thinking and it is more dynamic than the State of Presence. This is your mind, that is who you are in the mind.

When you are in the State of Presence, there are a few ways you can relate to the thinking process. In the first way, you are simply abiding in the State of Presence and the mind is silent or some thoughts arise and disappear. In this case, there is some gentle spontaneous thinking but you yourself remain unmoved in the State of Presence.

In the second way, you are in the State of Presence and you have an observing mood. You are noticing thoughts and consciously letting go of them. In this case, your attitude towards thinking in more active; you are observing it. It is not the State of Presence which is doing the observing. The State of Presence is witnessing which means it remains, always, passive. That which is observing, is the mind or rather the mind's intelligence, which is the deeper part of the mind. It is actively noticing thoughts and can create an attitude towards them. For instance, this intelligence decides whether to let go of arising thoughts or to co-create in the thinking process (conscious thinking).

In the third way of relating to thoughts, you choose to participate in thinking. In such a case, even though you are in the State of Presence, you still choose to participate in thinking. Here, it is your own will to think. All these ways of relating to the mind are valid and they interchange. In meditation, certainly, it is not your wish to think too much and to be involved in the mind. Some spontaneous thinking is natural but you do not intend to think actively. Therefore, you are letting go of thoughts, connecting more deeply with the State of Presence and Being. Meditation is like a time for prayer; it is a time of surrender, a deep and sacred moment in our life.

You are keeping the State of Presence and relaxing it in your mind, breathing slowly to the belly and letting the energy drop slowly towards Being. From time to time, you check your state in a very gentle way, in a way that you do not manipulate the state. You simply see and feel it. This checking is again done by your intuitive intelligence. Sometimes, you check consciously to know what it happening with you and to understand your state. Without checking, gentle checking, you cannot understand your state and neither can you grow. That's why it has to be done — in a balanced way, of course. At times, you simply know... there is a direct knowing of what state you are in, and checking is not necessary.

Coming back to the State of Presence, intensifying it in the mind, relaxing it in the head... holding and letting go. You are feeling the State of Presence like a space, a bright space of Awareness... surrendering into Being — into Not-knowing. Non-abiding where attention is direction-less but simply rests pulled by the Absolute. When we surrender, when we are deeply relaxed, we are naturally being pulled into the direction of the Unmanifested, the Source of Existence which is the centre of gravity, the centre of all. It is like falling into a deep sleep without dreams; something takes us into itself, liberates us from our Me... and we can rest so deeply! Meditation is the same, only the experience of rest is conscious. That's why our Me continues to exits, being a part of the experience. Here, our presence and our absence meet — Consciousness and that which is prior to Consciousness meet. We relax into Being, just being, Being and Awareness meet. Yes...

We are breathing slowly to the belly. During the exhalation we are pushing slightly the breath so our belly becomes flat, and we inhale gently, expanding our belly. At times, we breathe more intensely and at times more gently, relaxing.

Just sitting means: Non-doing. It might sound simple but it is not. Usually, when we think that we are in the state of just being, still, we manipulate our state. We are performing many different subtle doings within our state. Non-doing means to let go, as if we have become absent... and only Being remains.

We surrender into Being, into this sweetness and bliss of Being. In Whom are we being? What is this experience of Being, in truth? In reality, it is not ourselves that we experience but the universal I AM, the Beyond. Being is not us. It is the One, God, Existence: that which created us and now it receives us back. We are coming back home, awakening ourselves from the illusion of separation and re-uniting with the One... with God.

Without awakened Awareness we might experience, partially, this oneness within Being, but this experience cannot become solid and constant, for the mind will quickly come back, taking us away again from the Depth. Awareness, pure Awareness is a bridge between the psychological self, the psyche, the mind and the dimension of Beingness. That's why the State of Presence is so important. It is the foundation although it is not the end. Surrender into Being and the awakening of the Heart are our final goals. The State of Presence is a bridge. It frees us from unconsciousness.

You have to cultivate the State of Presence in every movement. In every situation you need to ask yourself "where is my I?" "Where is my Presence?" "Am I getting lost?" "Is it still at the background?" You have to remember more and more. The more the centre of wakefulness is awakened, the more it will remember itself spontaneously without you remembering it. It becomes automatic, as it should be.

There are two levels of self-remembrance. The first one, is an energy experience of the state itself. For example, you are lost in thoughts, trying to solve some important problems and not paying attention to the State of Presence. However, afterwards, you come back to yourself and you remember, through your subtle memory, that the state has not been lost - it has been vibrating.

The second level of self-remembrance is a function of your

intelligence. For instance, suddenly you direct your attention to the State of Presence and become aware of it. So the second level of self-remembrance is more personal. Here, it is You who remembers. In the first case, the remembrance is impersonal — the state remembers itself. When stabilisation in the State of Presence takes place, the remembrance is constant. It means that the first level of remembrance is constant. The second level of remembrance (where you remember the state) cannot be constant because it would be unnatural. You cannot constantly remember any state. From time to time, you must allow yourself to be spontaneous. In the functioning of the human mind and intelligence, there always has to be a place for the spontaneous activity of the subconscious mind. Otherwise, you would go insane!

But during cultivation, when you want to become established in the State of Presence, you do have to remember it as much as you can. The stabilisation is not equated with the constant personal remembrance of the state! You are not stabilised in the State of Presence by constant remembrance. Stabilisation takes place on the energy level. Through remembering, you simply activate the centre of wakefulness. When it is activated enough and your energy is mature, the stabilising moment takes place. The presence of a Master and Grace can create à shortcut.

We hope that you understand now who recognises the State of Presence. Firstly, the State of Presence recognises itself by its very vibration. Secondly, the creative intuitive intelligence of your mind is doing the additional recognition.

Please, bring the State of Presence to your mind. Feel it strongly and relax it in your head. At the beginning, you oscillate between the subject and the reality of objects. The experience of the State of Presence you might describe as pure subject. The moment you direct attention to the phenomenal reality, your Awareness starts to operate in the realm of objects; if you are not integrated, the State of Presence gets lost. In the perception of objective reality, you become exteriorised from the inner reality, taken away from the centre. In the cultivating process, you learn more and more how to retain the experience of the subject, while perceiving objects and being involved in activities. That is the purpose of this whole expansion of Consciousness. You are uniting the subjective and the objective polarities of Existence and, finally, you arrive at the state where the subject and the object are experienced as one.

In that moment, we can say that we are in the state of Oneness. It is one level of Oneness. The experience of Oneness is also multidimensional. Ultimately, the experience of Oneness takes place when there is a unity of Presence, depth of Being and fullness of the Heart. The Heart knows the Oneness in its own unique way and in its own divine dimension. In the Heart, the Soul meets the Heart of the Creator.

You are feeling your Presence in the head like a bright space of Awareness. With the breath to the belly you drop into the Beingness, you let go into Non-doing. You remain in the state of just sitting without any focus or direction of attention, in the state of Non-abidance.

We might ask where the meeting with the Unborn takes place. Only when we understand the different aspects of the I Am, can we have a clear insight into this subtle area. It is within the Being aspect of the I Am, that the meeting with the Unborn takes place. The State of Presence, the flowering of attention or the centre of creative intelligence is born in time. It is the essence of Manifestation and the essence of Consciousness. The Unborn, the Absolute is not in the manifested reality, but below the field of Consciousness. The Absolute is the unmanifested energy of the Source. It can be realised only through the Being aspect of the I AM.

When the Being aspect of the I Am meets the Absolute, when the inner Gate opens up, one shifts to the state of Pure Rest. This state is beyond manifestation and beyond consciousness. Here, the Unborn is met. It is important to understand that you meet the universal I AM only within Being. Not through intelligence, not through perception but through Being... and through the Heart. The Heart, ultimately, is one with Being. It is a dimension of Being, for the depth of the Heart is beyond emotion. In the Heart, the Soul dissolves into the Beloved, into Being of the Beloved. The Beloved, the Creator, is the unity of Absolute Rest and Love. Love of the Beloved is her Beingness.

Just being, you merge with the One, you merge with the Wholeness. It is through Non-activity that you merge, reaching the Oneness. Reaching God takes place through Non-doing, through letting go... through being so deeply relaxed that you simply disappear. Dwelling in the State of Meditation and the depth of appreciation are not the same. Appreciation of the Inner State and the experience of it, are not the same. Appreciation is, in truth, a fruit of understanding which is the meeting of intelligence and sensitivity.

Your intelligence has to grow, your sensitivity has to deepen in this process. You must wake up to the fact that you are meeting your Self, your own Soul...you are merging with the realm of Ultimate Sensitivity, which is the Light of Creation. You are not simply sitting. Your sitting has to be awakened. You have to awaken not only to the inner experience, but to the understanding of this experience as well. We can call this the second level of Enlightenment.

See how amazing the experience of I Am is. So many lifetimes you have been searching for it! How could you now take it for granted? See the value of the Inner State; feel gratitude to the Existence which allowed you to enter the dimension of Silence, Being, Awareness and Love. You are blessed...

Feel your Presence, intensifying your Awareness. Relax it in the head and relax in Being. Slowly breathing to your belly, drop into the state of just being, just sitting. You have been lost for so long in the dimension of forgetfulness, identified with the personality and with the mind! You have not existed, in truth, living like a shadow, like a ghost dreaming in the reality of appearances. Now, you are emerging, out of sorrow, into the light and all the shadows vanish. The darkness cannot live in the presence of Light. Now you are being awakened to your own self. You have matured. Now you see clearly that the awakening is about you. It is your personal meeting, personal encounter with the Truth that is intimate and so close to you...

You do not care anymore about becoming anybody else. You do not want to become Buddha. You are becoming yourself, your own Self. You have matured, you have clarity, for clarity has been given to you. It is not you who gave rise to this clarity - it has been given to you. You have received a gift, so be grateful. So many are lost in ignorance! Your responsibility is to follow the path of light which you already see. It is your own light. With sincerity, continue your practice and your inner journey until the moment of reaching complete Peace and fulfillment. It is not far...

There is negative evolution and positive evolution. Negative evolution is concerned with getting out of suffering and leaving the state of misery and forgetfulness. When you are awakened to your own light, the evolution does not stop but it becomes positive. Evolution is a never-ending expansion into Wholeness. It cannot have an end, because Wholeness itself has no end — it is bottomless, infinite.

Now we will direct our attention to the centre of the I Am which is our Heart. The Heart is the beginning and the end. It is the Heart which seeks and it is the Heart which has to be found in the end. It is the Heart which suffers, which needs to discover its inner silence and connection with Being. It is the Heart which has to awaken Awareness in order to free itself from the mind. It is the Heart...and what is this Heart? Who are you in the Heart? You are feeling it now...

Put your hands on the chest, put your hands on your Heart. Breathe deeply to your chest, feeling the Heart. The Heart is your true centre. It is your final and ultimate centre. It is in the Heart that you meet the Heart of Creation, which is the Beloved, the Friend. Who created your Heart? Who is holding your Heart? It is the Creator, your eternal Parent. She gave birth to your Soul. It is She who wants you to evolve, to come back to her womb and to return to her Heart.

Feel your Heart. Let it merge with your Being. Let it merge with the whole of who you are. You are like a child in your Heart. You are a child and you will always be a child. You are a child of the Beloved, child of the Creator. Feel it...

To meet your Creator you have to cry. The tears in your Heart will wash your Heart, so it becomes innocent, as it always has been. As you have to wake up to the State of Presence and to Being, so you have to wake up to your Soul, which is in the Heart. You are a Soul — this is your true image, the divine spark from the eternal fire, which journeys in the dimension of time towards the Timeless.

Feel your Heart and allow it to become one with the State of Meditation. You are silent, you are deep... You are moved; you are touched by the Beloved; you are seen by the Friend... and you are blessed.

### GRACE PEACE LOVE

# IV

# TRANSMISSION
# OF
# AWAKENING

# Transmission 1
## India: 22nd October 98

Beloved friends, welcome to the Place of Inner Silence, which is the destination for every Soul in her eternal evolution towards becoming one with the Divine. You are invited to make a next step in your evolution where you can transcend the fundamental limitation, which is the identification with the mind. You are returning to your eternal identity, to the I Am - the clear experience of Consciousness prior to thoughts, prior to the movement of the mind...

The process of awakening from this limitation of perception where one is the mind, where one is fully identified with the arising of thoughts, is quite complex. It requires the activation of certain faculties within you. First one has to activate Awareness. The essence of Awareness is attention. Attention is the closest point in you which is conscious and present. It operates in a split of a second so you cannot capture it, but you know it directly. Crystallisation of attention creates the bridge between the unconscious and mechanical mind and the depth of Being, which is the original stillness of Existence and with which we are eternally linked but temporarily disconnected.

The I Am is made of Awareness, Being and Heart. That is the true meaning of Sat-Chit-Ananda, the full reality of Brahman. Sat is the depth of Being, which is beyond Awareness. Chit is Consciousness, which in its pure form represents the State of Presence or non-dual Awareness without object, and Ananda is the happiness of the Heart, our divine flavour.

Our meetings are based on Meditation. As Satsang has been designed traditionally, the element of practice is missing strongly. The way we work here is a particular combination of the Buddhist and Advaita energies, but the main Energy which comes through during our meetings is beyond human traditions. It comes from the higher source of Universal Intelligence or Guidance.

In each of our meditation sessions we will be working with the awakening to the complete experience of the I Am. We will be exploring the three aspects of the I Am, activating them and uniting into one experience, the holistic experience of who you are. These meetings are very practical. With the technology of Consciousness that we are using, each of you can be awakened. That is the truth. But only if you sincerely and diligently co-operate.

It is only if you devote yourself fully and surrender to the Path, that you will succeed without a doubt. We represent here the universal understanding not a human tradition or a master. The presence of the Divine channels itself into this human dimension to accelerate the process of evolution — it wishes to help its creation. It wishes to help you, for you are in a state of sorrow, whether you know it or not... you are disconnected from Reality, you have no roots. Living in a complete dream and illusion where love cannot enter, your Soul cries for help. And this help is given to you, but you must co-operate.

To regain the inherent connection with the Light of Creation is the task of evolution. This evolution takes place in time. Time is moving within Timelessness and the timelessness is embraced by the Mystery, which is God. Now, within the dimension of time we create the spiritual path through which we wish to realise that which is beyond the field of time. The spiritual path bridges the state of ignorance or forgetfulness with the state of awakening or remembrance. The spiritual path ultimately is an illusion but this illusion is the Reality of human dimension and, therefore, must be respected.

Please, before we begin our meditation, take a comfortable position so you can sit without moving too much and you will be able to focus inside. During meditation we bring certain energies which represent discipline, mindfulness, concentration, determination and strength. These are the male qualities, the warrior qualities that are absolutely necessary to cut through the unconscious inertia of the mind.

Beloved friends, what is meditation? It is nothing! It is to be at the zero point. It is to abide within the vortex of the Now, the essence of the Now, which is your own existence. The ability to rest in the Now is the foundation of sanity. Meditation is a state of Being and, simultaneously, the process of deepening the experience of the Now. Before we can speak about the depth of the Now, we must learn how to go beyond the mind, which is the past and the future. Next, we need to learn how to surrender into the state of Being, which is the Now. Being or Now itself is beyond the present moment. The present moment is the immediate past already. That's why the Now cannot be grasped, but you can become it!

We begin with connecting to the breath in the belly. Please, breathe slowly and deeply. There is no way of reaching any steady state of consciousness, unless the energy is transformed and deepened. Because the centre of energy is in the belly, we emphasise breathing into this area. The awakening is not only the function of intelligence. The intelligence is a movement and, in itself, is unable to retain and give continuity to any experience. Energy is the primal force upon which Existence is founded. Therefore, energy has to be harmonised and adjusted in order to uphold the continuity of the inner state.

We begin our meditation with the basic principle that there is nothing to be reached. There is no goal. The goal is to be where you are, so the goal has already been attained! But because you tend to lose the connection with this very experience of Being, the need for pulling back arises. With this understanding, we relax into Being, remaining, however, watchful of the mind and letting go of thoughts as they arise. The combination of resting within the Now and a certain quality of attention will allow you to place yourself in the area of existing, where you actually precede the coming of thoughts.

The art of Being, the art of Non-doing is very subtle. Non-doing is not merely a lack of activity but an energy experience of stillness. This Non-doing is your presence, your very amness, the positive experience of being truly alive. Non-doing is not

manifested by your passivity. You have to create it! You must
expand into Non-doing. Something much bigger than you must
be there, to receive your presence within itself. This is what you
might afterwards translate as being in a state of rest, or simply
calm. Some meditators are not able to see the whole depth of
the State of Meditation. They usually say, "we were in a very
calm state." A great deal of sensitivity and intelligence, in truth,
is necessary to understand the real depth behind the experience
of Being. That's why we speak so much. To whom do we speak?
To this very intelligence which is listening and cannot grasp the
full meaning of this teaching yet. We create your intelligence!

We let go of the mind and we let go into Being. With each
inhalation you are very attentive and with each exhalation you
let go, surrendering vertically into Being. As you are dropping
into the experience of Being, with a certain sense of curiosity,
try to see what it is that is happening to you. What it means,
in reality, to Be. What does it mean? Let this knowing come
to you, as it is directly experienced.

As you breathe be attentive. You are creating the continuity
of attention. The mind is accepted as it is. Do not create a desire
to stop thinking. You have not created this mind, why would you
wish to eliminate it? Simply do not identify with it. You are
ignoring the mind, neither participating in it nor fighting with it.
Breathing into the belly and relaxing into Being.

You have a weight. Your Soul has a weight. The moment
you let go of any doing, your energy is moving down towards
the direction of Complete Rest. The Source, the invisible dimension
of Beingness is pulling you into itself. Like a tree, you are
growing roots into the dimension of Beingness. You have been
like a leaf and now you become solid as a strong tree, a mountain
that cannot be moved by the mosquitoes of the mind anymore.

You are in the process, so be patient. It is a process of
dissolution into Wholeness. It takes time. But it cannot fail! You
are sitting like a tiger in the middle of a jungle waiting for its
prey. With each exhalation you are letting go into the nakedness
of this very moment, into the Unknown. In the absence of yourself,

you meet your true presence. In the absence of the mind you
meet the I Am. Who is meeting this I Am? It is your Soul, the
one who dwells in the middle of your chest...

* * *

There is the Path of Grace and there is the Path of will. Advaita
is the Path of Grace and Buddhism is the Path of will. Although
Advaita is called the path of Self-knowledge, in reality it is the
path of Grace. Self-knowledge, in terms of having an insight into
our true nature, is not enough to bring a radical transformation.
The misconception of this tradition is the idealistic vision of the
Self. According to their concept, it is sufficient to recognise the
Self in order to become it - as there is only the Self. But it is
not true and many have suffered from this unsolvable contradiction.
The Self is the only reality but in our dimension is Realised by
the Me. This Me has not been seen and comprehended,
unfortunately. The Me actually becomes one with the I AM. It
is not the I AM, but this which becomes united with the I AM.
   Therefore, realisation of the Self is a process and not simply
an instant Illumination. This was the main contradiction the
Advaita masters were caught in. At one stage they had to deny
even the act of Enlightenment. If one becomes Enlightened, it
means that the Self, just a moment before Enlightenment, "was
not the Only Reality!" The very co-existence of the Self and
ignorance is a contradiction if we follow their way of thinking.
The true power of Advaita is the power of Transmission. The
Enlightened State has been transmitted generation after generation
by the presence of Masters and the esoteric energies belonging
to this tradition. However Transmission is not always enough
in order to manifest the state of Self-realisation. The disciple
must be ready in their energy system, intelligence and maturity
of the Soul. For that reason, co-operation and the element of
practice is so important!
   Without Grace transformation is not possible; without will,
without effort Grace does not enter. That is the law. One has
to do all that is possible to help the process of awakening...and
we can do a lot! Why, do you think, we have been given this

enormous amount of energy? Why have we been given our Heart and intelligence? Is it just to sit around and wait for Enlightenment to happen? No, it is our responsibility of co-creation to use them in order to evolve... We represent Grace itself, but simultaneously we are giving you a tool, with which you yourself can work and accelerate your own awakening. So please, co-operate. Grab firmly onto your destiny in your hands and grow...

We are returning again to this Mystery, which is the direct experience of oneself Now. Although you experience yourself Now, indeed, this experience is not necessarily complete. It is not true, what they say, that we are all Buddhas and it is enough to realise it. Buddha has to be born. This experience of the Now, this experience of our own existence within the Now, goes deeper and deeper as evolution continues further and further. This evolution reaches deeper and deeper into the Mystery. One dissolves more and more into the Universal I AM and this dissolution has no end... it is endless. There are two sides of evolution. One is the side of ignorance, the darkness of forgetfulness. Here, we are trying to get out of the mud of unconsciousness and negativity. The other side of evolution is already within the Awakening. One is already a part of the Wholeness, but the evolution continues. There are more secrets. It is not only about getting out of suffering as Buddhists imagine. Here expansion takes place within the already present Happiness.

In our second meditation we are going to explore the nature of Awareness. Awareness is the tool of going beyond the mind, so the surrender into Beingness can follow. Awareness is the light of knowingness which can go in many different directions, different corners of reality. Awakening is the area where this Awareness is no longer identified with any particular direction, but is experiencing itself. The awakened Awareness is self-aware. The source of Awareness, in our particular body, is in the brain. The centre of wakefulness is in the third eye, in the middle of the brain. In the case of an ordinary person, this centre functions at the minimum... just enough to survive — paying attention to the environment and being able to use the intellect efficiently. If we wish to reach the inherent purity of consciousness, we must free ourselves from identification with the subconscious activity of the mind. Awareness must be activated.

Bringing attention to the mind we ask ourselves the question, "what is this which is immediate?" What is it in the mind which is instantaneous? This is the object of our exploration - that which is instantaneous, prior to thought. That which is instantaneous in the mind is its very essence, the centre of Awareness. You can feel it simply as the sense of Me in the mind. When you hear the noise behind the window, attention is immediately activated. But what is this attention itself, without any object? Can you feel it?

Within the movement of the mind is a precious seed, which is attention. Attention is the closest point in the mind, it is the nearest touch of Awareness. That's why, you experience difficulties in recognising it. It is simply too close to You.

We become aware of the mind, observing the mind. The mind is simply the movement of thoughts. We begin with looking carefully at the nature of thoughts. What are they made from? They are made from nothing. Thoughts are empty of any substance. They are expressions of consciousness carrying certain information. A thought cannot be retained - it can be only repeated. As we have been looking at the mind, now we make a gentle step back to recognise the One who is aware of the mind. Certainly there is something which is present behind the mind, isn't it true? We could call it the centre of observation. When you sit in a watchtower looking around at the landscape, your position is in the centre. If you weren't there, how could you make the observation? Find the inner watchtower in the mind. It is the foundation of sanity.

When the centre in the mind is found, attention becomes aware of attention and you are beyond the mind. The vortex in the mind, the empty centre of the mind is beyond the relative movement of thoughts and mental impressions. That is your true identity in the consciousness. To observe the mind is not enough - one must recognise the observer.

Now instead of observing the mind we will practice "conscious thinking." Please, start to think intensively about any subject you wish to choose. Think fully in a contemplative way... When you think consciously, you are present, you know that it is you who is thinking. We would like to ask you to discern, to distinguish the Me who is thinking, from the thinking itself. Gently pulling back, you try to recognise the thinker. When you recognise the thinker, the sense of Me behind the thoughts, you simply hold into it and stay at this place. At this stage you can let go of thinking.

This point where the Me is aware of Me in the mind, is called the State of Presence. If you are experiencing it, centre yourself in it and simultaneously relax in your head. It is an experience in the head. There are some seekers who refuse to keep the energy in the head, for it is against their concept of "no-mind." Because of this attitude they remain unconscious, being unable to make any real progress. It is only when the energy is in the mind, that this mind can be transcended. If you simply ignore the mind, it will remain as it is - in the state of chaos. The energy we speak about is not one of thinking but one of Presence - the light of attention.

The State of Presence has a quality of a centre and space at the same time. It represents these two qualities. When it refers to itself through intelligence, it crystallises the experience of itself into a centre. When it relaxes and is not self-referring, it dissolves into space. For that reason, in Buddhism they speak about the Great Mind which is like a vast infinite sky without any obstructions. This Great Mind contains all thoughts and the whole of reality without being touched. That's why, in Buddhism they speak about the non-existence of phenomena. They say that they are neither existing nor non-existing. These are the philosophical and metaphorical descriptions of this inner realisation.

You are being initiated into the essence of the mind. It is a secret knowledge so, please, appreciate this information. It takes many lifetimes to reach this understanding and realisation.

With breath into the belly relax into Being now. Please, remain focussed! If you experience pain or discomfort, do not react mechanically. Use them to focus even more! Being and Awareness, third eye and Hara, sky and earth....they meet within You. The State of Meditation is a beautiful combination of inner stillness, motionlessness of Being and clarity of Awareness. If this clarity is missing, the State of Meditation is too dull; when the stillness of Being is missing, even if the clarity is there, the State of Meditation lacks certain essential depth and rootedness. The State of Meditation, as you see, is not a simple state, but a very rich inner movement within the Unmoved.

The essential question to be asked is: "what is it from the State of Meditation that one can bring into life, into activity?" The answer is: the State of Presence. The centre of Awareness can be retained in all situations. Our task, apart from recognition of this state, is also stabilisation in it. In that way, it can finally become one with our life and not just an experience we have from time to time. Many are looking for experiences. But we wish you to Become the Experience, to become the I Am.

* * *

Sitting for a long time in one position is not natural for the body. But often we have to do things which are not natural in order to become truly Natural. It is like a medicine, to be used when needed. We can tell you pleasant things about Enlightenment and have a enjoyable time but will it help you? Because of compassion we introduce the element of discipline and practice. It is not hard discipline, it is not Zen discipline - just a basic amount of discipline, which is truly essential.

Let us relax into Being. In Being attention has no horizontal direction but surrenders vertically into Non-doing, into Rest. When attention rests in an ordinary person, it becomes unconscious. When attention rests in meditation, it merges with Being - it is still conscious but in a state of rest. That is the meaning of Non-abiding. In Buddhism they say that the Great Mind has no abiding place. Where could it abide if nothing exists beyond its frontiers? We live presently in the realm of the Manifested. We are closed within the perception of time and space, like birds in a cage. The biggest riddle for all real seekers is: where is the way out, where is Beyond the cage? Where is the secret way to the Beyond, where is the unmanifested? How can one find the unmanifested if the only reality we experience is the manifested? Where is the Gateless Gate? The answer is not a concept but an experience. This experience is itself: Understanding...

The Beyond is hidden within the Now. The Beyond is the essence of the Now - it is the Now itself! The Now in truth is not Here. It does not exist in time and space. That's why, the Now is not the present moment. The present moment is the past already! The Now cannot be grasped but can be attained through surrender. At that moment, we become received by the depth of the Now and we find ourselves on the Other Side, the other side of the Now, which is not Here. Everyone wonders how a Buddha can be recognised. Everyone is looking for some special signs, behaviors and powers... but Buddha cannot be recognised for his/ her state is not Here, it is Beyond. "The beauty of his garden is invisible and ten thousands sages could not find him." The only way to find the Buddha is to become one — to disappear into the Beyond...

We relax into Now, into this which is beyond understanding. Each moment is a moment of surrender, letting go. Each moment is a moment of meeting. Only because we live in time, can the Unborn be met. The State of Enlightenment is not merely a State, the experience of it is arising in time - it re-appears as the subsequent experience of the Now arises. The Soul as she exists in time, is continuously meeting the Ultimate. It is not a State - it is an eternal meeting...

Reality can be divided into the unmanifested which has its gateway within the Hara and into the manifested, which is Consciousness. When one reaches the Absolute State, the pull from the unmanifested takes away the will to live in the manifested. One becomes fully disidentified on the energy level. The meeting point between unmanifested energy and manifested reality, is the Heart. When the Heart centre is awakened, on the energy level, one moves from the unmanifested to the middle point, which is neither in nor out — the meeting place between the inner and the outer.

The Heart is the place where our Soul is situated. Being awakened to the unmanifested does not mean that one is awakened to the Soul- the Soul may still not be aware of herself.

You bring your attention to the Heart centre in the middle of the chest, with the intention of becoming aware of the Soul. The Soul is your unique and individual flavour in the Heart. Who are You? Someone is experiencing the hardship of meditation in order to reach a better way of living. Who is this one? Someone is seeking happiness and is tired of suffering. Who is this one? Someone here wishes to return home and to reach the place of ultimate security, which is God. That one is Real! It is not simply the movement of impersonal consciousness, nor is it merely the mind. It is You and it is your challenge to discover what it means in reality.

We put our hands on the Heart feeling it deeply. Becoming intimate with who we are, with the innocence and simplicity of our Heart which is always pure. The mind has accumulated the dust of experiences and created our adult personality. But the Heart has remained the same, the child of God, the child of the Beloved. Breathing deeply to the chest, we tune into the presence of the One who resides inside of the chest - our own Soul. Let it speak....

GRACE PEACE LOVE

# Transmission 2
## India: 20th November 98

Today we will have one meditation instead of three shorter ones. It is a more advanced Satsang. The teaching will be directed mostly to those who recognise the State of Presence, which is Awareness without thoughts. The recognition of Awareness without thoughts is very important. We can call it the first awakening.

As far as the state of pure Awareness is concerned, there is awakening and there is Enlightenment. Awakening is recognition of the State of Presence or witnessing consciousness. It takes place when Awareness recognises itself without an object. Enlightenment is simply stabilisation where the state does not leave us anymore, it no longer becomes lost.

The term Enlightenment, although one word, refers to various states of awakening. There is not one Enlightenment, there are several kinds of Enlightenment. There is Enlightenment to the State of Presence, Awareness without thoughts; there is Enlightenment to the Absolute State, which is a condition of pure rest realised within the Being aspect of I Am. Next there is Enlightenment of the Heart, which is a separate dimension of awakening; and there is Enlightenment to the Soul, which, reflected in all those states, recognises herself, her eternal identity within the Heart centre.

Apart from Enlightenment to the Inner States, there is the whole process of enlightening of intelligence. Enlightenment of intelligence is as important as Enlightenment to the Inner States, because it is the recognising intelligence which gives meaning to any state. Enlightenment of intelligence is even more difficult than Enlightenment to the Inner States. It takes many lifetimes of evolution for the intelligence to grow so it can comprehend the subtleties of reality, both the inner and the outer.

There is the inner world and there is the outer world. The inner world is the perceiver, the outer world is the perceived. That's why, the psychic and psychological reality can be seen also as the outer, because it belongs to the perceived. Normally one lives only in the external reality and in the psychological reality, being disconnected from the inner world. Later, evolving, one discovers the inner dimension. When the inner is discovered, one oscillates between the experience of the inner and the experience of the outer. Only when the Inner States are complete, is the necessity of practice transcended. At this point, for the first time one experiences the unity of the inner and the outer, one sees the inner and the outer as one. The inner and the outer are terms referring to different ways of looking at reality; in truth it is One Reality, it is God.

The awakening happens through the subject, it is not happening in the objective reality, it happens through the subject. The subject or I is a gateway to the dimension of awakening. That's why the question, "Who am I?" is the foundation.

Why does awakening take place within the dimension of subjectivity? Because the relative I Am is a reflection of the Ultimate. The Ultimate reality can be called pure subjectivity, pure I. In India, in Indian mysticism they used to call it "I I" state, the Ultimate "I." The Ultimate "I" manifests itself as an individual in order to experience various states of forgetfulness and awakening. It is not the whole of the Ultimate which experiences forgetfulness, but only its individual expression or angle of perception. The relative Me becomes lost in the perceived, in the dream of life, in the dream of becoming. Afterwards, through the process of awakening it comes back to itself, it discovers the condition of pure "I" and finally merges back with the Ultimate. The cycle is complete.

Around you, you can notice many different sounds. Your consciousness can become aware of different happenings in the outer world; music, people are walking around, dogs, birds. Everything is being recognised through the only tool that you have, which is Awareness. Awareness meets the outer reality through the gateways of senses, ears, sense of smell, eyes... sense of touch, hot, cold, smell, taste, that is how you are encountering the dream of living, the Lila. But who is the one who perceives, who is the one who experiences the dream of life, this dance of appearances?

Consciousness has a certain choice on a deeper level: either it directs itself completely to the perceived, to the outer reality, or it directs its attention towards itself, towards the subjective reality. It is a revolutionary discovery that one can experience oneself as if in separation from the totality of external reality. One can experience oneself in complete aloneness. The person who is ignorant is an outcome of what is perceived, thought and experienced in life. When life brings satisfaction, one is happy, when life brings frustration, one is unhappy, and so forth. We derive our happiness from the external reality. Our emotional, mental and physical bodies are constantly looking for satisfaction in the outer and contentment, because longing for happiness is our primal instinct, the engine of evolution, the engine of life. For this reason, the turning in of attention to the inner, internal reality is a desire of very few Souls at this stage of their evolution. One has to be mature to see that happiness can be found inside and is not related to the outer.

Your Awareness allows you to perceive the outer. All these noises around you are recognised thanks to Awareness. Awareness looks outside through the gateway of senses. But what is this Awareness itself?

There is the relative silence and there is the unconditional silence. Meditators who are attached to the relative silence hate noise, they cannot meditate when there is noise; they feel disturbed, because they are looking for relative silence. This Awareness which is aware of noise is absolute silence. Awareness itself cannot be disturbed. It does not matter whether one sits on the top of a mountain or in a marketplace for this Awareness is, as such, untouched.

With this understanding, we bring into focus the State of Presence, the point where attention becomes aware of attention,

Awareness before thoughts. It is an experience in the mind, in the head, in the brain, in the third eye. We recognise it and hold into it. Even though we hold into it, we are relaxed within it.

To recognise the State of Presence, a certain profound self-referral has to take place in the mind. This self-referral carries an element of tension; attention and tension, they are similar. In order to transcend this tension, one has to simultaneously relax within the State of Presence. Relaxation at this stage is only in the head. You keep State of Presence and you relax with it in your head, so it becomes like an open space. If you relax too much, you will lose the State of Presence. If you do not relax enough, you become tense. When attention becomes aware of attention, there is tremendous energy in the brain. It is too much, that's why, one has to relax with it. How does one relax? Letting go, Non-doing. The moment you are Non-doing, the energy relaxes. Self-referral is doing, it is a necessary doing, through which the essence of Awareness is recognised. When it is accomplished, one can drop into Non-doing. This oscillation between doing and Non-doing is the art of being in a State of Presence and the stabilising process.

Around the State of Presence, you might notice a subtle movement of intelligence. It is not only that you are thinking something, there's a very dynamic pulsation of intelligence, which revolves around the centre of Awareness. The State of Presence is in the centre, it is the essence of the mind. Around the State of Presence there is a very fast and subtle movement of intelligence, which allows you to know that you are in a State of Presence. Apart from the subtle movement of intelligence around the State of Presence, there is a certain feeling. We can call it a mood, within which you experience your mind. Your mind is always coloured by a certain mood, certain feeling.

The State of Presence, as you see, co-exists with a subtle thought and with a certain feeling. There is also a certain sensation, because the State of Presence is an energy experience, which affects the brain and is being sensed almost in a physical way.

There are a few ways in which you can experience your mind

during being in the State of Presence. You are sitting in the State of Presence, you might notice that some thoughts arise in the mind, even though you are not involved, they arise and they disappear... and that is all right. The next way of experiencing thoughts is that you are aware of the arising of thoughts, you pay more attention to them; and the third way of experiencing thoughts is when you are actually thinking.

Remaining in the State of Presence, try to introduce some thoughts into your mind, try to think about something and notice that even though you are thinking, it does not disturb the State itself. You have to understand that "who you are" is multidimensional, you are not one thing; different dimensions, compartments of you co-exist as one organism.

Bring into focus the State of Presence, relax it in your head and let go of thinking, let go of any conceptualising. Simply relax and, with the breath into your belly, you relax even more allowing the energy to drop into Being. Observe yourself carefully, observe what happens, how the energy behaves, how it goes downward, expands and embraces the whole of you; it is no longer only in the head, it is around you.

Unless the State of Presence is firm and relatively steady, you cannot completely surrender into Being, because the moment you relax too much, you become unconscious and the mind overpowers you. That's why you have to always keep a certain amount of alertness in your mind, attentiveness.

Bring into focus the State of Presence. You become self-conscious as Awareness in the mind, like you are turning a light bulb on in your head. When it is clear, you relax it in your head, so it becomes like an open sky. This Awareness is beyond any limitations; it includes all possible realities and, itself, is beyond any object. Within this Awareness any dream can happen, any possible reality can become manifested, but this Awareness itself is always beyond, always untouched. That's why self-knowledge liberates, self knowledge is freedom.

In meditation you learn more and more that you are not a physical body, that you don't have any form; but of course in our particular manifestation, Awareness is born within this body. That is the paradox, that Awareness, which is born within the body transcends this very body. Consciousness channels itself through the body in order to experience this particular world, the dimension of time.

The moment you direct attention to attention and recognise it as pure I, the State of Presence, it feels personal; but when you relax with it, it is all-pervasive, it is no longer personal, it becomes universal. This is how the personal and the universal are inter-linked.

Through the breath into your belly, allow relaxation to go deeper into Being. When you experience enough concentration, enough integrity within the State of Meditation, there's no need to come back to the head in order to activate the Presence. But if energies of the Inner State get clouded, vague, immediately pull back to the head, activate the State of Presence, so it becomes clear, and from the point of this clarity, you again relax into Being.

Clarity, at this point, for most of you, is much more important than absorption into Being. Clarity liberates. Liberation from the mind is much more important than surrender to Being. Surrender to Being is a luxury for those who are already liberated from the mind. You will not find teaching anywhere, which explains clearly the movement within the I Am. It might sound simple, but it is a very high teaching, very subtle, through which you can know who you are and how you behave within your inner world.

From one side, you are crystallising attention, stabilising in the State of Presence, which frees you from the mind. From the other side, you learn the art of Non-doing, of Being, the art of surrender to the zero point of Existence, which is Being, which is the Absolute. In this way you are pulling out from the dimension of becoming and reconnecting to the Timeless, coming back to your source.

Now put one of your hands, the left hand, on the Heart and bring yourself to the State of Presence, clearly recognising

Awareness itself. What is this Awareness itself? It is Me in the mind. It is the nearest point to you, all other things which are happening in the mind are on the periphery, outside the view, various reflections outside the centre.

With a gentle breath into your belly, relax into Being. Being is called Parabrahman, the ultimate rest, the foundation of all realities, the unborn, the underlying primal energy of isness, it is underlying all, you relax into it.

## GRACE PEACE LOVE

# Transmission 3
## India: 27th December 98

Spiritual Path is nothing but a science of reaching the Inner Realm. It is the process which bridges the realm of forgetfulness, the realm of ignorance with the realm of remembrance where one knows who one is, fully, beyond the illusion of personality. Personality is b  a shell, an outer appearance, a mask covering the essence. The teaching, which is being presented here, does not belong to any human tradition. It is neither Buddhist nor Hindu, although it includes the insights of all great human traditions of Enlightenment. It includes the inheritance of collective consciousness...

When we speak about the spiritual Path, the first thought which comes to our mind is about the place of teaching within the collective consciousness. We ask always: "what tradition, what master and what religion is behind the message?" It is the way we seek security. We want to understand the spiritual message in the context of the Known, in the context of past knowledge. This tendency is understandable but dangerous at the same time. We should be very careful if we don't want to fall into a trap. One can lose the alive essence of the spiritual dimension which is truly beyond all that human kind has discovered. The spiritual dimension should be entered with the beginner's mind, the innocent mind, the pure mind, which encounters Reality directly without looking for any medium from the past. It is only in the space of Aloneness that the Divine can be met and experienced - in a space where you do not carry the burden of past knowledge.

Spiritual Path refers to something which is fundamentally simple, but complex at the same time. It is not complicated but complex. Unless the inner map of awakening is known, one can easily get lost. In the Inner Realm, there many states, many

"corners" and a rich variety of possibilities. There are also many
dead ends, where one can easily get lost, one can get attached
to that which is not real. In that way, one can become stuck for
a whole lifetime, which is the case with many seekers. If you
look critically at the spiritual scene you will see the sad truth,
that most seekers reach nowhere and attain nothing. Why is that?
Because the Clarity is missing as to what one is seeking and how
to reach it. Many get stuck in illusions, in this which cannot last...
and we are seeking that which can last, that which can become
our eternal refuge - the Real!

From a certain perspective, we are looking for security. There
is no security in this dimension. We are completely insecure here,
in quite a miserable condition. Everything grows and dies... one
cannot hold onto anything, in truth. Therefore, we are seeking
true security; not because of fear but due to sensitivity of the
Heart. On the Soul level, there is this deep longing in each one
of us, to find that which is reliable, which can be trusted... that
which can give us the Ultimate Security. We are seeking for the
Lover that shall never leave us, for the Creator herself, for the
Universal I AM. We wish to connect again with the Universal
Intelligence, which is Love. We are children born out of the Other
Dimension and now we are simply returning back home...

Before we begin our meditation, let us simply relax, letting go
of all concerns, anxieties. We are simply letting go of the mind
and of all the infinite information it contains. We allow ourselves
to be here in a relaxed way, so Reality can reach us. We simply
make ourselves available to the Now and to the Mystery which
lives within the Now. We are not only reaching the inner
wholeness, we are being reached by It as well. In truth, it reaches
us... but our responsibility or freedom, if you like, is to be
available... We have to surrender. This surrender is not emotional
but existential. We must surrender into Now, into the Heart of
the Now, which is the Mystery of God.

Let your mind be open like a space, not holding into what is
being said. Let words arise and disappear. There is nothing to
hold into; if there is any truth in these words, they will reach you

on the deeper level than the conscious mind. Therefore, relax and make yourself available to the Divine, to the Now and to the Spirit which comes through...

As usual, we must start from the beginning, that is, from ignorance. Ignorance is a state where one is fully identified with the mind, and there is no way one can experience any clear Me apart from the psychological movement. There is nothing wrong with personality or the mind. It is the lack of Awareness and the lack of Self within the function of the mind which is the problem. This that we don't know who we are, apart from thoughts and emotions, is wrong, for it is a fragmented reality.

Although we speak that, from a certain point of view, -the purpose of the spiritual path is to transcend the personal and to reach impersonal, the other way is also true. The human being, as a product of collective consciousness and one's own subconscious mind, is in truth impersonal. There is no one there, just a movement of unconsciousness. All thoughts, emotions and reactions can be easily predicted and the clear Me cannot be found. There is nothing personal here, only an illusion of being a person. In the process of spiritual awakening we are going beyond the unconscious impersonal way of existing. We are awakening that which is truly personal, which is truly intimate to us. We are approaching the sacred shrine within which, for the first time, we can say I Am. Not the mind is, not the psychological flow is, not this form is - I Am!

The I Am is nothing but the complete experience of oneself, free and independent from the mind. The I Am can be seen as an unconditional state of inner wholeness. I Am... The I Am is not given to you by birth. It is not necessarily your birth right to experience your I Am. It is not that you don't see it or you have forgotten it - it is not born yet. You have to give birth to it! You are giving birth to your I Am. That is the responsibility of individual and conscious evolution. If you see yourself as a Man or Woman of the Path - know what your responsibility is. This knowledge is your clarity, and clarity is your only security on the Path. You are responsible for yourself. It is not enough to hear spiritual news - your destiny is in your hands... the task of growth is in your hands.

This responsibility belongs to your Soul and is a direct reflection of your blueprint or destiny. You are responsible for your own awakening - that is a noble and sweet responsibility. Awakening is not something out of your reach. It is not something which relates only to the Great Buddha. It relates to you, to your everyday life and can be brought fully into Your reality! Awakening relates to you and we wish that you will be soon able to relate to it as well...

The problem with the teaching here is that we cannot give you answers unless there are questions, and there are no questions! If you are ready to formulate the right question, it means that you are ready for the answer; and in truth the answer is already there and must only be formulated. But there is this lack of ability to formulate the right question - one simply does not know what to ask. So, we are giving you here not only answers, but something much more important: we give you questions! Through these questions, you begin to question your reality and you begin to question yourself. Slowly you start to see that "you are not yet!" So far, you are only a part of the collective consciousness. You are an individual version of the collective mind! You are impersonal. In order to BE, to exist as YOU, you must start to question your reality. This questioning is an indivisible part of the awakening process.

Spiritual Path is a lonely path. It is not that you become a part of some spiritual club or sangha and you will call yourself "a member" of some kind or "a spiritual person." It is all false! Inner Realm is a realm of aloneness: there is only you and the Ultimate. That's why, you must have the courage and maturity to enter this realm. To surrender the false in order to reach the true. The foundation of a spiritual seeker is sincerity. The lack of capacity can be understood and it is nobody's fault, but the lack of pure and sincere intention in the Heart is a law characteristic of a Soul. If the Heart is sincere the spiritual Light reaches the Soul in this way or another. If one is not able to succeed using one's own effort, Grace brings Transformation. In this case, the Divine does all the work and the Soul is pulled into the Light. But there has to be this openness in the Heart, the true longing, honesty to one's own Soul. That is the code of honour in the world of the spiritual search.

The true seeker is not playing spiritual games. The true seeker is not looking for "Enlightenment" but for himself/herself and there is a big difference. It is exactly this difference which reflects our Sincerity. Enlightenment is merely an idea in the mind, full of projections and power games. If one seeks for oneself, one shall never fail, for the direction and the motives are right...

* * *

The Inner State, we are aiming at, we call the I Am. The I Am is not a simple state. It is composed of three qualities, three colours of Rainbow: Awareness, Being and Heart. These qualities need to be awakened and unified. Awareness is in the mind. The centre of Awareness which we wish to awaken is the State of Presence or the non-dual Consciousness. It is placed in the middle of the brain, in the third eye. The third eye is activated through attentiveness and gives birth to pure Awareness without content. Being is responsible for the experience of calm and rest. The centre of Being is in the Hara. Awareness transcends the mind and Beingness brings us the state of rest and unity with Existence. The third quality is the Heart, the gateway to the Divine and the essence of sensitivity. The Heart, we could say, is beyond meditation. Meditation, as it is traditionally understood, does not reach the Heart. But in our meditation we include the Heart. If the Heart is apart from the experience of the I Am, the energy of it is still fragmented. The I Am is very rich, vibrating, peaceful, deep and sensitive. It ultimately includes the Soul, its divine essence.

* * *

We begin our meditation where you are guided into the inner experience, making your own effort to have the right experience.

Our work here is multidimensional. We invite the energy of Grace, the Beyond, we share the energetic presence of the Master and through the proper guidance we direct your effort to your own awakening.

We sit in a comfortable but solid position; we make a short bow as a civilised way of entering the dimension of meditation; in this way we express gratitude, humility and respect to the Inner Realm.

We connect to the direct experience of oneself by becoming present to our own existence. This experience is already there, but it unfolds in the process of evolution, until the point of final completion.

We begin to breathe into the belly to deepen our energy and to focus the mind. It has been discovered in ancient China, in Taoism, that one cannot truly reach well-being unless the energy system is transformed and integrated. For that reason, Zen also emphasises so much breathing into the Hara; as Zen has its roots in Taoism. It is really important to breathe like that! We breathe slowly and deeply, completely exhaling the air and inhaling naturally in a way that the belly expands a little.

Our first meditation is about Being. We are learning how to reach it and how to understand this experience. In order to reach Being there must be certain letting go... Living within separation we are unconsciously holding into our identity, into crystallisation of the ego. Now we are simply letting go, dropping into the ultimate relaxation, which is Being. Letting go, letting go; dropping any doings, dropping any will. Being cannot be explained but you have to intuitively understand it and, above all, to experience it with the utmost clarity.

With each inhalation you are very attentive and with each exhalation you let go, dropping into surrender...

You are fully accepting the mind as it is. You do not create the desire to stop it, but you do not feed it either. You are not paying attention to the mind; you pay attention only not to be lost in this mind. By ignoring the mind and directing your attention into Being, the expansion takes place and the mind becomes transcended indirectly. No one ever conquered the mind directly. It can be done only indirectly: by creating an opposing force. On one hand, you ignore the mind and on the other hand, you invest your attention into a different area of experience than thinking. In this way you move deeper than the mind, beyond the mind. You find yourself more and more in a place that is not touched by thoughts. This place is called the experience of Being. It is an energy experience, which you translate as: calmness.

There are many meditation techniques but Meditation is one. Meditation is not a technique but a State, the state of just Being, Shikan-taza. The experience of Being cannot be grasped... it simply is present. An average person, fully identified with the mind, functions like a living computer, disconnected from Being... Is such a person really alive?

We continue to breathe, remaining very attentive and very... relaxed. Dropping into Being and encountering its infinite depth of Mystery. If you experience certain restlessness or boredom, do not allow these energies to distract you and take away from the vertical reality of the Now. Remain centred and watchful. Sit firmly like a mountain, unmoved within the dignity of inner stillness.

* * *

A certain element of discipline is absolutely necessary in meditation. Learning the art of meditation should be combined with the development of inner discipline. Not to move when it is not necessary, not to react immediately to the pain and discomfort can give one a lot of strength and energy. The minimum of discipline is simply an expression of common sense and wisdom. Because something is fundamentally off in the way the human mind operates, we must create an energy of focus and enormous mindfulness to transform our consciousness. This is the way we make the next step in our evolution.

Now we will speak about Awareness. Awareness is the light of knowing behind every experience. Without Awareness there is no knowing, there is simply nothing - a deep sleep state. When there is no Awareness, there is no Me and only the original state remains. Normally, Awareness is merely a function to bring into the light of knowing the phenomenal reality of appearances, but what is Awareness without any object, without content - what is Awareness itself?

One of the few pillars of Enlightenment is recognition of the State of Presence, which is Awareness without content. This awakening of Awareness takes place in the mind. As you see, the term mind not only designates the mechanical invasion of thoughts. Awareness is also generated in the mind as well as Understanding.

We direct our attention to the mind. We become aware of all that is occurring in the mind. An intelligent question to be asked is: who is experiencing this mind? Who is behind the mind? Who is Me? Who is the thinker and the observer in the mind? Is anybody home? Or is there only the mind?

We would like to ask you to recognise pure I, pure Me behind the mind. You are not the thoughts - thoughts are merely happening to You, you are behind them. But how can you recognise it? You have to pay attention. You need to direct the light of Awareness towards the very subject, which is Me in the mind. All this may sound complex but is elementary, in truth. It is a kindergarten in the realm of spirituality. Not knowing the Me, the I, cannot be regarded as a sane situation. We are bringing essential sanity to you, where you can simply be clear about your own identity!

Please, put yourself in a position of watching the mind. Normally, one is only thinking. Now you become aware of thinking. Stay like this and contemplate what it means to watch the mind...

When you are watching the mind, more space is created in the mind, certain openness... You are not merely thinking - you are somewhere behind thoughts. You are experiencing some distance from the mind. This distance is the beginning of awakening. But let us again ask you this annoying question: who is watching the mind, who is aware of thinking? You may say: "it is me and I am in the Heart." But is the Heart watching the mind? The Heart does not care about the mind. There is something else watching the mind, and it is in the mind. The observer is in the mind. Many of those, who teach about the no-mind concept, have not understood this simple truth.

As you are observing the mind, gently pull attention back to itself. In this way you will be able to recognise the observer, which is simply yourself.

Breathing into the belly, we are letting go into Being. Through this letting go, the State of Meditation is manifested. The State of Meditation is a unity of Awareness and Being, peace and clarity.

* * *

The State of Meditation is very extraordinary and special. One may think: "I will sit quietly for one hour to feel better." But the truth behind the State of Meditation is much more profound. You are experiencing yourself, out of the life's context and external identifications. You are experiencing yourself out of the social context, your role, your name and any kind of self-image. You are experiencing pure Intimacy with your own existence.

Returning to the zero point, returning to the subject, returning to the I... This I is not an outcome of thoughts, it is not a self-image. This I does not change... and it is a paradox, that although we change all our life, growing and evolving, there is something in us which does not change, our essence.

We relax into the Now, into this ocean of Beingness which cannot be grasped, but one can consciously surrender to it. You are not relaxing into your body or mind, you are relaxing into the Beyond, into the ocean of Beingness. That into which you relax is beyond the frontiers of your physical form, beyond your personality and beyond your separateness. It cannot be grasped, but it is the Ultimate...

True Meditation is a religious act. It does not concern the tranquilisation of the mind, nor does it aim at the freedom from suffering. True Meditation is a process of re-uniting with the Light of Creation. The Light of Creation is Reality; it is below, above and surrounds us from all directions... and only It Is! All else is but a shadow of Reality.

Meditation is a scientific process of annihilating you. You might want to be enlightened and to reach the Super-Consciousness, but what you are heading to is your disappearance. You are simply vanishing... but you are vanishing not into nothing - you are vanishing into Wholeness...

Next intelligent question: who is truly the one who arrived at our meeting? Who is enduring the pain in the knees in order to bring more peace into the mind? Who wishes to be happy? Who is longing to escape from sorrow and human sadness? This is not the same question as "who is observing the mind?" The observer is not the essence of you. The observer is merely our centre in the mind, in consciousness. Your true identity is the Soul which, by the design of a human body, is located in the middle of the chest. Our next meditation focuses on the spiritual Heart centre, and on the discovery of the Soul.

What is the Soul? It is the unique, individual flavour of Me which is experienced in the Heart. The Soul is using the mind, she is using Awareness and is resting in Being, but herself is dwelling within the Heart. The purpose of the awakening of the Heart is not merely to generate feelings of compassion and love, but essentially to recognise the light of our Soul.

Generally speaking, there is Enlightenment to the Self and there is Enlightenment to the Soul. The Self represents the unity of pure Awareness and Being. The Soul represents the essence of Me in the Heart. They are not the same, although they complement each other.

We begin breathing to the Heart. We cannot discover our Heart unless we pay attention to it... The Soul, which is in the Heart, is like a child. If you look at yourself deeply, you are just a child. You are not a child of your physical parents but of the Divine, of the Universal Mother. This feeling of child like quality in the Heart has been lost; we have become too adult, too gross in the way we experience our Heart. But this child is still there and it has not changed! It is always pure and always innocent... it has certain desires, longings and fears. These feelings are real and need to be acknowledged for they come from the Soul, not from the mind.

We put our hands on our Heart, breathing to it. As you see, in our vision of Enlightenment we do not negate the Soul and we do not negate human nature. We don't negate certain essential vulnerability in our Heart which, in truth, is pure sensitivity. We do not negate the presence of desires and, above all, the desire to be happy and fulfilled in all areas, not just spiritual.

We work with our Heart in the context of the meditative state, where the silence is present and there is sufficient amount of Awareness. In this space, we are discovering the inner flower, our own Soul, our own Heart.

Feeling your Heart, breathing to this area, listening to the beautiful music which is present here... allow yourself to become intimate with that who you are in the Heart... This is Love.

PEACE LOVE GRACE

# Transmission 4
## India: 29th December 98

Beloved friends, welcome to our next meeting, which takes place not on the Earth but far away from the Earth, in the Dimension of Understanding.

You might think that this meeting is happening on the earth because you are able to locate yourself physically here, but that is an illusion. This meeting takes place in the Dimension of Understanding, which is the pure light of knowing, beyond this dimension and other dimensions. It is the Other Side of the Now that we speak from. It is similar to turning the inside out of the pillow cover. If you turn the Now inside out, what you will discover is the Other Dimension, where nothing happens. This Dimension exists eternally beyond time. It is called your Eternal Home which you have left, once upon a time, in order to adventure in time. We are not concerned here with the exact reasons why you decided to enter the plane of imperfection and forgetfulness, which is earth. You are Here! You are like children lost in the playground of the phenomenal reality. Now we are simply inviting you home. You have been alone enough and you have suffered sufficiently. Therefore, welcome to the Dimension of Understanding, which is Love — to the essence of the Now.

This meeting is slightly more advanced. Different seekers represent different levels of realisation and understanding, hence, we try to present various levels of Teaching. How can the advancement on the spiritual Path be measured? In truth, it is the depth with which one perceives the Now. Everything that exists is Now. Even the mind, even the dream state occurs within the Now. However, there is no depth in recognition of the Now in the dream state, it is a state of unconsciousness. Spiritual progress is measured by the depth with which the Now is experienced.

How deep can we reach it? The Now is like an Ocean. One can reach the depth of it or one can remain on the surface... and this surface is also Now, but shallow without depth.

Spiritual awakening is the awakening of Me. Me, at the beginning is completely identified with the mind. It is fragmented, shallow and unconscious. Through the spiritual awakening, our Me discovers itself deeper and deeper, until it reaches this holistic and all-encompassing experience of Me or I Am, which is self-contained, completely peaceful and rich, vibrating with love and beauty.

Let us repeat, for those who are new and for those who have been already coming. This knowledge is simple but has to be imbibed fully. The state we are aiming at, the state of completeness, the I Am, is composed of three qualities: Awareness, Being and Heart. We are awakening them separately and uniting into one flavour of I Am, into one experience. Awareness is generated in the mind and it frees us from unconsciousness of the mind, bringing us to the state of clarity, self-recognition and pure consciousness: Consciousness without content. Being is this quality of I Am which allows us to rest, to experience peace, calm and rootedness in Existence. The ability to let go of oneself into this profound experience of Non-doing: it is Being. There is the Heart which is the third quality, which is the divine flavour, the essence of who we are, the essence of our individual manifestation and the gateway to the divine or to the Heart of the Creator. These three qualities, the three colours of the inner rainbow, we are awakening and uniting into One Experience.

One of the most important faculties to be awakened is Awareness. Although, Awareness functions in each human being, it operates only in the phenomenal reality. It functions at the minimum, which is not enough to experience oneself holistically. Awareness, in a human being is identified with the movement of the mind, and with the perceptions coming from senses. One's consciousness is completely objectified, so to speak, one lives in an objective reality and there is no subject as such. It is like in a dream: there is an experience, there is suffering, pleasure and happiness, but there is no subject. All these experiences happen outside the heart of this very Me, which we are discovering. When Awareness is awakened, a new dimension of experience is added, where one experiences oneself apart from the perceived. Here, one experiences the subject. This subject is not just an outcome of life's events, but a reality into itself, which is independent or unconditional.

Because today we will be guiding this meditation in a more advanced way, if you are unable to understand some issues, please don't be discouraged. In such a situation, please, come next time where we will begin the teaching from the foundation.

* * *

This time we begin our meditation with the gentle Chi-Gong's exercise, which is the best way of working with the Hara, which is the energy centre in our body. We start this exercise with focusing on exhalation for a few minutes, until another instruction will be given. We are simply exhaling very slowly to the point where the belly becomes completely flat. During this exhalation we will be doing gentle visualisation, imagining that all impurities, tensions and blocked energies are leaving our body in the form of dark cloud. We are exhaling very slowly until the belly becomes flat and it is followed by the natural inhalation. Please, do this for a few minutes.

At this stage we focus on the inhalation. When you inhale, the belly expands like a balloon and you imagine that it is filled with energy. Do this very slowly.

That is enough. Now, we are rubbing our palms and putting this energy into our face and into our eyes, massaging the face gently.

We begin our proper meditation. The exercise we did is good to do every day, concentrating on exhalation for five to ten minutes and on inhalation for five to ten minutes. It is a very strong and helpful practice. We centralise ourselves in the sitting position, taking all dispersed energies and bringing them together into the experience of Being Now.

Meditation is a state of just sitting or just being. However, the depth of just sitting, the depth of just being can be reached only when certain faculties become awakened within us. For example, we need to activate Awareness and deepen the energy in Hara. So, you see, just being has a few levels and it is not a simple state. One evolves in Just Being, one reaches deeper and deeper the depths of the ocean of I AM, until the experience is complete. And what does complete mean? It means one is completely at ease, completely at rest and completely luminous with clarity.

Today's meditation is designed for those who have already recognised the State of Presence, which is Awareness behind thoughts, self-attention or witnessing consciousness. The State of Presence is the heart of spiritual discipline, the heart of meditative consciousness. There is a Zen saying, that "practicing the Way is seeing the Way." If you are not seeing the Way, you are not really practicing, but groping in the darkness. Seeing the Way is to recognise and being able to retain the State of Presence, Awareness without object.

For a few thousand years there have been quarrels between different Spiritual Schools whether Enlightenment is gradual or sudden. Some think that Enlightenment is reached through gradual effort and some think that it is a sudden miraculous event. In the second case, either one is Self-realised or one is not, and there is nothing in-between. Both concepts are true and false at the same time. There is an evolution within the Inner States but often they are being reached in a sudden way. They are certain events in our evolution which are sudden, but they are interconnected with the gradual process of growth and maturation.

The gradual approach is more true, closer to reality. Even in the case of Masters who had a sudden Awakening, like "Kundalini explosion," the evolution didn't stop. The gradual process of maturation was present before their awakening and certainly after. There are different stages of Enlightenment. Not everyone who reaches Enlightenment is in the Ultimate State. Therefore, it is more true to say that there is evolution, there is a gradual process through which one reaches deeper and deeper the depth of I AM. If you experience the State of Presence, it is already an awakened state, it is already an enlightened state. But you might say that this experience is simple and — not big... but it is special and it is not simple, it is a profound state...

We begin our meditation with bringing ourselves clearly to the State of Presence. Those who do not recognise the State of Presence, simply watch the mind and try to keep this Awareness which is watching the mind, attention in the mind. As you see, the State of Presence always carries the same flavour. Everything changes, thoughts come and go, but the State of Presence remains the same at the background of the mind. It has a quality of the timeless or eternal. However, even though it does not change as such, in each moment it arises. It is because you recognise it in the process of time. You live in time, in the river of time and in each moment you are being born to this reality, which is recognition and perception. So you are meeting the State of Presence in each moment — it is an eternal meeting. This meeting is called to see the Way. To see the Way is to meet your own Presence within the flow of time. The moment you lose yourself, you lose the State of Presence, you are not seeing the way, you are losing the way, you arrive at the state of forgetfulness. Therefore, to see the Way is to keep the continuity of the State of Presence. So it does not break, it is constant; it flows like a wide and powerful river.

The State of Presence can be understood or translated within you as the experience of "I" or pure Me, and that is fine. But this Me is not an ego, it is not self-image or an outcome of thoughts — it is an energy-presence which is felt. There is no other way to disarm the unconscious mind but through giving rise to the State of Presence. It is the only opposing force within the mind which can transform the function of the mind. It is not enough to observe the mind. You can observe the mind for one hundred years and nothing will change fundamentally. It is only the opposing force, which is the presence of pure Me that can fully transform the mind.

You are keeping the State of Presence, self-attention in the mind, becoming sensitive to its specific vibrations. You observe how it behaves, how it feels and you relax with it in your head. In this process of practice, you are doing two things: you hold it very firmly, so you won't lose it... and you are relaxing with it, letting go. Both are necessary. This naked Awareness can be called your eternal face, your true face. It doesn't have any characteristics, it doesn't have age, doesn't have any shape or colour, it is pure Awareness, the primal vibration of Consciousness.

Being in the State of Presence or non-dual Awareness does not mean that there is no mind, that the thought process gets erased. There are still some thoughts and it is really irrelevant whether thoughts are present or absent. Who you are is multidimensional. The existence of the State of Presence and the movement of thoughts do not contradict each other. They both constitute what we call the mind or consciousness. So in your meditation do not try to stop the mind, at all. Your most important task is not to lose yourself in the mind but to remain at the centre of Awareness.

Although the State of Presence has certain impersonal characteristics, it cannot be separated from the personal movement of intelligence. For that reason it feels like Me, because it is the closest point to you in the mind. This intuitive intelligence that circulates around the State of Presence relates to it at the same time. Who we are, in the mind, is composed of two centres. One, is the static centre of the State of Presence which does not change. Second, is the dynamic centre of our intelligence. This dynamic centre is always in movement, and it relates to both: to the State of Presence and to the gross level of spontaneous thinking coming from the subconscious mind. This intuitive intelligence is very important for it allows us to grow and to understand the process of awakening.

Whom are we speaking to here? We are speaking to your intuitive intelligence. This intuitive intelligence is listening and is trying to learn. Sometimes, it simply doesn't understand, and that is fine for this is a part of its growth.

Please, look into your mind keeping the State of Presence and become aware of the "scenery" around it. You can notice a subtle movement of thoughts, a certain vibration of intuitive intelligence and a more gross level of thinking which arises in the mind. Become fully aware of the scenery in the mind, for it is You!

A long time ago, in India, a concept was created that one is not a doer, that one is purely a Witness. This concept is coming from the awakening to the centre of Consciousness. When the State of Presence is awakened, the mind becomes witnessed from behind and moves to the periphery. The movement of thoughts is no longer in the centre. In the centre is this non-dual Awareness which is, so to speak, witnessing the mind. This concept, however, is not completely correct. This concept implies that one identifies oneself fully with the State of Presence and refuses to see the self-conscious movement of intelligence as being an integral part of Me. In this way we perceive the mind and its intelligence as something just happening on the screen of Consciousness, and not being Me. However, much more accurate is to say that they both constitute the reality of Me.

You are the witness and you are the intuitive intelligence as well... and, in truth, it is only because you are this intelligence that you can discover the State of Presence and are able to relate to it. You, as the intelligence, relate to the State of Presence. It sounds rather simple but it carries quite profound implications. You as the ego, you as the mind, you as the intelligence, you affect the quality of the I Am. There is a relationship between them. The State of Presence embraces the mind and the mind relates to the Presence. It is only because of this that you can experience different levels of absorption. You have a choice either to be absorbed in the outer or to go inside. You have the choice to surrender completely to the Inner State, giving this experience a new depth or to direct your energy more to the external reality.

We present here a New Psychology, which finally enables us to explain much more precisely the inner dynamics: the dynamics of I Am as well as of the intelligence which is indivisible from it. The traditional teachings, which have been created a few thousand years ago, did not discover how the Inner State and the movement of intelligence relate to each other. That's why, the psychology which has been proposed by them is unable to explain fully the inner processes and the process of awakening.

Please, keep the State of Presence for a few more minutes before break. Who is the one recognising the State of Presence? Who is the one who is appreciating the State of Presence? Who is the one who is observing the State of Presence? It is YOU as the intelligence, without this intelligence you would be dead... it is important.

* * *

We begin with the clear recognition of the centre of Awareness in the mind. If you do not recognise the State of Presence, stay with attention in the mind, observing the thinking process in a very acute and sharp way. The State of Presence is the inner sword which cuts through the illusions of the mind. Without this sword one is fully controlled by the mind. It is a very miserable condition because the mind is full of negativity, full of past impressions, which we do not want anymore but which keep coming back. But the most sad is not that one experiences the negativity of the mind, but that one doesn't know where the centre of identity is located. One doesn't know where one is, in truth, being completely identified with thinking. One is the mind, one is a computer — not a being yet. The State of Presence is precious and you have to believe it! Only when you understand it fully, can you begin the real work of self-remembrance. The State of Presence is useless as far as survival or well-being in the world is concerned. That's why, one has to be really intelligent to see the great spiritual importance of it.

We keep the State of Presence and we relax it in the head. When there is recognition of the State of Presence, it involves immediate self-referral in the mind, a certain crystallisation of attention. For that reason, you experience the State of Presence as a centre. But when you relax in your head, it opens up and it assumes the quality of space, as a sky, clear sky. This is what they mean in Buddhism by using the metaphor "the clear sky of

the Mind." This open sky of Awareness has no boundaries and
no limits, it is luminous, brilliant and illuminates all universes
with the light of knowing. This experience is not just in the head:
it pervades the infinite space. In this process of cultivation of
the Presence, one has to learn this art of keeping and letting go.
If you keep it too much, the energy becomes too tense. When
you let go too much, you will simply lose it. Therefore, you have
to keep it and let go, let go of it and keep, finding the exact
balance

Now, with slow breath into the belly you let go even more.
You are not keeping the energy in your head anymore but you
surrender into Being. When you let go, the energy by the law
of gravity travels downwards. Be sensitive and observe what
happens to the energy when you let go into Being. Keeping
Awareness in the head involves an element of certain subtle will.
There is still will... one is still not free from will. One can become
free from will only within Being. One can completely let go of
any doing only in Being... and this we are doing now: letting go
completely. But in this letting go, we still retain a certain inner
focus.

Again, we bring ourselves to the State of Presence, clearly
experiencing it in the mind. Relaxing with it in the head and
relaxing more into Being. Gently breathing into the belly, letting
go into Shikantaza, just sitting, without any focus. Shikantaza,
pure meditation is the combination of rest in Being and the clarity
of Awareness. It is a state of Non-doing.

How do we know whether we should bring ourselves in
meditation to the State of Presence, crystallising our attention or
whether we should relax into Being? Clarity is the only criteria.
If you feel that the clarity is missing and the energies of the mind
are unclear and vague, you have to immediately bring yourself
to the State of Presence. The centre of Awareness is like a light
dispersing all that is unclear and semi-conscious. When you reach
this point of clarity, where the State of Presence vibrates and you
are fully present, you can let go. From the place of having a clear
centre you relax, let go into Being again. However, when you
sit and there is a sufficient amount of clarity, there is this strength

of the Inner State, you do not need to go to the head. In such a situation, you simply remain as you are, resting in Being, for it means that there is already enough Awareness integrated. The Presence has merged with Being.

You have to experience, you have to create the continuity of Presence. This continuity can be experienced exclusively in the head or can be experienced in a way that it is integrated with Being. In such a case, the experience is not merely in the head but it is distributed to all areas of you... and even if you are not fully self-conscious, part of you knows clearly that there is a continuous experience of I Am. The experience is firm, solid and has the depth of calmness.

Our greatest wish is to bring you to the point where you believe fully, where you are fully convinced that Enlightenment relates to You! This "miraculous and magical" Enlightenment relates to you, and not only to the spiritual "supermen" who are worshiped by thousands of devotees. It is your destiny and you have to start to believe in yourself. To believe in yourself is to believe in your Self. When you believe in yourself, you look inside, being fully convinced that the light, the truth has to be there, because where else could it be? It is in you and when you experience it directly, it is nothing but the Self. It is nothing but the flavour of awakening which has been there all the time.

At the end, as usual, we are bringing in the experience of I Am, which is a combination of Awareness and Being, the vibration of the Heart. This time, we simply put our hand on the Heart, remaining in the state of Shikan-taza, in a state of just Being. Being gently open to the Heart, allowing the energies of the Heart to become a part of the State of Meditation. We are also listening to music allowing it to become a part of the holistic experience of I Am. Feeling the Heart and letting go into Being...

## Conclusion

It is very interesting to see that the Soul who is the experiencer of all, can negate herself. That's why, the concept of the no-soul or no-self has been created in Buddhism. The Soul, who has reached the original state the Unborn, the Emptiness and who has become completely one with the universal I AM, can negate her own existence! She can say: "I am not." The Soul can assume that there is only the Universal Impersonal Existence. For that reason, the awakening to the Soul is the most subtle for she is closest to us, she is our nearest identity.

From the view point of the Soul, even Emptiness, even Awareness, even the Inner State and Inner Peace are external, so to speak. All the Inner States, from the perspective of the Soul, are merely an "environment" within which the Soul exists. The Soul is the closest to us. But the Soul cannot discover herself fully, unless this perfect environment of Awareness and Being is created, which is like a spotless mirror. It is possible to discover the Soul without awakening to Awareness and Being, but this experience cannot go deep, it is more emotional. It is possible to be in touch with the Soul without practicing Awareness and Being but one is unable to apperceive the depth of the Heart. In such cases, there is no quality of depth, no quality of rest... and no continuity of Awareness-intelligence.

Even when the energy of the Heart is present, this Heart cannot rest inside, for it is disconnected from Being. The Heart which is not able to rest within, can express itself only outside, which is beautiful but lacks the completeness. The depth of the Heart is not an emotion but the pure experience of I Am, the divine subjectivity. The Heart is resting in the Heart. It is pure Love which is not an emotion but a condition of Being. The Heart even though it is Love, does not know that it is in the state of Love. The energy of the Heart, one with Being is resting in itself and through itself in the Other Dimension, merged with the Divine.

GRACE PEACE LOVE

# Transmission 5
## India: 14th January 99

Beloved Friends, welcome to our next meeting. Welcome to the continuation of our inner search for clarity and completion. We wish to arrive finally at the place where everything feels right, where we can relax in the arms of Truth which is the Universal I AM or God...

Spiritual Awakening does not concern perception, but it is about expansion within Being. The quality of Beingness expands within our individual I Am, and through Being, within Being we become one with the Creator. Spirituality is not a therapy. We can say that it is the Ultimate Therapy, by the power of which one is cured from the sickness of separation, and one returns to the state of Unity.

What does it mean to experience oneself in the realm of separation or ignorance? It means that our sense of Me, which is common to all of us, is experienced out of the context of the Universal I AM, out of the context of Totality. It lives in a virtual reality of itself! It lives in a closed cage of ego. But we do not wish, at all, to eliminate Me. Rather we wish to add to the sense of Me the higher perspective. Through this higher perspective our Me experiences itself, this time, in the context of Wholeness - its existence is embraced by the presence of the Universal I AM.

The state of ignorance is a very narrow perspective, where one is fully identified with the mind, where one simply is the mind. Here, the movement of thoughts creates our identity, our false identity. It is not the mind which is wrong, but the fact that we are lost in it, not being able to experience our isness in separation from thinking. The mind is simply a tool to be used, but it is not who we are. In our awakening process we are adding to the mind a clear and whole experience of Me or I Am. We are adding to the mind the experiencer of it!

Spiritual awakening is an awakening to the very clear experience of oneself, which is free from the mind. We are not eliminating the mind, but adding our own existence, as being already present beyond the mind.

In order to experience the state of inner Wholeness, the I Am, we must awaken certain faculties. Firstly, we need to awaken Awareness. Awareness is in the mind and in the case of an ignorant person, it is identified with thinking. When Awareness is awakened, it is experienced apart from thinking. It is Awareness of Awareness, free from any psychological or physical objects. The non-dual Awareness is one of the pillars of Self-realisation. The second faculty is Being. Being and Awareness are different. Being allows us to rest within - it is below consciousness. When Awareness and Being meet, there is a simultaneous experience of peace and clarity. The third faculty is the Heart. The Heart centre is the gateway to the Divine and the abiding place of our Soul.

Meditation as it is being taught traditionally, awakens Being and Awareness. The systems of meditation available nowadays, however, do not differentiate between Being and Awareness. The process of awakening is not fully conscious and the right conceptual tools, that could allow us to understand the internal reality of the I Am, do not exist. In the traditional approach the work with the Heart is definitely lacking and even if we could find some teaching speaking about generating feelings of love and compassion, they do not point to the Soul, which is the essence of the Heart.

Awakening to Awareness and Being brings us to the state of Liberation, state of freedom - complete inner silence and rest. But when the Heart is not awakened, still, the wholeness is missing. The inner beauty, sensitivity and the fragrance of Divinity is lacking. From the other side, if we work only with the Heart neglecting Being and Awareness, the Heart is experienced out of context. One cannot reach the depth of the Heart if the depth of Being is not present. In such a case one is constantly disturbed by the mind and one is unable to rest within. The ultimate experience of the Heart is not merely to feel it, but to Rest in it fully. Now we hope, that you see clearly the importance of these three elements and how they complement each other...

At this point the concept of Wholeness, for most of you, remains on the level of abstraction. You may not know whether you wish to invest energy to reach something, when you really do not know what it is! But along the Path it will become more and more clear, as you mature and grow in understanding and the inner experience. That which links you with your future completion is an immediate intuitive understanding below the conscious level. Enlightenment is not merely an event in the future. It is already happening as you enter the Precious Path and, as you progress, it simply reveals itself more and more, until it is complete. There is simply more and more light, more and more happiness. It is an unfoldment of the I Am which is already present. In other words, you are meeting yourself more and more. You are being revealed to yourself by the power of evolution, which is the universal movement of Intelligence.

Spirituality is not a game. It is not about becoming a follower of some kind or about getting a new name. For many, spirituality is simply an extension of ego. It is how ego decorates itself, by becoming spiritual. Some seekers dream about becoming a master or guru, which gives a feeling of power and makes one a centre of attention. All of this is, however, a complete illusion. True Spirituality is humility; one returns to the state of being nothing and nobody. This nothing is not negative but positive. This nothing is open like a sky - it is pure understanding.

* * *

Our meetings are based on guided meditation. Sometimes we sit silently but in most cases you receive guidance. You are guided into the inner experience and into Understanding. These meditations are not too hard but they require some focus and discipline. We encourage you not to move during meditation and to sit in a solid way. If you experience discomfort in you body or mind, try not to react but remain still outside and inside. It will help you to concentrate. The motionlessness of the body helps to reach the motionlessness within.

We make a short bow as an expression of respect to the Divine. We are entering the inner shrine of the Self. We are invited to the home of inner silence by the One who created All.

We close our eyes and fully accept who we are in this very moment, without aiming at any particular goal. Full acceptance. Full acceptance means to be in the Now. But within this acceptance, there is an understanding that we can still go deeper into the Now, that we can deepen the very experience of our own existence. Complete understanding includes full acceptance and the knowledge of what one needs to do. It seems like a paradox but it is simply the reality of the one who entered the Path. The I Am reaches the I Am through the I Am until it becomes the I Am.

We begin with slow and deep breathing into the belly. In the case of most people, the energy is too much up and disconnected from the Hara. For that reason, slow and deep breathing like this is essential. It is not a technique - it is wisdom.

Simultaneously, as we are breathing slowly into the belly, we are continuously letting go into Being. We are here in this extraordinary process of learning: how to Be. Being is not given. That is again a paradox, but Being must be created and awakened.

You are not in conflict with the mind. You are fully accepting the movement of thoughts in your mind. But don't allow yourself to get entangled in the mind. Neither participating nor opposing it - that is the art! Letting go into Being and slowly breathing into the belly. You don't need to stop thinking in order to experience yourself as being already beyond the mind. Just relax...

With each inhalation you are very attentive. You must be extremely attentive. Attention has to be like fire burning inside you... and with each exhalation you relax into Being. You are using two very important polarised energies. You are using the masculine energy of will and attention; and you are using the soft, gentle and sensitive feminine energy of surrender, letting go into Being.

With each inhalation you are very attentive and with each exhalation you are letting go into Being; into Being no one, into Being without any identity, into Being a space of Being... and dying to the past.

Who am I? What is it, which is sitting here apart from the mind? If we take away the mind from you and erase your memory, what will remain? You cannot give it any name, but you can live it. You can meet it in this very moment, in this intimate embrace of your very own self, but for that you must go beyond the mind. The mind is only a shadow of that who you are. With each moment you are letting go into Being, into the nakedness of your identity prior to thoughts.

You are very attentive, letting go of the mind from moment to moment and surrendering into Being. Be patient. If there are some difficulties, accept them in the understanding that you are planting seeds for your future. A ten thousand mile journey starts with the first step. You are entering the Inner Realm, the secret dimension which is not perceived, at all, by anyone. It is a secret! Please, respect it.

How do you experience Being? There is still the mind but something is added, which you might translate as "being calm," certain expansion of energy, certain stillness, the touch of I Am below the mind. Just Being is the highest meditation and, in truth, the only meditation. Shikan-taza, just being, just sitting... In a state of just Being everything is embraced: the voice you hear, sound of the ocean, song of a bird, the wind on your face, warmth of the sun... and your own mind as well. Here, one is Connected. For the first time one is connected to Existence. Being is the very Heart of Existence.

* * *

One has five senses to connect with the outer reality: eyes, ears, nose... etc. We constantly look through these five windows fascinated by the landscape outside. And the sixth sense is the mind, which also perceives the outer landscape of ideas, thoughts and mental impressions. One lives through the connection with the outer. An average person is unable to even conceive of the.

possibility that one could experience oneself just as pure I, pure Me, which has nothing to do with the outer. This disability represents the basic neurosis. That's why everyone is in a state of deep suffering. It is not even conscious suffering, the mind does not always recognise it, but the Soul is in pain!

Who am I apart from what I see, I touch, I hear, I smell, I taste and I think? Who am I? Who am I in this intimate encounter with myself at the core of my identity? That is the right question. If you don't have the right question, how could you discover the right answer? We give you here the questions and the answers, for most of you don't really have questions, and even less the right ones. Who am I? Am I only a dream character playing a role of a human being and personality? Am I a crystallised ego made from the continuity of some meaningless memories and mental impressions? Am I just a shadow? Or is there someone inside who allows me to say: I Am?

Now we will speak about Awareness. Awareness is everything. But the awakened Awareness is a dimension of knowingness without the "outside." We are searching for the state of self-awareness, the essence of Consciousness, which is our dignity. Development of Awareness is the only way to free yourself from the mind, which is your relative enemy and your future friend. The essence of Awareness is attention. Wherever you direct your Awareness, attention is involved. Thinking, for example, means that attention is lost or identified with thoughts. When attention is awakened, it experiences its own presence in separation from the psychological movement. In India they call it "witnessing consciousness" and in Zen: "clear mind."

How do we awaken this Awareness? Meditation develops Awareness; it teaches you one-pointedness of the mind. You learn how to create continuity of attention by watching breath, observing the mind or repeating mantra, for instance. In this way attention grows. But the awakening itself is in another dimension. We speak about the situation when attention is not directed anywhere, but to itself. It looks back and sees its own face. This is what we are doing here.

For a few moments focus on your third eye area. Your eyes
are closed but looking up to the place in the middle of your
forehead, inside of the skull, you imagine that you are seeing this
point. Remain like this for a few moments. You will feel a strong
energy impact. This practice aims at the activation of the third
eye, which is the centre of wakefulness.

Now, we are becoming aware of thinking. Direct your attention
to the mind. To be aware of thinking is quite interesting. Who
is this that is observing the mind? It is you certainly, but what
does it mean? Who is this you? Unless it is clearly recognised,
it remains on the conceptual level. Observe the mind with a sense
of learning and curiosity. This mind which has imposed itself
upon you, is now being simply observed. It is no longer an
obsession, but an object of observation.

While observing the mind, become also sensitive to the observer.
There is the mind, there is the observing of the mind and there
is the Observer. The observer is Me. Pay attention to this which
is immediate. To this which is so close to you that you are unable
to see it. It is like touching your own nose! It is you! Pay
attention to it. Gently withdrawing energy from the mind by
observing it and directing attention to the observer.

Sometimes it is difficult to observe the mind because the mind
is in a state of chaos; it is invaded by many, not clearly formulated
thoughts, and one is unable to keep any sense of centre in the
mind. To make it easier, this time we introduce one thought,
which you will repeat like a mantra but with a different purpose.
The mantra will be: "attention in." This thought is just a thought,
a mental object in the mind and should be seen as such. You
will be repeating this mantra without caring about its conceptual
meaning. Repeat it very slowly, in a contemplative way, being
fully present and alert. While you are repeating this mantra, feel
that it is you, who is doing it. It is not just the mind thinking
- it is you. Isn't it true? Who is saying this mantra. What is
this Me behind? Feel it! The sense of Me behind the mantra
"attention in." "Attention in... attention in... attention in..."

The moment you recognise the sense of Me behind the mantra,

you can let go of the mantra itself and keep only this Me. The sense of Me when recognised represents self-attention. It is the same. We call it Me, for it is our identity in the mind. Keep this Me and relax it in your head...

The State of Presence, self-attention, is the centre of Awareness. To arrive at the state of Pure Awareness is one of the pillars of Enlightenment. Firstly, one needs to recognise it and secondly, one practices self-remembrance in order to become established in this state. When the State of Presence is constant, the mind is fully transcended and one has the centre of Awareness in all circumstances. This practice is to be done not only during sitting but in all situations; in walking, eating, talking... That is the real practice.

At this time, with the breath into the belly we relax into Being. In this relaxation, in this letting go we observe how the energy behaves; how it gravitates downwards in the direction of Being and Stillness.

* * *

It is a paradox that even though we are simply ourselves, still, we have to meet our own Self, our I Am. This paradox is contained in the wisdom of evolution. It has its purpose and its reason... This is an adventure of Consciousness, which enters many different forms and ways of expressions, journeying in time. Until the point when it meets itself, it meets its own light and dissolves into God, the Source of all.

Evolution is universal. You might think that your growth represents an individual evolution but it is only relatively true. From the higher standpoint, this evolution is impersonal and universal. It is the evolution of Universal Spirit which is discovering itself - through You. You are simply an angle of perception, a particular individual flavour of that which is not individual but universal.

You are giving birth to yourself, which means that you are taking responsibility for your life and for your growth. Spiritual awakening is your responsibility; the responsibility of co-creation with the Universal Spirit. If you delay the inner work, you simply postpone the great moment of becoming whole... and this postponement is itself a state of suffering.

The I Am, as it has the centre of Awareness and Being, so it has the Heart. The Heart of I Am is the Soul: your true identity. It is located in the middle of your chest, in the spiritual Heart. The spiritual Heart is a gateway to the Heart of the Creator. Here, the individual Heart and the Universal Heart meet each other, giving rise to the sublime experience, which is beyond unity and separation. The essence of the Heart is called the Christ Consciousness. That is the secret of Sufi Masters intoxicated with the Divine. They are not merely in a state of peace: they are drunk with God!

The awakening of Awareness and Being gives rise to the experience of inner stillness and Samadhi, but the wholeness is still lacking for the Heart is not present. The sensitivity is missing, the vulnerability and the softness of the Heart is missing. Love is simply lacking.

We begin, therefore, paying attention to the Heart. Please, start breathing this time to the chest energising and feeling this area. Notice, that we enter the Heart in the context of the State of Meditation, that is, in the context of inner stillness and silence. Now we have the necessary foundation to explore the dimension of the Heart. We continue to breathe in the Heart.

What is the Soul? Similarly, as with the I Am, the Soul is not necessarily present. She must be awakened in order to be experienced. So far, she is in a latent state, in a dormant condition. What the average person experiences as oneself is the shadow of the Soul, which is the ego or the mind. The Soul is your intimate identity in the Heart. Feel your Heart, feel yourself... put your hands on the chest. Who is putting your hands on the Heart? It is the Soul herself which is putting her thirsty hands on the Heart in order to discover herself! She wishes to wake up, at last, to her own light.

The tool we are using to work with Awareness is attention. The tool to deepen Being is surrender. The tool to awaken the

Heart is Sensitivity. Be very soft, delicate inside and feminine... wake up to the fact that you do have a Heart! The Heart is made from pure energy, which is sensitivity and Love, in truth. This love is not externally oriented. It is reality into itself. There is Love and love's expressions. Love itself is not an emotion but the energy presence of the Heart Centre. It is like the I Am - it exists in itself without translating its presence through the outer. This love is your Soul...

In the Soul-less plane where we live, which is the collective human mind - we are discovering the Soul. The forgotten flower within us, the inner Sun... and with the help of the Divine it is done...

With each inhalation we feel our Heart, the sweetness of our Heart; with each exhalation we relax into Being, into Non-doing, into Wholeness itself...

LOVE PEACE GRACE

# Transmission 6
## India: 31st January 99

Welcome... to the dimension of inner silence, inner stillness and inner wholeness which is the Other Dimension, the Other Side of the Now. The Now has two sides: one is the earth dimension and the other is the Divine Dimension, the dimension of Wholeness, eternal perfection where nothing changes, nothing evolves and nothing is lacking...

When you... when your Souls have, at one stage, decided to incarnate, to journey in time - a state of forgetfulness replaced your timeless self-knowledge. The state of forgetfulness was given to you, by the power of which you experience this dimension of time as if in separation from the Other Dimension. Why was the state of forgetfulness given to you? So you could experience the joy of remembrance! At one stage of evolution, when you are completely tired of forgetfulness, when you are really tired of suffering, when you are simply tired of being a separate Me, a separate entity - you begin to question your situation. You give rise to the conscious evolution which takes you again to the state of Oneness, where you return home to the womb of Universal I AM or... God.

This is how it looks from the Universal Perspective. You might have come here to practice meditation, to calm down your mind, but the reality of this meeting is much deeper; it has metaphysical Depth. The voice that you hear is coming from your... Future. When you reach, at one stage of your evolution, the Other Dimension you will know that only IT exists, and all else is but a shadow.

Spiritual Evolution is about returning home to the Other Dimension, to the state of Wholeness. This mechanism, this science of how to shift from the state of forgetfulness to the State

of Remembrance is called the Spiritual Path.  Spiritual Path has
certain laws which have to be comprehended, which must be
respected.  These laws refer to evolution of consciousness and
evolution of energy.  Consciousness and energy, they are two
sides of who you are.  Consciousness is nothing but recognition
of energy - where energy and knowingness meet.

The state of spiritual wholeness, which is truly beyond all you
can imagine, does exist and it is to be reached; it can be reached,
but there are not many who want to reach it.  Let us be clear:
there are not many seekers; there are many who think that they
are seekers, but there are few, almost none, who are really seeking
the Light.  What most call spiritual search is taking place purely
in the realm of Maya.  They do not want, at all, to transcend Maya
— they are in love with Maya.  What they truly want is to find
security and contentment within their limitations, within their
limited perception of reality, within their fragmented and ignorant
self-identity.  No one wants to die to the Bigger Me, to the I AM
- to that which is the Only Reality.

Those who are truly seeking, shall arrive home.  Why?  Because
when the spiritual search is real, it always comes from the Soul.
When the desire for peace and completion arises in the Heart,
and the intention is sincere — the support from the Beyond comes
instantaneously.  One simply receives help from the Divine itself,
from our Parent, who is God...

Let us be practical and explain what awakening is about.  Just
as an ordinary person is identified with the mind, identified
completely with the emotional and physical bodies, so there exists
a way of Being where one is Beyond these bodies and the mind.
This state we call I Am, a holistic and unconditional experience
which is constant in someone who is fully awakened.  The question
arises: how to shift from identification with the mind, from this
chaotic, semi-conscious and deeply disturbing state, to the way
of existing which is free from the mind - to the complete experience
of I Am?

This shift requires, first of all, awakening of Awareness.
Awareness is a key for everyone who is at the beginning of the

Path. Awareness, whose heart is Attention, is itself the only way beyond identification with the mind. That's why, Awareness must be awakened. The next element indivisible from the shift into I Am, is the ability to rest in Being. It also has to be awakened. Awareness and Being are two sides of the I Am. For that reason, Absolute Meditation is aiming at the awakening of these faculties.

The purpose of meditation is not a temporary tranquilisation of the mind; a temporary pacification of neurosis; the purpose of meditation is to reach a state which is permanent, which exists beyond sitting, standing or walking. Be clear about it. At the beginning you may experience the State of Meditation only in a sitting position, but afterwards it enters your life and finally - it becomes you!

Slowly, please, prepare yourself to enter the State of Meditation. How do you prepare yourself to enter the State of Meditation? First, express to yourself a clear intention that you want to surrender into the Now, whatever it is, that you will have the courage to let go of your mind, to let go of your fears, anxieties, concerns revolving around your separate self and protecting your well-being in this dimension. Simply let go of all of this and have the courage to relax into your existence, in order to experience, regain, the lost part of yourself which is under the water of the mind.

Gently connect with your Heart, connect with your Soul in the Heart. Connect with that which brought you here and ask yourself a question: what it is that you want? Why are you here? Not, what your mind tells you, but what the deeper part of yourself whispers to you... Ask yourself in your Heart: "why am I here? What am I looking for? What is it that can make me feel complete, fulfilled and right?..." As you connect with your Heart, with your Soul - through this very Heart express your longing, to the Divine, to be helped. Ask, within your Heart space, for help. You are asking that which you cannot see... but you have no choice but to trust it's existence. Existence of that which created You, which created your Soul, which brought you here into this cage of Maya,

into this dimension of ignorance where you don't know, you don't
have a clue - who you are or what you are doing here! You are
just like a child asking your parent for help... and you do have
a parent; you are not an orphan...

* * *

We begin our meditation with a short bow. We are entering the
inner Shrine, the temple of inherent purity which is our True Self
- the Guest we are meeting now.

We start with slow and deep breathing into the belly... we are
breathing into the belly not merely to focus the mind, which is
a meditation technique, but for energy reasons. The belly... Hara
is the centre of energy. It has to be deepened; it has to be
transformed in order to be capable of containing the higher state
of consciousness, beyond the body and mind. So please, breathe
slowly and deeply, at the same time relaxing into Being, relaxing
into the Now and learning what it means to Be.

Sit, please, in a very disciplined way; don't move if it's not
necessary. Don't listen to your mind which wants to escape from
the situation of non-activity. Remain motionless. If you experience
pain, try first to observe it; do not react. Sit like a mountain,
with determination, as if your life was dependent upon it.

You see, as normally, most of you are identified with the mind,
you are nothing but this very mind. Your sense of identity is...
equals... thinking. But, through the simple act of breathing into
your belly and relaxing into Being, on the energy level, you
expand... your sense of identity expands. There is still thinking
but somehow you experience yourself more, there is more of you
and this is called Being. We are adding the quality of Being to
you. Stopping of the mind is not necessary - adding of the quality
of Being is necessary!

You are doing a few things simultaneously: breathing into the
belly which involves a certain gentle effort and you are attentive,
not to get lost in unconscious thinking. You have to be attentive,
all the time returning to the breath... being attentive and breathing
is what you do. But apart from that, the true key of this practice

is letting go into Being. This relaxing into Being is more passive...
you are using more gentle energy, feminine energy of surrender.
Being is very, very subtle and gentle. One has to be very, very
sensitive to recognise it and to... learn how to be in harmony with
it. So you are attentive, you are breathing into your belly and
letting go into Being, encountering it in each moment and mastering
the subtle art of how to Be.

You will have a short brake... still keeping inner focus, not
allowing the mind to take you away from the subtle connection
with Being.

* * *

Our first meditation was about Being, about expansion into Being
as well as understanding what Being truly is. The second
meditation is about Awareness. Awareness is the sky and Being
is the earth. They are two sides of the same reality of the I Am.
For that reason, they both need to be activated, awakened and
integrated.

What is Awareness? Awareness is the light of knowing. If
there is any recognition, any perception, Awareness is involved
for it is due to Awareness that knowing arises. Awareness is the
light of consciousness, which makes any experience possible.
That's why it is an essence of our life.

There two kinds of mindfulness: one is the mindfulness of
object, second is the mindfulness of subject. When mindfulness
refers to itself, it refers to the subject which is the mysterious
Experiencer, the One behind the field of experiencing.

Where is the centre of Awareness? Where is the centre of
observation? It is in the mind. When you are aware of the breath,
the centre of observation is involved. The centre of wakefulness
directs the energy of intelligence towards the breath, becoming
conscious of it. But it is more difficult to become aware of
thinking; it is more difficult to observe the mind. Why? Because
the centre of observation is simply too close to the thinking
process. To observe the breath is fairly easy for there is distance,
but to observe the mind... one cannot create the distance, one
doesn't know where to locate oneself in this act of observation.

As we speak, please, direct your attention to the mind, become aware in the head. So you see, in the mind there are two things: first, various sensations, thoughts, mental impressions, images which you recognise on the screen of consciousness... and second, the very Awareness behind, which allows you to be aware of the mind. Learning how to observe the mind, you are simply activating, triggering this Awareness, freeing it from unconscious identification with the mind. This Awareness, in the case of the average human being, is functioning at the minimum. It is not aware of itself; it is used only to perceive various objects on the screen of consciousness, lost in mental and empirical reality. So, what we want to do, is to separate this Awareness from mental activity. We want to give rise to the experience where Awareness is aware of itself, without any object.

Normally, Awareness needs an object in order to create recognition. There are many kinds of objects: physical, mental, emotional... but what is this Awareness without any object? What is this Awareness which is aware of Awareness only? That is more difficult, more subtle... One has to learn how to turn attention In, how to turn attention back to itself, back to the centre of Awareness. Awareness without an object is the heart of meditation.

As you are observing the mind, do it very sharply, with great intensity and, at the same time, becoming sensitive to this amazing fact that there is something in your mind, which is beyond the mind. There is something which is observing the mind and which is not the mind, which is not (the) thinking. There is something which is... prior to thought, before thought. Become sensitive to it and try to recognise it, gently turning attention back to itself...

A person who is aware of the mind is an aware person; a person who is aware of the observer is a self-aware person. This self-awareness is the first step of awakening. Here, for the first time one is aware of oneself not as a mind, not as an ego, but as pure I, Atman, Awareness itself.

Be very focussed. It is an important practice. When we sit just with Being, it is easier to sit, for you are more grounded and calm. When you go into the mind, you may feel restless because of booming disconnected from Being. Be aware of it and don't lose focus. Observe the mind sharply. You are Awakening! You are leaving behind yourself, a human machine, a human thinking robot and you become a conscious being. Like a snake leaving its skin behind, you are shifting into the Future, to the place where for the first time you can say: I Am, not only the mind is...

To help you, we will change the practice a bit. Now, instead of observing the mind, as it arises, you will be thinking about anything you wish, but doing it consciously. Being present and contemplative, you are thinking with full involvement... and, as you think, become sensitive to your very Me who is doing this thinking. Become sensitive to the Thinker. Try to distinguish and separate the thinker from thought. When you think consciously, when you are involved... when you've got a problem to solve, you are certainly present. It is not merely the "mind" thinking; You are thinking... and who is this Me who is thinking? You must find this out...

When you think consciously, there is a quality of attention. To whom does this attention belong? It belongs to the Subject, to the I, to the Me. This Me is a feeling behind thought. It has continuity. Thoughts, they come and go, come and go... the Me, the thinker, has a continuity of presence behind the mind. This should help you to recognise the essence of the mind. Look for this that has continuity and on which you can rely, in terms of having a constant experience. Please, pay attention to the One behind the mind....

The moment you do recognise the Me behind thoughts, simply take hold of it, keep it, stay with it and let go of thinking. Stay only with the Me... and as you keep it, relax with it in your mind. There are simultaneous elements of relaxing and holding in the work with the State of Presence or self-attention. Holding and relaxing... relaxing with it and keeping it firmly in focus. And what is this Me? What is the centre of the mind, which we call the State of Presence? It is Me certainly, but what kind of Me is it? It does not have any face... it doe not have any form... it does not have any identity, any memory, any age or sex; it is simply Me - pure Me.

Ego is like smoke from a candle, Me is the very flame. You might be surprised but human beings do not experience Me; they experience a shadow of it, which is ego. Here we are discovering Me; we are discovering who we are beyond the mind...

At the present moment... with the breath in your belly, again, you relax into Being, allowing energy to gravitate downwards according to the law of gravity - into the direction of the original stillness. Be focussed. If you are not able to sit for one hour without movement, you will not reach anywhere. In the past, one had to renounce everything: going to the monastery, sitting for years, suffering physical discomfort and pain... not being emotionally fulfilled, not experiencing human love... only practicing Dharma. You don't need to do that, but you must do something! If you are not able to suffer for one hour, if you are not able to sacriface and remain motionless... it means that you don't have will, basic will which could take you home. This discipline is not for the sake of discipline; it is common sense. It is compassion...

We relax into Being, into the ocean of Beingness, into the vastness of Existence. The heart of reality is Now. The Now is a secret. It is very, very intimate, very close to who we are. It is so close that we miss its existence. How can the Now be experienced? Through Being only! Being is, itself, the Now.

Awareness frees us from the mind, from unconsciousness. It gives us a sense of self in the mind, a centre in consciousness and in intelligence. Being allows us to rest, to surrender, to let go and to be received by the vast hands of Existence, which is Beingness itself.

This art of Being has to be practiced. What most of you experience at this moment, is merely a touch of Being; this experience can go much deeper. The depth of it relates to the expansion and deepening of energies within the Hara. This energy, the body of Being, becomes more and more subtle, more and more refined, so it can receive a deeper and deeper experience of Beingness. It is the evolution of energy. One has to sit. Sitting meditation is so important! One must sit every day; one needs to do retreats; one has to learn How to Be - one has to surrender...

* * *

We make the last effort, bringing ourselves to the vertical reality of the Now... to that which is so fast that one cannot grasp it but one can Be it. In the middle of this vast universe, which you experience through five senses and through the mind, there is this You, your very Soul. Your Soul is not just an outcome of what you experience, it is a reality into itself and the foundation of the Soul is the I Am. Your I Am is a reflection of the Universal I AM, which is God. It is a reflection and a golden gateway to God itself... to become one with that which created you. This oneness is experienced on the energy level, on the level of Beingness.

You are relaxing into Being, enjoying the space of Being, seeing the sweetness of this experience. It is sweet to Be! Isn't it? It is sweet to Be, but nobody sees it! To enjoy most people need a noisy "techno-party" because they are dead! They don't have even a touch of Being. You have to become completely quiet inside and sensitive to experience Being... and when you re-connect with this ancient energy, for the first time you experience Existence, not as a concept, but as Reality.

As we sit with Being, we put our hands on the Heart, which is in the middle of the chest. From our human perspective, we can experience Awareness, Being and Heart separately. We can feel only Heart without Being; we can feel only Being without Heart or we can experience only Awareness. The Other Dimension is a total complete unity of Awareness, Being and Heart. It is all melted into one, unified universal taste of I AM.

So, as you sit with your Being, you are breathing into your chest, adding... adding to your Being the subtle vibration of the Heart, the gentle, sensitive and beautiful vibration of the Heart. In this way, the energy of Being changes, becomes transformed, something is being added: a new quality, the Divine nectar flows into Being from the depth of the Heart.

With each inhalation, you are feeling your Heart, and discovering what it is that you feel in the Heart. With each exhalation you relax into Being, within the experience of which the energies of the Heart are already combined.

The foundation of I Am is Awareness and Being, but I Am also has a Heart in the middle. This Heart is the seat of the Soul, the essence of our identity and the only link with the Heart of the Creator, with the Divine Dimension. This link is Inside the Heart; you are journeying into the space of the Heart discovering the depth and the fundamental unity with the Beloved.

### GRACE PEACE LOVE

# Transmission 7
## India: 4th February 99

Beloved Friends, welcome to our next meeting, which is a meeting
with your own Self. In our meetings you make various efforts
to support the process of spiritual awakening. Your efforts are
constantly assisted by Guidance, which offers you clarity and
understanding.

We are going to explore the most important subject of our true
identity. How can you meet yourself, the essence of who you are,
beyond the outer and superficial layers of personality, beyond the
movement of the mind and fluctuation of emotions? Today we
would like to focus on this fundamental question which has been
asked for a few thousand years by different sages and spiritual
seekers: "Who am I?"...

The question "Who am I?" is very important, but what is even
more important is the understanding that the answer to this question
is multidimensional. Usually, when you are asked the question,
"Who are you?", there is this immediate contraction and feeling
of being stuck, for you simply do not know the clear answer. In
search for the answer, we are trying to find "one thing" which
would fulfill the criteria of being "ME." But, in truth, who we
are, is multidimensional. Who we are is simply composed of
several different but complementary qualities.

As we evolve on the spiritual path, we discover more and more
of who we are; we discover the complexity and the richness of
the I Am which is our identity before the mind. Of course, the
question, "Who am I?" points to something which is before
thinking, which is before the mind. The purpose of this question
is to shake a person from their usual identification with the mind
and personality. In this way, the person looks inside, trying to
discover something deeper than self-image... and what is it, this
that is deeper?

One cannot understand it unless the complete I Am is manifested. In Advaita Vedanta, when they speak about the Self, we might assume that it refers to one area of experience, to one reality which is common to all awakened beings. In this way either one recognises the Self or one does not, and there is nothing in-between. But, in reality, the Self itself is multidimensional and is not always revealed fully to the awakened being. That's why, we have created the Inner Map of Awakening: to bring clarity into this sublime area. One can experience some aspects of the Ultimate or one can be fully awakened, merging with the Wholeness. The level of Self-realisation reflects our own expansion and growth into "who I am."

Awakening to the Self does not mean that suddenly one remembers what one has forgotten. It is the whole expansion of energy and Consciousness; one becomes wider and wider, reaching deeper and deeper the heart of Reality.

The teaching, which we represent here is not a traditional teaching. It goes deeper into the understanding of the complexity of the inner world and the process of awakening. Listen carefully because this information is important, it will help you to understand yourself. The growth, the expansion into the Inner States and Understanding should always accompany each other. If there is no understanding, the experience of I Am is dull and without depth. We grow in understanding and in sensitivity; we meet the Eternal with our own intelligence and our own Heart.

The question, "Who am I?" can be answered on three levels. If a person, who has strong energy in the mind, is able to recognise the State of Presence, for this person the centre of identity is in Awareness. Therefore, this person would conclude: "I am the Witness, I am pure Awareness." It is an experience in mind. The mind itself has many layers: on the surface, it is just thinking, but deeper, it is the source of Awareness — it is Awareness itself. Awareness is generated in the mind; without mind there is no Awareness, there is nothing. In the case of a feeling type of person, who does not have a strong mind but deep connection with the Heart, the answer would be different. Such a person would find the centre of identity in the Heart, of course. This person would not be able to understand that one can place the centre of identity in the mind. Finally, in the case of a person who has neither strong mind nor much connection with the Heart, but is able to tune into the inner calm, to the inner rest, to the stillness within, the answer would be again different. This person would translate his/her sense of identity as Being. This person would answer the question "Who am I?" by saying: "I simply am, I am just Being." For such a person the experience of oneself is deeper than the mind, Awareness and emotion. Simply Being.

These three answers are correct. They represent the three qualities of I Am. The complete I Am is not one thing, but is composed of three colours of the inner rainbow. Awareness is in the mind free from thoughts; the Heart, feeling of the Soul is in the middle of the chest; and finally there is the state of Being, where one simply rests within. In Hinduism they call it the Ultimate Reality: Sat-Chit-Ananda, Being, Awareness and Heart. This is the complete answer to the question "Who am I?"

In our meditation, the Absolute Meditation, we are simply awakening these three qualities, going beyond the simplistic and linear conclusions drawn by the past traditional teachings. This meditation is based on the clear perception of the multidimensionality of I Am.

* * *

We will begin our meditation trying to reach the experience of I Am deeper and deeper, more and more complete. We keep the spine straight, sitting in a strong position, in a way that we do not need to move. We sit with full determination, letting go of the mind which is the past and which is fear. We are surrendering to the Now.

Our first meditation aims at the deepening and awakening of our connection with Being. We begin with slow and deep breathing into the belly; with each inhalation we are very attentive; with each exhalation we relax, letting go into Being. At the same time, we are discovering the true meaningfulness of Being. What it means to Be.

You are not fighting with the mind, at all. You discover your existence below the movement of thoughts, deeper than the mind. Awakening is not merely a function of understanding or a result of an intellectual insight. It is directly connected with the transformation of energy. If energy is not transformed, one is unable to experience the complete "who I am." Therefore, breathing is essential — breathing into the belly. This has been the discovery of ancient Taoism. Taoism, in many respects is much more practical and realistic then the idealism of Hindu spirituality, although sometimes it may lack metaphysical depth.

You are not only breathing into your belly; it is just a part of your activity. You are continuously performing a conscious surrender into Being, letting go into the vertical reality of the Now. If you merely concentrate on the breath, you can become a martial art adept, but not a meditator. You will have a strong Hara, but you will not be someone at peace, resting in the bliss of the Inner State. The conscious surrender into Being is absolutely essential. You are simply dropping yourself into Being, into being nothing; into this space of isness which is the true heart of the Now.

Be focussed and be at ease. You have to be focussed, for if you are not focussed, you are dispersed, you do not exist as a centralised being. The mind is in a chaotic condition and the energy is restless, fluctuating in a disturbing way. Focus brings all these elements together, and it is only when you keep yourself together, that there is a possibility of surrender into Being. Only when you have the Self, can you surrender into the Non-Self.

In this process of practice, in this process of meeting yourself and inner growth, we wish you to go beyond the myth of Enlightenment. We wish you to be free from the arrogant concept of Enlightenment which has been stimulating the egos of so many seekers. Behind the concept of Enlightenment, there are many power games and emotional manipulations. We have the image of Enlightenment as taking us beyond our human nature and giving us some supernatural abilities. Because in our minds the Enlightenment is so high, one does not dare to think of reaching it. We think that only special beings or "avatars" can accomplish it. There is too much nonsense and self-image manipulations in the spiritual scene.

Enlightenment is something natural; it is simple and complex because there are layers of Enlightenment, but the complexity of reaching it refers simply to the natural and ordinary, in its essence, process of growth. One becomes more and more peaceful and connected with the inner silence, more and more rooted in the Universal Wholeness, more and more absorbed in Reality. It does not make you anything special — you are simply at peace with Existence and with yourself...

If you experience a certain energetic connection with Being, certain strength in your energy, certain amount of calmness and concentration in the mind, you can let go into Non-doing. You can let go of focusing on the breath. Let go into pure Being, which is non-activity, exploring the dimension of Shikantaza, just sitting, just being without any direction. Here, attention is simply resting, in no-direction — just being.

* * *

What is the function of ego? There are two kinds of ego: the intelligent ego and the unintelligent one. The unintelligent and unconscious ego is lost in the mind and disconnected from Awareness, Being and Heart. But there is also an intelligent ego, which is exploring the deeper dimensions of Me, which is awakening Awareness, which is discovering its own Heart and which is surrendering into Being. That is the intelligence of spiritual ego. Ego is a function. It is not who we are, it is a part of us. Who we are is deeper. Ego is a tool of intelligence, but who is using this tool? The one who is using this tool is deeper...

We relax into the Now in a very focussed way. There are two elements of the Path. One is the Self-knowledge, this that they called Gnyana Yoga and the second is our effort, discipline and the practice itself. In certain traditions, the emphasis is on practice. One is doing the practice in hope of reaching one day the promised goal of Enlightenment. Usually it never comes true. The second approach, the approach of Self-knowledge, comes from the assumption that when one looks inside with complete clarity, one should discover the whole of I Am, and, therefore, become fully Self-realised. Unfortunately, this does not work either, because even if one has the transcendental insight, one is unable to retain it. Self-knowledge is not enough to oppose the inertia of ignorance, for ignorance itself has a strong power of unconsciousness.

Ignorance has the power of the past, certain habitual tendencies of the mind. For that reason, the Path of Practice and the Path of Self-knowledge have to go together. One needs to practice but at the same time inquiry has to be involved. One has to look inside asking important questions and discovering the Self. What is this that is eternal? Who am I? One needs to make various attempts at trying to discover oneself in a true sense, to find out, to wake up from this dream. If one only practices, the light of intelligence is not present and the process of growth is dull, devoid of the transforming power....

We use our intuitive intelligence, at all times, to discover who we are. We investigate in an intuitive way, not intellectualizing: what is it that is deeper than the mind, who am I, what is my true identity beyond becoming, beyond the body and the mind? From the other side, we are cultivating... cultivating Awareness, deepening our energy and bringing together all necessary elements. This that we say to you is pure wisdom. This that is being revealed to you is not a theory but Clarity. Why do so many get lost? Why does almost everyone is lost? Because this Clarity is missing.

Our second meditation is about the quality of I Am which is called Awareness. Where is Awareness? It is in the mind. When you are not aware of Awareness itself, you experience Awareness as thinking. A very fast process of recognition of different objects: mental, physical and emotional. But Awareness itself is beyond object. Awareness itself is called self-awareness. The heart of Awareness is attention, when attention becomes attentive to attention, here, the non-dual Awareness is born. The centre that is responsible for the birth of true Awareness is the third eye, which is in the middle of your brain. Unless it is activated, one simply cannot experience Awareness free from thoughts.

To help this process, we bring our energy to the mind for a few moments. Please, focus on the point in the middle of your forehead and slightly inside the skull. Your eyes are turning up into this direction. Stay like this for a few moments, please.

Now you relax... keeping energy still in the head. Now you experience more energy in the head, more presence. If you don't have enough energy in the mind, you will remain unconscious. You see, "being in the mind" means that one is thinking constantly, one is living like a computer, but to have energy in the mind is something else. To have energy in the mind means that one is attentive, there is an energy of presence and mindfulness.

Look into your mind, into your head. Is there anything that you can call "I," apart from coming and going of thoughts and mental information, which are changing all through life? Is there anything that is immediate? Before a thought comes, is there anything already waiting? Is there anything, which carries the same flavour all your life and that can you recognise as Me? Or does such a thing not exist??

The fundamental principle of spiritual exploration is that one is always looking for this which is immediate, instantaneous. There is no time, it is already there! The real seeker searches only for this which is already present, which is Now! The object of our search is the closest to us, for it is the subject. We are trying to find the zero point, this which is so fast that one is unable to grasp it, but It Is.

So, when you are looking in your mind: is there something which is immediate, instantaneous, which is fast like thunder? This which is instantaneous, is attention itself; this attention is I, or atman, or pure Me... When this attention is recognised, it does not have any object, attention is subject, it is I. However, when one is so identified with thinking, with perceptions, one does not have enough inner focus and clarity to make this recognition.

The foundation, one of the pillars of awakening, is recognition of attention without thought, self-attention, and making this experience constant. In the case of a person who is Self-realised, this self-attention never leaves — it is constant. In India, they called it: witnessing consciousness. Witnessing is an experience in the head, in the third eye. It is an energy behind the mind, behind thinking — the vibration of the centre....

Now we will make our next practice: observing the mind, observing thoughts, as they arise and vanish at the screen of consciousness. When you observe thinking, you are observing this that you are not. This does not mean that thinking does not belong to you, it is simply not your centre. A thought cannot be the centre, because it has a momentary existence. It cannot be retained; it can only be repeated over and over. So, observing the mind you are observing what you are not. The one who is behind the observing, is who you are. The whole trick is to find out who is observing or who is the one behind the observing process; simply to make a step back in Awareness. When you observe the mind, Awareness becomes stretched, as if the muscle of Awareness was stretched, and there is much more spaciousness arising in the mind. You are not just thinking automatically, you are aware of arising thoughts. But who is aware of arising thoughts? This you must find out, and there is no technique that can replace your own awakening! Look directly...

At this moment, with this Awareness in the mind relax into Being. You can connect gently to the breath in the belly... letting go and in this letting go being very focussed, very concentrated. Not allowing the pain in the body to disturb you, sit like a mountain... relax into Being.

The energies of Beingness are originally below the conscious level. They are not conscious. But you become conscious of the experience of Being because Awareness is there. Without Awareness you return to the deep sleep state without dreams: no Awareness, only pure Being remains. In our practice, Awareness and Being meet, this meeting is called I Am. We are expanding you into a deeper identity. You are letting go of identification with the mind, you are leaving the skin behind, becoming a new being, a whole being. You become a being that does not belong to the human kind anymore, but to the Universal Consciousness.

There is a way of existing, where you experience yourself holistically, with extraordinary depth, with extraordinary sensitivity of complete Awareness. In such a state, you are beyond the mind in unity with the I Am. It is your choice whether you wish to reach this state. If you really want to attain it, you will attain it and there is no power which could stop you! Why? Because you are in harmony with evolution and evolution is itself the light of Creation. Unfortunately, this sincere desire is rare and that's why most seekers reach only fragments of I Am. Look into your Heart...

\* \* \*

Part of us lives in the external reality; the reality of objects, we are constantly connecting to, through the five senses and through the sixth sense which is the mind. In the middle, there is this I Am. It has nothing to do with the perception of the outer, it is in the middle, it is I Am, our dignity and true identity. Ignorance refers to the fact that a particular individual is not aware of the I Am, this person is only an outcome of what is being perceived, thought and experienced. In such a case, what is present is a constant psychosomatic moment, deprived of I Am. The I Am is not present, unless it is being given birth to. That is our work, awakening of I Am, of that one who is in the middle: the King who sits on the golden throne, in the middle of this physical form.

Awakening is not about being someone special... it is about being sane, about being real, for the first time, and the foundation of being Real is I Am. You relax into the dimension of Beingness, letting go into the Now, like a drop of water letting go into the ocean, merging and yet, at the same time — remaining a drop of water. What is this drop of water? It is your Soul. The Soul is your true identity, as an individual. She is the divine flavour of your unique individuality, which is placed in the Heart.

The primal instinct of the Soul is to reach happiness, complete contentment. If you look inside your Heart, you will see that this is the truth. You wish to be happy and not to suffer. That is your Soul's wish.

* * *

As usual, in our last meditation, we are adding the element of Heart. We become aware of the Heart centre, breathing to the chest, adding the sensitive and so precious energy of the Heart to the experience of Being. With each inhalation we are feeling our Heart, with each exhalation we relax into Being. Put your hands on the Heart in a soft and loving way. To the Chit, which is Awareness and to the Sat, which is Being, we are adding Ananda, which is the Heart.

Awakening is not, as some assume, to become an impersonal Consciousness. In reality, it is to become completely personal within the vastness of the impersonal Universal I AM. When one merges in the Universal I AM, this experience is both, impersonal and absolutely personal. It is experienced through our own Soul, which is in the Heart and through our own intelligence.

This happiness which you experience, the deeper you go into I Am, it is your happiness, this happiness belongs to your Soul. The child returns home to the house of its Eternal Parent, to the house of God. The child was wondering, wondering in the land of Maya, in the land of ignorance for a long time... and now is coming back. The child has learnt its lessons. It has been enough, to live like this in the state of forgetfulness, in the cage of a separate ego. One is ready to return home, to the womb of Timelessness, which is the only Reality.

## GRACE PEACE LOVE

# Transmission 8
## Israel: 16th March 99

Beloved Friends, we welcome you to our next meeting. Welcome to this place which never changes and which is inside you covered with the dust of ignorance, covered by the mind. We will be uncovering this place, discovering this place within us. Digging deeper and deeper into how we experience our own existence in the eternal Now.

We start with breathing into the belly. Slow and deep breathing. When you breathe deep into your belly, like a tree you are rooting yourself in the earth of Beingness, on the energy level. You are letting go of the mind, of all that has happened today, yesterday and before - of the entire past. Just being here, naked and exposed to this present moment with whatever it can offer you.

We are used to living through the mind. There is nothing wrong with the mind as such. The mind is simply a tool to be used. It is the tool to think, to understand, but we are not this tool. We are the one who is using it. Because the mind has become so important, it almost seems that we have become it. In this way we do not experience ourselves otherwise than thinking. That is neurosis or simply madness. This madness does not relate to the content of your mind as such, but to the very way this mind operates within you. There is no control over the mind, it has its own momentum of ignorance and unconsciousness.

As you relax into this moment, you are learning like a child again what it means to experience yourself, not as a thought, but as that which is much deeper and direct. It is already here... We breathe into the belly slowly and deeply, being very attentive; not allowing ourselves to be lost in the mind and taken away from this very moment. This is what we do.

In order to experience yourself fully, you need to develop

certain faculties. There are two main faculties that you have to activate within yourself. One is Awareness. Awareness must become stronger, more clear and focussed. It is only Awareness which can free you from forgetfulness and unconsciousness. The second faculty, which you are awakening, relates to the energy expansion within your Hara, through which you can be rooted in Being.

How is it that one person sits and is immediately experiencing deep calm, connection with Being and rest, whereas, another person cannot have this experience? The other person is restless, disconnected from Being and experiencing only the mind. The reason is that, in the first case the energy is more balanced and deep within the Hara. That's why breathing is so important. Let us breathe, letting go into Being...

We sit in a firm and solid way like a mountain. It feels as though nothing can move us. We are breathing into the belly slowly and deeply... Returning to the I Am, to the pure experience of yourself before thinking. The I Am is simply your original form, pure light of the Soul. This light is not visual. The highest, the purest light cannot be seen, it is not visual. It is not outside the one who perceives it, the seer. It is the I Am, it is the subject, it is not the object. As you are breathing and as you are focussed in the present moment, you are constantly returning to the zero point, to the Now where your I Am live, and you are meeting its everlasting presence.

There needs to be an element of curiosity, self-discovery. You are not merely sitting to be quiet. You sit to meet yourself, your own existence, the light of I Am... for only there you can truly rest.

With each inhalation, you are very attentive and with each exhalation, you let go into this which cannot be seen but which Is. To let go, there is no need to do anything, you simply let go. To let go means not to do, to drop... to drop the weight of yourself into the place of non-activity. That is real surrender.

* * *

We know that to sit in meditation is to be in the Now. When you hear the sound of a car on the street, is it Now or is it already the past? There is only one true experience of the Now; that is the I Am. All else is in the past. The I Am is you and the Now is you. That's why, coming closer to the Now, is coming closer to the I Am, to your true centre. What you are trying to do, is to root yourself in the experience of your own existence, which has nothing to do with thinking or perception of the outer reality.

Before a thought arises in you and before you perceive anything, you are already there, aren't you? This that is already there, is the essence of meditation. The One inside, the One who makes any experience possible; the One without which all vanishes. That One is the Soul, your innermost identity, that which never dies and is never born. The Soul does incarnate into the body, but the Soul herself is not born. It is the body that is born, it is the mind, the personality that is born. That's why the deeper you go into yourself, the more you have this amazing realisation that you are not in the body, that you are not in the world and not in time. You feel that you are not from Here, but from somewhere else. Your mind is not able to tell you where you truly abide, but the feeling remains.

We tell you where you are coming from precisely. It is the voice of the Higher Intelligence which tells you this. You are from the I AM, the Divine dimension... you are abiding, in reality, within the Heart of Universal Consciousness, the Heart of the Creator. In truth, only this exists.

The Divine exists. It is beyond time, beyond the universe, beyond all that can be imagined... but it exists. That is the good news, otherwise there would be no hope. Going inside you are finding this ultimate tune, through which you can become again one with the Source and the Light of Creation. You are returning home.

You might not believe it, for you are still a part of the collective human mind, which is recognising only the gross level of reality. It only believes the profane, the mundane, not being aware of our true roots. But even though you might not be fully convinced, as you evolve on the Path, clarity comes to you, and one day it will be your own understanding and perception of reality. We are now planting seeds for the future.

During the first meditation we have been exploring the Being part of the I Am, that which allows you to rest within. The second part of the I Am is Awareness. The awakening of Awareness is the foundation of all true spiritual disciplines. The awakening to Awareness takes place at the point where attention becomes one with attention and there is no object. It takes place in the mind for Awareness is generated in the mind. Without the mind there is no experience.

We direct our attention to the mind. Attention is coming from the mind and can be focussed on many different objects. But when it is directed towards the mind, it comes closer to itself. That's why it is difficult to observe the mind. Thinking is simply too close to the centre of attention. If our eyes are touching the mirror we are unable to see our face... distance is necessary.

You observe the arising and disappearing of thoughts. You are intensely aware of what is happening in the mind. When you are watching the mind, you may find it difficult, for you don't know where your location is within the observing process. To watch thinking, you need to remove yourself from it. You need to step back. But where is this place, from which perspective are you out of the field of the mind? This place is the centre of the mind or the State of Presence. It is your Me in its pure form that is watching the mind, trying to disidentify from it and to pull back to itself. This Me experiences difficulties, for it does not know itself and the place of its location. This Me is awakening in you to itself.

Watching the mind, do it with a sense of self-discovery. You really want to feel, to recognise the One behind the mind. Isn't it the most urgent and important matter? By pulling gently back attention to itself you are meeting that which is the closest to you in the mind. The Atman.

This time you can let go of watching the mind. Instead of observing the mind, you participate in its activity. You are going to think fully and consciously, choosing any subject. Be creative! The moment you hear the signal "stop" - the thinking stops and you remain with the thinker.

Stop!

You begin to think again in a very contemplative way, being fully engaged. When you think fully, it indicates that you are behind. For who is thinking? Certainly yourself. When we say "stop," thinking is cut off, but you remain. Please, recognise it!

Stop!

This that remains, which is instantaneous is the centre in the mind or simply Me. This Me, the centre of attention needs to be kept. It is your true face. The face without form, the formless identity, the face of Awareness... pure light of Awareness. No form and no age... you must have courage to see your true face. If you look into the mirror and you don't see any reflection, you would panic, wouldn't you? But in truth, you don't have a face or your face has no form. This face that you see in the mirror is a temporary contraction into the matter, a cosmic joke.

With the quality of Awareness and crystallisation of attention, we relax into Being. We connect gently to the breath. When you sit, you might experience certain restlessness, in the mind and, above all, on the energy level. You feel discomfort, agitation and boredom. It is because the complete I Am is not manifested yet. However, you are in training. It is not only the present experience that matters but the whole preparation for the birth of the I Am. That's why, you should still remain disciplined even during difficulties. Stay unmoved inside and out. Have the attitude of a warrior. Sit like a tiger: completely relaxed and fully alert.

You continue to breathe, letting the experience of Being manifest itself. You cannot force it but it enters into you. Relax into the purity of the Now as it arises.

You can look at spiritual discipline as a way of bringing temporary relief from the lower aspects of this reality. Or you can see it as a Great Vision offering you a real goal — vision of completion. If you do have this vision, naturally you fully

accept the necessity of training. There is a goal if you wish to
have it. This goal is the complete realisation of the I Am, the
inner wholeness. At this place you are simply whole, from the
bottom up to the top. Nothing is missing there, for the I Am is
present. This is the experience of Happiness. This happiness
is unconditional, not dependent on any outer element, happiness
which is inherent to the Soul.

To reach the spiritual goal one has to make some sacrifices.
One has to practice... one has to dedicate an important part of
life-energy to the spiritual dimension. That is the law of this
dimension.

We relax into Being, into the sweet experience of the Now.
We relax into this familiar taste, the taste of Being. With our
tongue we taste many dishes, but what is the taste of the tongue?
With our being we experience ten thousands things, but what is
the experience of Being? We relax into it. We relax into the
ocean of Beingness, the dwelling place of all living beings.

* * *

As we rest in the ocean of Beingness, let the waves of this ocean
reach higher and higher, until our Heart is touched. We make
several deep breaths into the Heart, into the chest. Putting gently
attention in the Heart, we remain connected to this sensitive
space.

There are three gateways to the realm of God. One is the third
eye, the second is the Hara and the last is the Heart. Through
Awareness one realises this part of God which is pure
consciousness. Through Beingness, one realises the Source, that
which is eternally at rest. Finally, through the Heart, one realises
the Divine-Love aspect of the Creator. When the Heart is not
awakened one is unable to experience the Divine.

Please, put your hands on the Heart, continuing to breathe
gently into this area. You remain like this in unity with the Heart.
You cannot force the Heart to open up. You cannot force the
Heart to love. But you can simply be with your Heart as with
a dear friend, and only then it begins opening like a flower.

Free yourself of all concepts and ideas about love for otherwise, you will not be able to experience your Heart in a genuine way. Be with your Heart and it will teach you about itself.

As there is the outer Beloved so there is the inner Beloved. The inner Beloved is your own Heart. Remain with your Heart, let it vibrate the energy of sensitivity and warmth. As you touch your Heart with your hands, you are tuning in, becoming intimate with this space inside.

Only in your Heart you can become fully one with your Soul. One can be in a state of perfect Awareness and still not have a Soul. Meet yourself... discover your own Soul. After being separated for such a long time, you have a chance to realise directly the intimate light of your everlasting identity. It is in the Heart. Become one with your Soul...

Remain with your Heart... remain with your Being...

Remain with That who You Are.

PEACE LOVE GRACE

# Transmission 9
## Israel: 18th March 99

Welcome again to the dimension of the Now which is beyond the dream of personal life, beyond the illusion of time.

We begin with breathing into the belly and simply relaxing into the Now. When you relax into the Now, it is not that you relax your body or that you relax your mind. It is not what you relax that matters but where you relax into. You relax into the Now. The ultimate tension is not in the body or the mind. The ultimate tension is the disconnection from the Now. This is the basic tension and this very tension we relax, by connecting to the Now.

As you sit, you are very attentive. You keep on guard against forgetting yourself in the mind. When you forget yourself in the mind, you, in reality, forget the Now. The Now exists before the mind, so if you wish to experience it, you need to learn to be before the mind yourself.

From our perspective you are dream characters and dream figures; therefore, you are trying to find a way out of this dream, to the place where you are no longer dreaming but you experience yourself, you experience reality, which is the Now. So in your personal dream we tell you: breathe into your belly and relax into the Now, deeper and deeper. Have courage to let go of the mind, have courage not to protect yourself through the thinking process, have the courage just to be Now. There is nowhere to go, in truth...

How do you experience the Now? It is not what you experience around yourself, different sounds, and sensations - it is your own presence, your own I Am through which you experience the Now. The Now is an energy experience within yourself — that which is the Nearest. Before a thought comes, it is already there. It is your Being. Being is not thinking or feeling — Being is Being.

As you breathe, you are very focussed and you surrender. You drop into the space where you don't do anything but you Are. As you meet, as you encounter this space, you experience this that we call: Being. You become more and more familiar with the taste of Being... and your mind understands this experience as well.

It is a secret, Being. Nobody knows it because it is too subtle. When you are born, as a child all your energy goes outside, and this is how you live all your life. The energy goes outside through thinking, through emotions and perceptions. You become fully identified with the dream, with the illusion of this movie in which you are playing the role of somebody, the main role in your reality. When you come here, to Satsang, to meditation, it is a sign that on some level you have matured, you have grown up, to the extent in which you allow yourself to realise that there is something more than to perceive things, something more than thinking. There is something which is much closer — the I Am, the subject. You start to go into the direction of your eternal home. You don't know how to enter this inner home. You have many concepts and many ideas, but the actual experience is not clear yet, so you are learning how to enter the inner space and you grow in understanding of what this experience is about.

From one side, you are letting go of the mind more and more. You learn how to Be, without relying on the mind. From the other side, by letting go into Being, you are actually meeting this inner space. You are merging deeper and deeper with it. This is the process of expansion into the I Am, the ultimate process of awakening, emerging out from the thick and unconscious dream state of ignorance, into the light of clarity and happiness which is I Am.

You are breathing and letting go into Being. You are very focussed, very alert and very... soft. Because you understand that there is nothing to attain, apart from being here, you naturally relax more into this moment. But within this relaxation you remain very focussed, so the mind will not take you away from this surrender.

From one side, you are discovering yourself, you are discovering the depth of the Now. From the other side, you are creating yourself, you are giving birth to yourself. You are coming out of the cocoon. And what is this cocoon? It is the collective unconsciousness of which you are a part. By encountering yourself you become an individual, a free spirit which lives in its own light, which does not need the borrowed light from others.

Meditation is an art. You don't wish to create in your mind the desire to attain anything as such, for this would take you away from the Now; but, at the same time, there is a process of deepening. Although you are not seeking for anything outside this moment, you deepen the experience of the Now. It deepens itself, which is evolution.

Constantly you are bringing yourself to the zero point, to the subjectivity, pure I before thought. As you bring yourself to the zero point, from the zero point, which is your Presence, you let go. Through this letting go, the deepening takes place.

There is a place, a dimension from which perspective your life and this earth is truly meaningless, without substance. Certainly it has value, because otherwise it wouldn't be here in the first place, but compared with the Other Dimension it is Lila land, illusion. But there is a way out. Living in this primitive dimension on the earth, in your physical body, having so many troubles to survive and never being able to become fulfilled emotionally, you may not believe that there is a way out of sorrow. But there is a way to reach the other dimension through the secret entrance, which is within you. We are showing you the way, how within your experience of yourself, you can find the Secret Gate, the door within, the golden door, the gateless gate... and you are invited to enter this dimension. At that moment, you find yourself on the other side of the Now, which is Reality... at that moment, you meet your Soul, you meet the Divine.

We are breathing and relaxing into the Now. The experience of the Now takes place, on the energy level, within the Hara. That's why breathing helps so much. On the energy level, there is more of you, you become bigger. There is still the mind, there

is still thinking, but You are somewhere else, you have expanded.
You start to rest below, beneath and beyond the mind. In this
way, you experience simultaneously the mind and that which is
beyond the mind — the realm of Being. You become more whole.

You are very focussed. We wish, we wouldn't have to tell you
to be focussed so much. We wish we could tell you: just relax.
But without the energy of focus you would not have a sufficient
amount of attention to be in the present moment, and you would
get lost in the subconscious mind. So be focussed... From this
place of focus, you let go into the space of Being that is underlying.

* * *

We return to the I Am, to the One inside, who is sitting here and
listening. When you listen, when you hear, you know that you
exist. But what is it that exists, that is listening? It is inside.
It is looking through the windows of eyes, ears, nose, tongue,
touch, but it itself is inside. The one who is inside cannot be
easily grasped, because it is not a thing. We cannot make an
image out of it. We cannot pinpoint it like any object, a chair,
for example. It is a subject. The subject is a flavour, a feeling,
an energy state, reflection of God. We cannot grasp it, but it can
be clearly experienced. It cannot be fixed as a concept but you
can become it. This is the reason that you are born: to discover
and experience clearly the One who incarnated into this physical
form. Your ancient Soul identity, your Me in a form of pure light.

In order to experience yourself clearly, however, certain elements
need to be corrected or "repaired" inside you. Because of the
specific path, human evolution has taken, certain elements in our
energy system and in our mind are out of order, not reflecting
the purity of our Soul in the consciousness. For that reason, the
way you experience yourself is fragmented, where many aspects
of your wholeness are simply disconnected.

Our second meditation, as always, is emphasising the Awareness
aspect of the I Am. Awareness is that which allows you to know
anything, the light of knowing behind the perception. The light
of attention... the light of consciousness. It is only when this light

of Awareness is fully bright and activated, that you can free yourself from unconscious identification with the thinking process.

When you have been relaxing into Being, Awareness has been already there. That's why we spoke so much about being attentive. It is important to know that the experience of Being can be recognised only through Awareness. But where does this Awareness come from? Now we are discovering the source and the centre of Awareness. The place where Awareness is experiencing itself without any object.

When we use Awareness, we direct it toward many different areas. It is through its reflections in the objective reality that Awareness can be manifested as knowing. In order to experience Awareness itself, free from its outer expressions, the light of attention has to turn back to the place from where it arises. Here, the State of Presence is born.

We begin with bringing attention into the mind, because Awareness is generated in the mind. We become aware of the thinking process, putting ourselves in the observing position of the watcher. We observe the mind with intense focus and discipline. In the watching of the mind we have the basic sense of distance, certain aloofness and disidentification.

First, we notice the illusory nature of thinking. The thoughts are empty of any substance. They are as phantoms or ghosts in the mind, but because we believe that they are real, they take away our freedom.

Who is producing these thoughts? Thoughts arise from the subconscious mind without our control. But to whom are these thoughts happening? Who is the experiencer of the mind. What is this Me behind the mind?

By feeling and intuitive understanding that thoughts are not you, you are pulling gently back to the discovery of the I, of the Me behind. The first step is disidentification from the mind, which is Vipassana. The next step is self-discovery where you are no longer watching the mind but you turn attention to your Me, you are recognising your very Me, the centre of the mind. Any act of perception originates from the centre. The centre is

Me but the Me is not aware of itself and, therefore, becomes lost in the periphery of the mind.

You must have this essential curiosity to discover this Me, certain important interests. Meditation is more than sitting calmly. Without the element of self-knowledge there is no depth to the inner experience. You must be certain of who you are, who is the One, the I in the middle of your world.

Observation of the mind is a very good beginning. But the problem is that the watcher is not aware of itself, therefore, is unable to find its location in the mind. For that reason, the activity of watching cannot be retained fully, from moment to moment one finds oneself lost in the mind again. It is only when you have a clear location within, that you can fully pull out of the mind. This location is in the mind, but is beyond thinking. It is nothing but the State of Presence, the energetic centre of consciousness. It is the pure Me... you are this location!

Our next practice in order to discover the Me in the mind, is conscious thinking. This time, you will be thinking consciously, being fully present in the thinking process. Instead of observing the mind, this time you are using it... you participate in it being fully engaged.

When you don't participate in the mind consciously, the mind is spontaneously active on the subconscious level. In such a case, the subconscious Me operates. When you co-create thinking, the intuitive intelligence is present. The intuitive intelligence can either observe the mind or co-operate with it. The intuitive intelligence involves the presence of Me. When you think consciously, Me is doubtlessly at the background. Try to feel it, gently turning attention back to itself, to the centre. You have to be sensitive enough and centred enough to recognise the thinker. The thinker and the observer are the same, only the functions are different.

Conscious thinking, when the intuitive intelligence operates, is something in-between the subconscious mind and the awakened state. It is almost awakened for Me is already present, but one is not yet able to stay with this Me and to recognise it in its own light. One is still unable to discern Me from the thinking process. That's why, you have to pay special attention to the sense of Me. Isn't the sense of Me mysterious? The moment you recognise the sense of Me in itself, you must hold into it strongly, keeping it as your own centre in the mind. At this stage, you can let go of thinking. When the thinker is recognised, thinking can be dropped. When you retain your Me, the one who is present behind thoughts, it is no longer used to create conscious thinking. It is now experienced in itself.

By the very presence of Me, the centre of Awareness, the function of the mind gradually transforms. The light of Presence enters the vague, unclear and unconscious energies of the mind and destroys the darkness. One second of light ends a thousand years of darkness.

You are retaining the State of Presence, keeping it and relaxing it in your head. When the State of Presence, which is the pure Me in the mind, refers to itself, it has a quality of a centre; but when it relaxes in itself, it reaches a space-like condition of openness. This experience originates in the brain and is felt in the third eye area, but, simultaneously, it has no limits and, like an open sky, is clear and infinite. It is brilliant and luminous, serene and bright, free and empowered. Such are the qualities of pure Awareness.

At this stage you relax more, no longer keeping energy in the head. Connect to your breath in the belly and let go into Being, into Shikan-taza. Let the energy of Awareness gravitate downward toward the Hara, toward the belly, toward the centre of gravity which is the place of absolute rest within. Not within you... simply Within. Let go into Being, remaining, however, centred and alert in this experience. It is very important to cultivate attention even in the process of deepening the experience of Being. Without enough attention, relaxation into Being can dissolve the essential amount of Awareness, and one becomes again lost in the subconscious mind.

As you drop more and more into Being, the energy experience of the Inner State changes. Observe what happens to your energy.

It is no longer centralised in the head area but encompasses all of you. You become embraced by the holistic experience of the I Am. That is the proper State of Meditation. It is not located in any particular centre in your body, but is all around you from top to bottom. Here, Awareness and Being meet. As you have the feet, so you have the head; as there is earth, so there is sky, and the space between them is the experience of the I Am.

Between Absolute Rest which is the unmanifested energy and the flowering of Awareness which is the State of Presence, there is the whole experience of the individual flavour of the I Am. This experience is a combination of the unique sensitivity of your Soul and the totality of the Universal I AM. Here, you may discover the true meaning of Non-abidance, which is the permanent condition of an enlightened being.

* * *

Please, make one last effort to centre yourself in the I Am, in spite of difficulties and tiredness. Beginning your practice you need to use your will and concentration to keep yourself at the centre, because the habitual tendencies of the mind are exactly the opposite. But the longer you are on the Path, being in the I Am becomes more and more natural, while not being in it seems strange and unnatural. How could one not be in the I Am? Where else could we be? Not abiding in the I Am is truly a neurotic situation. The experience of the I Am is the ultimate intimacy. You are simply intimate with your own existence. You drink the nectar of your own being and through this you become whole.

As the I Am is composed of Awareness and Being, so it has the Heart. This time we devote our time to explore the dimension of the Heart. Please, direct your attention to the Heart centre, at the middle of your chest. Breathe into your Heart and put on it your hands to feel it stronger.

Connect to your Heart. This is the true meaning of Prayer - to be connected to the space within the Heart. When this connection is created, one is in a state of Prayer. Prayer is not an activity of the mind. It is a state of the Heart. The Heart is Love. There are expressions of Love and there is Love itself. Love can be directed towards many different areas and objects through the medium of the emotional body, but when not directed anywhere, Love rests in its own splendour within the Heart dimension. This is the experience of the Divine, which is the Heart of the Creator.

Feeling our Heart, we direct its energy inside it. We activate the energies of the Heart opening them up and we enter into this dimension. We enter into the dimension of Love. Love is not an emotion but a dimension, a state of Being within the Heart. Here, the energy vibrates in the utmost sensitive and beautiful way. One becomes deeply moved.

Within the Heart space we are feeling our own Soul. The Soul is not the mind of Me, but its very Heart, the essence of sensitivity, the ultimate centre of Me. That's why, it feels special to touch the Heart. Doesn't it?

We are discovering our Heart within the context of Meditation. Not in an emotional and superficial way, but rooted in the inner silence and the clarity of Awareness. We do not tell you how you should feel and what you are supposed to feel. We point directly to the reality of the Heart.

Be with your Heart, feel it and be sensitive to it, so it can reveal its secrets to you. Stay with your Heart, with the Beloved inside. Embrace your existence, the I Am and in this embracement dissolve.

## PEACE LOVE GRACE

# Transmission 10
## Israel: 24th March 99

Welcome to our next meeting, which takes place in the Timeless dimension of I AM, which is Reality.

We relax; we simply relax. There are two important questions: who relaxes and into what one relaxes? The question about "who" relates to your own Soul, to your own Me; the question "into what" you relax relates, in truth, to this very I AM, to this dimension in which you are invited.

Meditation is an art of letting go of oneself into that which is much bigger than our individual Me, into this infinite space of Wholeness which is above, below, everywhere and beyond.

Before you let go of yourself, you have to exist, you have to recognise your own existence and crystallise it into the true identity of the Soul. You crystallise it through giving birth to pure Awareness, the State of Presence, the centre of attention and you crystallise it within the expansion into Being, within your individual I Am. The individual I Am is like a crystal ball, completely pure and clear. The crystal ball exists within the universal crystal ball, the infinite crystal ball, which is God.

The individual I Am has a unique flavour of the Soul. In truth, it is the Soul herself experiencing herself within Wholeness. The radiation, the shining of the Soul creates a relative space of individuality. Individuality is not contraction of ego; it is as a wave within the ocean of God... one with the ocean and separated from it, separated and one...

We relax into IT, simultaneously keeping a sense of centralised identity, sense of attention and presence which holds us together. In this way, we create an opposing force against the mind, which is the past and we are able to surrender into the future which is emerging Now.

We relax. We don't relax the body, we don't relax the mind, we relax the I Am. We relax the One inside, the light of the Soul which knows that it exists. It lets go into the Infinite.

Being individuals, living within the borders of our separate Me, we wish to return to that which created our Souls. We are learning how to dissolve. The dissolution is a love affair with the Ultimate, with the Beloved. That's why, it is not a momentary event; it takes time, because Love needs time... to flower... to create affection and movement of emotion. For this reason, we dissolve slowly, not being in too much of a hurry. We appreciate this time of waiting and coming closer... Sometimes, we oscillate our whole life between complete surrender and coming back to our Me, and again into surrender. Until the final point when the lover and the Beloved disappear and what remains is the Mystery.

We relax. We bring this TRUE relaxation, not a shallow, not a primitive relaxation of the body and the mind — a true relaxation of the I Am. Within this relaxation we feel both: we feel the One who surrenders and we feel the Mystery of that into what we surrender; that which we cannot grasp, that which we cannot see, that which is fathomless...

To understand, fully, the true meaning of what is happening in meditation, a tremendous amount of sensitivity is required. Otherwise, one is simply experiencing calmness, which is another name for not being disturbed by the mind... it is no longer a love affair, but a dull abiding within the Now. That is fine, but still one can go further into the understanding of this very meeting with the Now... with the Ultimate. One can hear the music which nobody hears; one can smell the fragrance which nobody is aware of...

We relax. We are not doing, we are undoing, we are canceling ourselves as we arise within the Now. We merge with the inner space. We are no longer who we thought we were. Our past identity is far away. We merge with the inner space. We have no name, we have no form, we have no sex, we have no memory, but - we Are. We are not human beings; we are this very light which allows us to know that we are.

We bring the energies of the I Am into focus, to experience ourselves in a solid way, crystallising the State of Presence, being present fully as intelligence and letting go into the inner space of relaxation, true relaxation, dissolution. When we dissolve we do not stop existing but our existence is a part of something bigger: of the Wholeness.

Look carefully at the one who dissolves and see that the essence of that one is in the Heart. It is the Heart which dissolves. Our individual heart dissolves into the Universal Heart, the Heart of the Creator. We just let go. No effort, no memories, no identification, no name... this is the experience of the Soul.

The Soul cannot experience herself unless she dissolves. She can experience herself only within the Universal I AM, because she exists only within the Universal I AM.

We relax. Our I Am and the Universal I AM are one I AM. They are made from the same light. This light is called Love.

GRACE PEACE LOVE

# Introductory Talks

## Transmission: 19th November 98

Welcome beloved friends, to our next meeting which takes place in the plane of Understanding, where Intelligence, Love and Being are one. You are invited to enter the Inner Realm. The Inner Realm exists and can be accessed. The outer reality is but a shadow of the inner realm. The inner realm is not a psychic realm. The psychic realm is the outer realm. The inner realm is a dimension of pure subjectivity which is eternally beyond the dream of becoming, the dream of time.

With the "technology of consciousness" that we use here, we can easily take you in, within yourself, but your co-operation is necessary. There has to be desire in your Heart to meet yourself, to meet your own light.

Most of the energy that you invest is directed toward physical and emotional security in the external reality. How can you go in? There is no more energy left to go in. All energy goes out. In order to go in, you have to renounce, sacrifice a certain important amount of energy that is normally dissipated for your personal well-being.

You have to direct this energy in so you regain your wholeness, your connection with who you are, before your role in the outer reality. Most seekers fail in their search because they are not sincere. They are not looking for themselves, they are looking to fulfil their projections about Enlightenment or spiritually. They build up their ego, instead of finding their true nature. It is easy to find who one is. It is easy to reach inner completion and inner peace, if there is a desire in the Heart and certain capacity in the mind.

The Inner State we are aiming at, we call here the I Am. The I Am is who you are before thinking, before identification with the mind, with your psychology. When one is identified with the mind, one is the mind, one is not alive. In order to become alive, one has to get out of the mind to find one's own integrity below, beneath, beyond the mind. The art of meditation is an art of being beyond the mind. Meditation is not a short experience or an accidental experience. It is a transcendental state that exists objectively. We are simply accessing it, tapping into this dimension.

The challenge of this teaching is to bridge the state of complete forgetfulness, complete ignorance, unconsciousness, in which an ordinary person is immersed, with the dimension of awakening where one is free and complete. How to bridge these two completely separate worlds is the challenge of teaching.

That bridge between the world of unconsciousness, which is an ordinary state of human consciousness, and the supreme flowering of consciousness, which is the Buddha mind, is called the Path. The spiritual path is clear. It is a scientific path. Each step is clear. There is no mistake, no accident, no miracles, a natural unfoldment of evolution.

We would like to initiate you into the true spiritual path, not into an illusion of spiritual path. Following the true spiritual path, you know what you are doing and where you are heading to. You understand your state and all the steps in-between.

The process of awakening is both negative and positive. The negative part relates to the various tools that we are using in order to get out of the mind, to cut through the mechanical and unconscious identification with the thought process, to get out of the prison. The positive part of the awakening process is the whole discovery of "who I am" apart from the mind and the deeper and deeper experience of I Am. The positive and negative support each other in this process. You need to learn how to get out of the mind and you need to discover who you are apart from the mind.

* * *

## Transmission: 20th November 98

Our meetings are not about teaching you a technique of meditation.

They are about initiating you to the New State, to the State of Meditation, and the State of Meditation is I Am. State of Meditation is beyond techniques. Technique is just a tool to deal with the unconscious and ignorant mind and has to be dropped sooner or later.

Absolute Meditation is not a technique, it points directly to the inner experience. When we use a technique, there is always a split between the present moment, present effort and the future experience. In our way of practice, there is no split. Each moment is a manifestation of inner truth. Each moment itself is manifestation of the goal.

There are two kinds of practices. One is dualistic, where we make various efforts in order to reach, hopefully, some realisation or awakening in the future. From the other side, there is the non-dualistic practice, where one investigates into the Now, where one is meeting oneself in each moment and in this meeting one is growing. This meeting goes deeper and deeper into the nature of the I Am.

Our teaching does not belong to any particular tradition. It is teaching beyond traditions, holistic and universal.

* * *

## Transmission: 1st December 98

From our perspective, the ultimate perspective, you are simply travellers in time, making a magical circle through the process of evolution until the point where you return fully to the original place, to the timelessness.

Being born on the earth, for some time you enjoy the state of forgetfulness where you do not know who you are, and you experience yourself as if out of the universal context, in the realm of ignorance.

To experience ignorance is your choice. It was your choice, the choice of your Soul certainly, not a conscious choice. Ignorance or forgetfulness offers certain interesting experiences, but ultimately leads to suffering and frustration. That's why you undertake a spiritual path, in order to bring this ancient memory of who you truly are beyond the dream of being human, a personality, a persona, a mask.

In our meeting we are giving you different tools thanks to which you can transcend the state of forgetfulness, which is like a trance, and you can wake up fully to your eternal identity. This waking up is not just a function of intellectual remembrance. It happens within the energy. It happens within the Heart. It happens on many levels. When all these faculties are awakened, you remember yourself fully.

Ignorance, or the ordinary state of a human being, is a situation where one is completely identified with the psychological self, with the movement of the mind; one is disconnected from pure Awareness and from the depth of Being and Heart. In order to transcend the state of forgetfulness we have to create a bridge with the state of pure Awareness, pure rest within Being, and we have to enter our own Hearts to discover the beauty within.

Being is that which links you, which roots you in Existence, in the un-manifested; this that allows you to rest, just to be. All trees and mountains are in a state of Being, completely one with Being. Humans, because their intellect has grown too much, are in a mysterious way pulled out of the state of Being, from the rootedness in reality. This overuse of intellect causes a certain painful separation from Existence. That's why our first meditation works with Being. We learn again what it means to be and how we can be.

How can we learn to be, to rest? We are constantly moving. Our mind is moving, our energy is moving. Our body is moving. We don't know what rest is. We experience the state of rest only when we fall unconscious, when we take drugs, when we listen to the trance music, when we fall asleep or — when we simply die. For that reason, learning how to be is extremely important. It is a foundation of sanity.

Awareness is in the mind. The heart of Awareness is called self-awareness or self-attention. It is a point where Awareness recognises itself without the medium of thought. Everything you do involves Awareness. Awareness is perception...but although everything involves Awareness, this Awareness is lost in the perceived, lost in the objectified reality. This Awareness does not recognise itself. One of the elements of spiritual awakening, one of the foundations, is awakening to the self-recognising Awareness without thought. Some call it "witnessing consciousness" or "pure consciousness." Some call it "observing the observer." Some call it "thoughtless state." We call it here the State of Presence.

The Heart, which is a gateway to the Divine and the seat of the Soul, is the centre of sensitivity and beauty. It also has to be awakened in order to fully experience the Inner State.

Before we speak about the awakened state, the biggest issue, the biggest problem is that most seekers do not realise what state they are in. They are not aware of their ignorance. They are not aware that their state, in truth, is painful, very incomplete, very fragmented. It is a dream state. To become sensitive to ignorance is a part of the Path. It is essential to really understand how miserable the situation is when we are identified with the mind. Only from this clarity, the true sincerity and dedication to the Path can be born.

Human being is not a given creature. It is a task. Human being is in quite an interesting situation, because it has left the animal kingdom, which is unconsciousness and has not reached yet complete Awareness. It is in-between. It is neither resting in unconsciousness, nor resting in consciousness. It is-in between. This is the cause of our suffering. That's why we have to evolve, we have to make the next step in our evolution.

Suffering has a purpose, and one of the fundamental purposes of suffering is to force us to evolve, otherwise we become stagnated. We become stuck. In this way we remain all our life glued to the same ignorant state of consciousness.

\* \* \*

## Transmission: 3rd December 98

Meditation is not simply a state of consciousness. It is a process of cooking energy, bringing it to the right state, the right frequency or vibration. When energy is fully brought to the right frequency, right state, the need to perform any particular meditation is transcended, and one is at all times in the complete Inner State. If meditation is done properly, at one stage of the Path, it has to be dropped, so one can return, to ordinary life. One can transcend spirituality. Spirituality is like a medicine against ignorance. When this medicine is fully absorbed it can be dropped. Spirituality belongs to the ego as such. The Natural State is beyond the division between the mundane and the spiritual, it simply is. A mixture of ordinariness, humility and sacredness - that's what the ordinary natural state is.

* * *

## Transmission: 5th January 99

Beloved friends, welcome to our search for clarity - spiritual clarity, clarity of the inner experience and clarity of understanding.

Spiritual growth includes many different stages, where consciousness and our being shift into the deeper experience of reality; and includes evolution of understanding where our intelligence understands more and more the meaning of our life and of our evolution.

There are certain schools which negate the mind, which speak about "no-mind" and try to cut off any kind of inquiry into the nature of truth. These schools are too extreme. Of course, the essence of spiritual discipline is the state prior to thought, deeper than the mind, but it does not mean that the mind is to be negated. It is to be embraced, included as an inherent part of who we are and this mind also has to grow. Intelligence is a combination of intellect and Heart, sensitivity and comprehension.

Our meetings are based on meditation and speech, dharma talk. The main purpose of these meetings is to create a shift of consciousness, where one can fully abide in a state deeper than thinking. Ignorance is a very limited state where one is identified with the mind. One is lost in a mental realm, disconnected from Being, disconnected from Awareness and disconnected from Heart. Our meditation is awakening Awareness, connection with Being and awakening the Heart, in order to give rise to the holistic experience of what we call the I Am State. The I Am state is our inner home, our inner refuge.

One of the main misunderstandings in spiritual philosophies is the concept of elimination of the Me, negation of individuality. For example, the Non-dual philosophy, which exists in Buddhism and Advaita, speaks about the annihilation of Me, identifying it with ignorance itself. That's why, many seekers on the path are confused, because all along they experience a certain sense of Me. This sense of Me is experienced either as a feeling in the Heart, or as self-referral in the mind. But, in truth, self-referral in the mind and a certain intimate feeling of Me in the Heart cannot be negated. They are always present, and even the awakening or the expansion into the deepest state of Consciousness does not annihilate Me. It always remains as the essence of all experiences.

Without Me, without the Soul, which is the essence of our individuality, there is no experience, there is no awakening. There is an experience of "non-duality," because the non-dual state is an experience. It is an experience where one is united with the bigger, bigger I, with the universal I Am; but even though one is united, the Me remains. This is the paradox that one experiences. Still there remains a certain sense of separation which is natural and which is a part of who we are.

This that we call Me is nothing else but an angle of perception through which the universal I Am perceives itself. This angle of perception is valid and has to be respected. However, Me is something much more than what we call ego. Ego is a shadow of Me. Ego is simply a movement in the mind which can be disconnected from the deeper Me. The deeper Me, or the whole of Me, includes pure Awareness (Awareness free from thoughts), the depth of Being, the complete inner rest and the profound sensitivity of the Heart. This is the complete Me. So we can say that an ordinary person does not experience Me, but only a fragment of it.

In our process of awakening we do not eliminate Me but we are expanding it. We are embracing deeper and deeper layers of Me, until the point when the whole of Me is experienced. When the whole of Me is experienced, the Soul and the Universal I AM merge into one. A paradox, a divine paradox, but not a contradiction.

It is only the non-lineal logic that can comprehend what is happening in this process of awakening, where one transcends individuality but still remains oneself. The Soul cannot be negated. One can pretend that one does not see her; but one cannot escape from one's own Soul.

The Soul which dwells in the Heart has to be fulfilled. That is her blueprint, the goal of evolution. She must reach her fulfillment. When the Soul is fulfilled, she simply transcends this particular dimension evolving further, no longer in the human dimension. The Soul, in order to be fulfilled, has to reach completion inside and completion outside. The Soul reaches completion inside by expanding into the I Am and by growing roots in the inner dimension. The Soul becomes fulfilled outside by realising herself in her emotional body and by having some important experiences in life. She needs to express her creativity and complete all latent karmic desires.

What most people try to do, is to be fulfilled only outside, but one cannot be fulfilled outside unless the I Am is present. If one is not grounded in the I Am, if there is no centre of identity, the mind creates endless desires and the true desires of the Soul cannot come to the surface. Therefore, first we create the inner foundation, inner sanity where we are grounded and connected, resting within. Next, from the place of inner wholeness, we fulfil ourselves in the world, experiencing human love and creativity. Here, we have to be attuned to our Soul's true desires.

* * *

## Transmission: 21st January 99

Beloved friends, welcome to our meeting, which takes place in the dimension of Understanding far away from earth. It takes place in the dimension which is complete, where nothing changes, there are no seasons, there is no imperfection. There is just light of Universal I Am, the domain of the Divine. From that place, we are speaking to you in order to bridge your plane, your state of consciousness with our Reality.

From our perspective, what you are is a certain state of consciousness, which experiences itself in quite a limited way, which in spiritual language is called "ignorance." Ignorance is nothing else but a limited experience of oneself. Ignorance is real. Ignorance is a fact. Ignorance is where most people live and, precisely from that place, we have to begin our journey into the dimension of Understanding.

How do we bridge ignorance with the dimension of Understanding? How do we manifest your future wholeness? The technology of awakening is called the Spiritual Path. Spiritual Path is scientific, in a true sense of the word. There is no mistake, all is clear. There are certain laws within the spiritual path, which have to be respected and understood. Enlightenment is not a miracle. It is not that you will suddenly experience a change and you will be on the other side. It is not like this. There is a path, a gradual change of energy, understanding and consciousness. Until the moment that you cross the bridge fully and when you cross the bridge fully, you will disappear and what will remain is Reality itself.

We are not using spiritual slogans here. We describe the spiritual path in a very precise way and if it seems complex to you, it is all right, because reality is complex. If this teaching was not complex, it would not be a true teaching.

We are here not to comfort you. We are here to shake you up, to face you with not knowing, to create a Great Doubt in your mind, so you can grow. This growth into awakening, is the very expansion within the way you experience yourself. This experience of Me, this experience of I, this experience of myself simply expands.

The consciousness can expand, can grow in many different ways. For example, if you gather knowledge about the Universe, if your intellect grows gathering different information, understanding different laws of nature and so forth, it is the growth of consciousness in the objective reality. But the growth of consciousness, we speak of, is about the subject. It is how you experience yourself in separation from the outer, in separation from the mind, in separation from your relative knowledge. This Inner State, this inner complete state we call I Am. I Am is a state without object. It is pure subjectivity, pure aloneness, the self-contained state of wholeness.

The I Am state cannot be experienced unless one develops tools on how to go beyond the mind, because identification with the mind, the identification with the thought process, keeps one in a very narrow state, very limited fragmented state. That's why, one of the foundations of the science of meditation, the science of awakening is development of Awareness, is growth of Awareness. Awareness is a light which transcends, dispels the clouds of unconsciousness in our own mind. Awareness is a tool of freedom from the mind. From a certain perspective it is a goal, but from the higher perspective it is a tool.

The goal is what we call Beingness, which means complete inner rest, which is deeper than Awareness. Of course, a certain element of Awareness has to be there, otherwise you would not be able to recognise the state of Beingness, but Awareness is a tool. Beingness is the goal. Within the dimension of Beingness which is the ultimate pure rest, infinite rest without any movement, there is a secret Sun, the Heart, or the Divine dimension.

The gateway to the Divine dimension is our own Heart. That's why, opening of the Heart, reaching the depth of our own Heart is a part of this process. To conclude: the I Am, we are aiming at, is a unity of Awareness, Being and Heart; our meditation is dealing with opening these faculties that allow us to experience it fully.

The purpose of spiritual path is not liberation but Wholeness. In certain spiritual teachings liberation has been emphasised, which has a negative connotation. The Wholeness is positive, Wholeness is beyond liberation for it includes imperfection and includes human nature with its limitations as well.

* * *

## Transmission: 28th January 99

We would like to make it clear that our meetings are not meditation classes. Our meetings are about Awakening, about coming back home, about returning to the state of unity with the universal I AM or our inherent wholeness.

What is awakening? What is this mysterious Buddha state of mind? What does it mean to be enlightened? We hope that soon you will reach clarity in these matters, as you will grow in the inner experience and in understanding. There will be more and more clarity, so you will fully understand that Enlightenment is about you. It is not about someone special, it is about you and it can become a part of your daily experience.

What is this awakening about? It is nothing but about giving birth to the state of consciousness, which is free from the mind and which is our true abode. It is about shifting from the narrow perception, narrow ignorant state ,where one is identified with the mind, to this vast holistic experience of I Am which is free from thought, but includes thinking.

Awakening is not about negation, it is about expansion, about adding and adding different layers of the inner experience until we become whole, united with Inner Light and peace. The state of I Am, at which we are aiming, is a holistic inner experience of I Am. I Am is composed of three qualities. These three qualities are Awareness, Being and Heart. In our meditation, we are working with these qualities in order to bring this experience of I Am completely. Awareness is a quality which frees us from the mind, which takes us beyond unconsciousness. The flowering of Awareness is a state of non-dual presence or self-attention. Being is that which connects us with basic peace, with the experience of rest. The Heart is our connection with the divine or with God.

Be clear that the purpose of meditation is not a temporary tranquilisation of the mind. The purpose of the art of meditation is to bring a state which is permanent, which is unconditional. That to which we refer by the term "State of Meditation" is an

unconditional state which exists objectively, and we are simply
tapping into it, connecting, re-connecting, becoming part of this
vast dimension of the State of Meditation.

The State of Meditation is beyond sitting, standing or walking.
It is simply beyond earth. This voice that you hear is coming
from the Other Dimension, from the dimension which is not
touched by the movement of time, from the dimension where
nothing happens. In that dimension, everything is already and
always has been perfect. This dimension is the place where you
originally come from, your home. Only you have forgotten and
we are bringing this ancient memory, so you remember who you
are. You begin to remember that in you which is always pure
and beyond evolution, beyond imperfection.

* * * *

# V

## QUESTIONS–ANSWERS
## AND
## SPONTANEOUS TALKS

# Questions–Answers

## Transmission: 20th September 98

**Q:** Why are there so few real seekers?

**Aziz:** Because such is the level of humanity. It is a question of evolution again. In reality to look for the Inner Light, is the desire of very few souls. Most, are like children, they still need to play with the toys of phenomenal reality. It's simply their level of evolution.

**Q:** What are the signs of a true seeker?

**Aziz:** A true seeker simply is, you can say, in Heart and in the mind completely devoted to the task of self-discovery. A real seeker is craving the Truth and will do everything to complete the Path. A true seeker must have the essential sincerity in the Heart and certain capacity in the mind. In most cases, either sincerity or capacity is missing.

**Q:** Is evil a function of the mind or is it something deeper?

**Aziz:** Evil is a function of the mind. Evil is, you can say, neurosis.

**Q:** Could you say something about the experience of light in meditation.

**Aziz:** The light, the word light is a metaphor, having nothing to do with a visual experience. The so-called experiences of light are related more to the psychic phenomena and not, at all, to awakening. True light is not a visual experience, it is an experience of pure subjectivity. Awareness itself allows one to see light in a visual form, but what is this Awareness without light, without object? It is beyond experience, it is pure experience. The awakening takes us to the dimension of pure subjectivity, which is object-less. To see a light means to be separated from this that we experience. Who is the seer? The seer is pure light!

**Q:** Sometimes I find myself in a state of Being, in a state which is very self-contained and full, and this state happens to me accidentally, with no planning. Can you explain to me what this state is?

**Aziz:** The experience you speak about is a mixture of Being and being "spaced out." We call it the mystical state. In this kind of state one doesn't have any particular thoughts but neither is there any clear centre of Awareness or Being. It is simply not grounded in Reality. There are many altered states of consciousness which have nothing to do with I Am.

**Q:** I really don't know what this experience of I Am is?!

**Aziz:** You don't know? Who is saying, "I don't know"? To find what the I Am is, you have to find what your Me is. The I Am and Me are inter-related. Your true Me is the essence of who you are, beyond the psychological flow. Because your Me is identified in the psychological flow, that's why you don't know who you are. So, in order to discover the I Am, first you have to discover Me, distinguish the Me from the mind.

The I Am is a new state which you don't simply explain, it needs time, you have to awaken more; firstly, you have to separate, create a distance from the mind. When you create a distance between you and the mind, you are closer to the centre, which is unchangeable. So there is an extension of Awareness, self-knowledge, and more and more peace and rest becomes manifested in this process.

Who is behind this mind? You are using this mind all your life, who is behind it? Who is the thinker? Can you explain who you are apart from thoughts? Who is behind these eyes? Who is looking at me now? Is there anybody home?

**Q:** It's a whole mixture.

**Aziz:** Yes, it's a mixture. You are unable to recognise any clear sense of identity which you could translate as Me. If you wish to discover it, you will, but you need to work for it. There is something in you which is pure, which is truly You, and that needs to be found.

* * *

## Transmission: 19th November 98

**Q:** I try to transcend myself, to go beyond, using the Maharaj's approach. It is as if I leave myself behind, like a pure witnessing state. But it doesn't have any juice, it's like I'm not there — and then eventually the Me catches up...

**Aziz:** First of all, you have to see that you can transcend yourself either through Awareness or through Being. Through Awareness you are pulling back to the centre of Presence, which is behind the psychological I; so there's certain transcendence. A deeper transcendence takes place through Being, which is vertical. It is deeper because it happens through Non-doing, through surrender. In the case of reaching the centre of Awareness, a certain element of will is involved, you can notice. That's why this transcendence is not pure, not complete. The ultimate transcendence takes place when one drops into Being. It is the true transcendence, for one becomes absent.

The Witnessing Consciousness represents a relative transcendence. One places the centre of identity beyond the psychological self, in the dimension of pure attention. It is transcendence but it is not annihilation, you are adding something, you are expanding beyond the psychological Me, but the psychological "me" co-exists with the State of Presence.

In India, they use a very interesting model. In Bhagavat Gita, for example, it is written that one is not a doer, one is the Witness. According to this model, ignorance refers to the illusion that one is doing something, one is identified with this Me in the mind. While, in truth, according to them, who we are is only the Witness. When one shifts the state of witnessing, one sees that the mind is just occurring by itself, and the centre of identity remains unmoved. This model is interesting, but certainly not complete. How reality looks is more rich, it is not so linear.

What we are trying to say is that in the mind you have two centres, one is the centre of the State of Presence and the other is the centre of intelligence, which is dynamic. The traditional model doesn't seem to see the relevance of the second centre. It is aware only of the static one, which is the Presence. Traditionally the movement of intelligence is not accepted as belonging to the real Me. But it is incorrect. The movement of intelligence is also Me, the self-referral in the mind is also Me. When you relax in the State of Presence and when you go beyond the idea of not being the Me, free from any preconception, you simply see reality as it is. What is reality? Reality of the mind is the co-existence of the State of Presence and the self-referring movement of Me. They are two and one, one system, they both create who you are. That's why Me and the State of Presence are one whole.

If you choose the State of Presence as the only real centre, you create an artificial situation, it is not real. It is a teaching device and helps when you are too much in the mind. It is your freedom in the mind to place your centre of identity in the thoughtless Awareness, but at one stage you need to go even beyond that. Your Me and the State of Presence co-exist... and Me, apart from the movement of intelligence, is also in the Heart. The movement between Awareness, Intelligence, Being and Heart create the complete field of Me. In this process we are not negating Me, although it may look like this. In reality, we are expanding Me, bringing it to the point of completion.

Now you can understand how important the model of awakening one uses is. The model reflects reality of the spiritual evolution and on some level creates this reality. Most seekers prefer to follow the traditional models, for it gives them security and sense of authority behind their search. Unquestionably, they try to fit themselves into the traditional models, not being able to think critically.

Let's say, for example, a Buddhist is conditioned by the perception of spiritual search which identifies Self-realisation with the freedom from suffering. Such a person, perceives reality only from the viewpoint of suffering or non-suffering. For some Buddhists, the proof of spiritual attainment is not the Inner State (which according to their model should also be impermanent), but the level of attachment and desires an enlightened being or any other seeker has. Attempting to disidentify, one tries to eliminate any kind of desires and attachments in order not to suffer. At one stage one loses the natural perspective; one becomes a fanatic of an idea! Pursuing an incomplete model, one can become easily handicapped, negating life, negating human nature and the positive evolution into the multidimensional wholeness of Me.

Those pseudo-religious people who walk around telling others that Jesus loves them simply follow, from our perspective, a wrong model of spirituality. We are doing nothing but giving you here more of a complete model of reality. It is not just a difference in expressing the reality of Enlightenment. It is a more intelligent model, a spiritual vision that bridges your past with your future. The kind of future you will reach is reflected in the vision you choose to follow.

* * *

## Transmission: 19th November 98

**Q:** In your meditation you use objects. First the object is Being, or breathing to the belly. Then the object is the third eye, or Awareness itself. Then the object is the Heart centre. But then you also say, rather than looking at the object, look at the subject, which is observing the object.

**Aziz:** Let us say that it is just a linguistic formula, then we call it an object. In truth, it is a subject. Third eye, if you look from outside, it is an object, but if you look at it from inside, it is an experience of a subject, there's a sense of wakefulness. When you direct attention to attention, it seems like an object, but, in truth, it points to the experience of the subject. If you don't experience your Heart, you are focusing on it in order to activate this area energetically. But when it is done, the Heart is no longer experienced from outside, but from inside, from within. It becomes you! So these three centres of I Am are subjects, they are three aspects of the one subject, which is called the complete I Am.

**Q:** But isn't the actual subject Awareness, attention?

**Aziz:** Some teachings say so but it is not true, it is not a complete subject. What you are aiming at is the complete experience of

Me. The Me is already there, but fragmented and unconscious. When Me is awakened, it can experience itself through these three centres. When we discover the State of Presence, the Me in the mind is discovered, the essence of Awareness. But this is not the whole of Me. Me also exists in Being. When you, from the State of Presence simply relax into Being, suddenly the experience of yourself becomes more holistic, it is no longer located in the head, it is all over. This is how the Me in the mind and Me in Being meet and they give rise to a higher ME. Even though the higher Me is awakened, it is still not the complete Me because sensitivity from the Heart is missing. In this way we evolve into the Heart, enlarging our Me until it contains our totality.

There are certain schools which only emphasise, as you said, attention, witnessing consciousness. For example, some speak about witnessing consciousness as the ultimate. But is it the ultimate? Where is Being and where is the Heart? It is only self-attention which witnesses the mind. Can you witness the Heart?

**Q:** You mentioned at the beginning of the meditation about the protective mechanism of the mind. Can you speak about this?

**Aziz:** The Me, your own Me, your individual Me, in order to survive in the world, has to protect itself. You have to think about survival, you have to think about your emotional fulfilment, you have to think about shelter, about your future... The self-protecting mechanism it is a natural mechanism, but it is a mechanism, it is simply a function, it is not who you are. This function has become too obsessive and out of control. Instead of controlling our security, it controls us! In this fever of protecting ourselves we have lost our connection with who we are. We basically constantly protect ourselves, trying to survive physically and psychologically in the world. But there is something more than survival. Spirituality, we can say, is beyond survival.

Certainly you cannot completely give up the self-protecting mechanism, because it is a natural function and it's necessary, but you can balance it, you can relax it, you can use it in a very wise, intelligent way. It is not always necessary to think about yourself, about your securities, you know. It is very often completely unnecessary. It is not only you who makes you survive. Existence, this complex and multidimensional organism of life, allows you to survive, creating reality for you as well. It is not you alone who tries to survive, life also takes care of you and has its own wisdom. You have to allow life to take care of you too...

So you simply realise this mechanism, use it in a balanced way. In meditation, you can be silent, you don't need to think about yourself, relax in trust. That's why we spoke about meditation as an act of courage. Certain courage is necessary to trust, to let go, because this self-protective mechanism is instinctive, it is almost animalistic. So we are bringing balance into it, we are not denying this mechanism, it's a natural mechanism.

**Q:** Maharaj speaks about contemplating the I Am in order to receive the whole knowledge of it. You also told me to contemplate I Am. Can you speak about it?

**Aziz:** Nisargadatta Maharaj was a great Master. He was the first who differentiated between the realisation of Pure Consciousness and the Absolute State. You will not find any other clear teaching making this important distinction. For Maharaj, however, the I Am was mostly the State of Presence. That is how he translated the sense of "I am," and he was encouraging to contemplate it, in order to realise that "I am not the I Am." The purpose of this contemplation was to go beyond I Am. He wasn't very fond of the I Am. His only interest was the Absolute, that which is beyond the I Am.

Our purpose is different, not to negate I Am, but to understand who we are. Contemplating the State of Presence, you become more and more clear of what it is, how it arises, how it functions, what the relationship is between the State of Presence, Being and Heart. You begin to know who you are and how you live in the internal reality, because internal reality is a movement, it is not a static state.

Contemplation of the I Am is a complex subject and we cannot speak about this fully now. There's many areas of the I Am, there is Presence, Heart and Being. All of them can be contemplated, all of them need to be understood in an intuitive way, to see how they relate to each other. For example, contemplating your I Am, you might notice that in activity the State of Presence is experienced more, while in meditation, Being is experienced more. It gives you insight into the mechanism of I Am, how it behaves in certain situations.

Maharaj himself, he had his own purposes, his own things in mind when he was speaking about contemplating the I Am. His main point was to go beyond the I Am, and, as we know, it is not always necessary, because for most, it is not their destiny to go beyond the I Am; for them I Am is the ultimate experience. Our emphasis is more positive, so to speak.

**Q:** Maharaj speaks about a sage who managed to completely disappear while playing the sitar and certainly there was nothing but the sitar in the sand left. Your approach seems also rather nihilistic. What about enjoying the horizontal dimension?

**Aziz:** No, our approach is not the same, that's why we speak about the Soul. In the traditional approach, the Soul is negated, it is emptied. We are speaking about the validity of the Soul. The Soul exists and the Soul has more things in mind than just dissolution into the Absolute. The Soul reaches the Absolute in order to experience perfect peace and freedom; but she still grows and expands in the horizontal reality or in the world. The Soul, in order to be fulfilled, needs to be complete emotionally as well as to have some adventures in life, some creativity. There are various Souls; for certain Souls dissolution is completion. That's why, you need to know yourself in order to live your life in harmony with your Soul's destiny.

In our teaching we speak about the awakening to Me. What is Me? It is not true that there's only sitar. Between the Absolute and the sitar, there is Me. The Me is subtle, but it colours all reality through itself. The Soul colours reality through her emotional body, through her mental body and through her Heart. This model of reality is different, for it includes the Soul.

* * *

## Transmission: 20th November 98

**Q:** I experience in meditation a state of Being, but still thoughts come?!

**Aziz:** The energies of Being are in the belly and around you, it is not located in any particular place. It is an experience of rest. When you notice that you are distracted by the mind, you bring immediately the State of Presence. It is not only becoming aware of thoughts, it is becoming aware of the centre behind thoughts, becoming aware of the observer of thoughts. When it is done, then you relax into Being. But when you are in your Being and you feel a certain amount of absorption and the experience is clear, there is no need to go into Presence. Some amount of thoughts don't necessarily disturb the process of sitting in Being. It is quite complex because attention is able to divide itself. Part of attention is dispersed into thinking, part of attention is in Being, and part of attention is able to recognise the State of Presence. It is the Economy of attention, the energy of attention gets distributed to different centres.

If you feel that there are too many thoughts and you lose yourself, you must crystallise attention in the mind. You have to bring it clearly to the State of Presence. Awareness of the breath cannot be constant, because it is not natural to be constantly aware of the breath. But resting in Being can be constant, remaining in the State of Presence can be constant, because these are the subjects, these are who you are...and being who you are, when it is awakened, is effortless. Watching the breath is just a tool. Being is the goal.

**Q:** Can you speak about Being. Is it like all over Awareness?

**Aziz:** No, Being is something else. When you sit in meditation, try and simply observe what it means to Be. Being is not somewhere. It is not something to be located or perceived. Being is an experience. It is not visible. It is simply an experience of rest and calm.

When you sit in meditation, suddenly you see that you are just sitting, you experience calm. What is this calmness? Where is it coming from? You are sitting in Being, it is already an experience of Being. You are being received by Being, and it happens through expansion in the Hara, in the belly. The centre of energy is in the belly, it needs to expand, needs to deepen. Afterwards one is rooted. You create roots within yourself. There is a pull from the centre of Being which is downwards, in the belly. That's why it is experienced through Non-doing. It is in the Hara. Hara is the gateway of Being. When you are Non-doing, you gravitate downward towards the Hara, and you reach rest. You are resting upon something. You don't know what it is, but you are resting. It is called BEING.

Pure Being is a deep sleep state without dreams. You are in a condition of pure Being. There is no Awareness but there is Being. And when you are awakened, you create a relationship with Being, you can experience Being while being conscious. This is what meditation is about.

**Q:** Why do you emphasise the Heart in the end of your meditation and not in the beginning or in the middle?

**Aziz:** In our particular meditation, we bring it at the end, because first we want to create a foundation of Being and Awareness. If you don't have Awareness and you don't have Being, the experience of the Heart can be only on the surface... and also, if you are identified with the mind, if you are disconnected with Being, you are in a very miserable state. So first you should attain certain peace, certain sanity, and afterwards you can reach also sensitivity in the Heart.

If you try to enter your Heart without the experience of peace, without Awareness, it will not give you happiness. It can even confuse you, because you will become over-emotional within the neurotic state, which is the absence of Awareness and Being. This is neurosis.

When you meditate, direct part of the attention to the Heart, breathe to the chest. Try to feel it also in daily activity: "where is my Heart?" It has to be activated. You have to breathe to your chest, as much as you can. You have to use different tools to awaken it: beautiful music which triggers feeling in the Heart, prayer. But the most important is to pay attention to it. This attention itself will open the Heart. This attention is energy. When it is connected with the Heart centre, it activates it.

So the Heart has to be awakened on the energy level, the energy of the Heart has to vibrate; and it has to be awakened on the feeling level, so you become intimate with your own Heart, with the sensitivity in the Heart. You feel yourself in the Heart, it is not just a feeling of the Heart, it is a feeling of yourself. When somebody speaks to you, there is always a certain feeling in the Heart. When somebody says something to you which hurts you, you feel it in the Heart. What does it mean to you? You have to contemplate it. What does it mean, this feeling in the Heart which follows any experience in life?

**Q:** You said that the State of Presence, when it is crystallised in the mind, is personal and when you relax it, it is impersonal. Can you speak more about that?

**Aziz:** This process of crystallisation is connected with your personal intelligence. Your personal intelligence is directing its energy towards the centre of Awareness. It is a personal act. It is your personal intelligence which does it. You are using will to do so.

When you are in the State of Presence, this energy of will, this energy of self-referral is still there, it has not disappeared. When you relax, it disperses, it relaxes as well, into the experience which is impersonal. There is always a certain touch of personal feeling, because you experience yourself, but this personal feeling merges with the impersonal experience. It is you and it is not you.

Any kind of relaxation relates to Being. Being is impersonal. Although we speak about relaxation of the Presence in the head, it is already Being. There is already an element of Being, and Being is impersonal. That's why the personal presence, personal self-referral relaxes into the impersonal, they are like two qualities of the same thing.

**Q:** This dream of manifestation, this Maya, to what extent is it a dream and to what extent is it real?

**Aziz:** It is one hundred percent real dream... (laughter)... It is a dream. It is valid. When you say a "dream" it doesn't mean it is negated or discarded. It is real. It is a Vision. You can see this universe and other universes as a vision coming from this ultimate subjectivity. A vision which has its purpose, its goals, but doesn't have a substance on its own. When you have a dream, the dream is real, but it is not you, it arises within you. Similarly this universe, it is not God from a certain point of view. It arises within God. It is not God herself, it arises within her. That's why we call it a dream. But calling it a dream doesn't mean we negate it.

When we say it is a dream, we are emphasising that there is something deeper. There is a dimension of subjectivity behind the phenomenal expression. This is the purpose of the word "dream" — pointing to something which is deeper, prior to it. There is the Timeless behind the Time. This is the purpose.

**Q:** Why do you call the Divine "she"?

**Aziz:** The Divine represents feminine energy. Of course the Divine or the Ultimate is neither feminine nor masculine, but it is perceived as feminine from the perspective of human psychology. From the view point of our human psychology the Divine or God is feminine. She represents feminine qualities. There is a statement in "Tao The Ching" which is a Taoist scripture by Lao-Tzu that "the gateway to Tao is femininity." Only complete surrender either into your Being or to your Heart, allows you to merge with the Ultimate. The surrender is feminine, but that into what we surrender is the Ultimate Femininity.

**Q:** How can I relax more in the head? The State of Presence is a new experience for me and I feel a lot of tension in the head, energetic tension.

**Aziz:** This will come in time. What you can do now is: the moment you are aware of the State of Presence, gently breathe to your belly and naturally you will relax. In such a case, you are attentive in the mind, but part of attention is already in the belly, connected to the breath in the belly, and what happens is that there is a certain drop of energy, the energy drops. It is no longer focussed in the mind. It drops. But because you want to be focussed in the mind, so you must do two simultaneous things: you are keeping the State of Presence and, on the other hand, being aware of your breath, you let the energy drop and relax. When you hold into the State of Presence, you hold it. In order to relax you have to let go of holding. A vertical letting go. This is how we learn to do it. It is simply a question of practice. Relaxing in your mind, relaxing in your head while keeping the State of Presence is not such an easy act, but you can learn and it will come more naturally later on.

At this stage when you relax too much, you lose the State of Presence. That's why you have to be careful. Holding and relaxing, holding and relaxing. This is how it goes. The more you are connected to the State of Presence, the more you can let go of keeping it. It keeps itself and then you can fully allow yourself to let go.

**Q:** What is the difference between Awareness of the Heart and Awareness of Awareness?

**Aziz:** It is different. Awareness of the Heart doesn't create tension necessarily. Why does Awareness of Awareness create tension? Because this Awareness, which may rest in the Heart, suddenly gets directed into itself and becomes like a ball of energy. When it goes into the Heart it is no longer self-centred. From the viewpoint of Awareness, from the viewpoint of the centre in the mind, the Heart is an "object." It is "external," that's why the energy of Awareness is not so concentrated. When Awareness turns upon itself, it is very concentrated. It is felt as tension.

**Q:** You said that Being is the primal energy. I think I heard you once saying that Being is Beyond Energy.

**Aziz:** It is not contradictory. It is the Primal Energy, prior to the movement of energy. Energy is a movement. Energy itself is a movement, but the primordial energy which is the Absolute does not move. It is pure isness. It is energy in the condition of rest, before it begins to move.

\* \* \*

## Transmission: 29th November 98

**Q:** You said that everything that we experience in life is registered in the Heart. Can you speak about this?

**Aziz:** Behind every experience of life there is a subject. The essence of a subject is the Soul, which is in the Heart. Any kind of experience which happens to the mind and to the body is going through the Soul, is being registered in the Heart, in a subtle way.

Whatever you experience in your life, if you are sensitive, you feel that it goes through the Heart. It is very fast and the mind can cover it up, but it is first registered in the Heart. For example, you enter a certain place and your Heart responds immediately; whether it is a place or a person you meet on the street, it is being felt·in the Heart. The Heart is a very sensitive instrument, the seat of intuition and, on some level, the centre of perception. That's why in some places like "music parties," with alcohol and drugs where the music is loud, the Heart has to close, not to be energetically harmed.

**Q:** If the mind is not there, is it only the Heart which remains?

**Aziz:** You mean when the mind is silent... Not necessarily. The Heart has to be awakened. There's a few ways of experiencing No-mind. There is No-mind which can be experienced as pure Awareness, free from thoughts. Another way of experiencing No-mind is when you relax into Being, there is a certain holistic experience, a combination of Awareness and Being. In both cases, the mind is absent or silent, but the Heart is not necessarily present. The Heart is only present when awakened. If the Heart is awakened and the mind is silent, certainly, the energy of the Heart expands and merges with the whole of I Am. In that moment, the experience of it is not merely in the middle of the chest, but all-over, it becomes the whole of you.

**Q:** Can you speak more about Prayer?

**Aziz:** Prayer. We can look at prayer from many different angles. Prayer, the deep meaning of prayer is Connection with the divine. When you go deep into your Heart, you find this connection; this connection is simply there but one has to awaken it. To be conscious of this connection is prayer itself. That is the deepest meaning of Prayer. It is no longer a verbal communication from mind to mind, but a profound feeling of intimate unity with the Beloved. Prayer is a love affair of the Soul with her Creator. Suddenly, you remember your divine Mother and you feel this knowing in the most sensitive place, at the depth of your Heart.

Another level of Prayer is more personal. When the Prayer, we spoke about, was more on the level of pure Soul, now certain personal elements are present. First, you must acknowledge in your Heart all that you feel, desire, long for; you simply acknowledge the human in you. From that place, you feel the Beloved and express all that you feel, asking for help and assistance. It is fine to use words if it is natural for you.

The essence of Prayer is this flavour in the Heart that links you with the Divine. Being, that is, abiding in your Heart can be called pure Prayer. Pure Prayer is the Heart itself. But there are different expressions of Prayer, like conscious communication with the Creator, feeling of gratitude; burning incense in respect to the Divine, offering flowers... Prayer is not formula but an alive expression of Love.

**Q:** Is prayer individual or is it impersonal, universal?

**Aziz:** It is individual and it is universal, both. It has Universal meaning but because it is unique to you, that's why, it is also individual, it is very personal. It is your own personal connection with the Divine. It is not that you realise an impersonal state. You realise your own personal relationship with the Divine. It's like you have a mother and you have a personal relationship, personal connection which is particular to you. Nobody can tell you how you should feel your Heart or how to feel your Soul. It's your own personal challenge; it is you who meets your own Soul!

**Q:** Which is more important in meditation, first to relax the body or to observe the sensations, the tension in the body?

**Aziz:** First, we don't teach so much about relaxing the body here, we teach about being relaxed, as such. In meditation, because you are developing attention, because you have to concentrate, your body can become even more tense at the beginning; and that is perfectly all right. Later, when you don't have to work so much with attention, you can relax more and this relaxes the body. But the deep meaning of relaxation is not to be relaxed in the body, it's to be relaxed in Being, and Being is not in the body.

When you sit meditation and, suddenly, you experience an absorption and deep calmness, this calmness doesn't pertain to the body. You don't know where this deep calmness is coming from, it is simply calmness, stillness, pure abidance... that is called Being. That's why we teach about relaxing into Being. So you relax into Being, at the same time you cultivate attention, you do both. The centre of attention is in the mind, it has to be crystallised, because if it's not crystallised, the subconscious mind completely takes you away into the dreamland. When you have no centre in the mind, you are just the mind. When you have a centre in the mind, you are free from the mind. When you are free from the mind, finally you can afford to relax into Being fully. If you don't cultivate attention and you want to relax into Being, what happens is that you become unconscious or fall into a certain state similar to dreaming. Attention and relaxation are two wings of the same bird.

As far as observing sensations is concerned, we do not teach this technique, for it is not directly related to Awakening.

* * *

## Transmission: 1st December 98

**Q:** After realising your oneness with the Beloved, is there still an experience of prayer?

**Aziz:** That's so. As long as you're alive, as long as your Soul is manifested as an individual, even when the oneness with the Creator is realised, the separation simultaneously is present. You experience both, and, in truth, only because you are relatively separated, you can experience the oneness. If this relative separation completely vanishes, you dissolve; it means your Me disappears, there's no more Me, there's no you. That's why, this separation has a purpose and it's precious, because it allows you to experience oneness. Because you are still experiencing separation, even after becoming completely one with the Heart of the Creator, you can still relate to this experience. This unity is being re-awakened in the flow of time; for that reason you can still pray, you can still feel, you can still... relate to the Beloved. This awakening is not fixed, it is reappearing from moment to moment — it is a never-ending discovery of the Mystery.

* * *

## Transmission: 6th December 98

**Q:** Can you clarify the energetic experience of the State of Presence? Is it experienced in the third eye or in the back of the skull? Can you speak about this?

**Aziz:** No, you don't need to locate it, it's better not to try to locate it. What you need to locate, is the State of Presence itself, as a direct experience; and where is it located physically, it is better not to concentrate on that, otherwise you can manipulate this experience. If you feel the State of Presence, try to become more and more familiar with the experience as it is naturally, as the centre of self-attention. Remember what the state is, what the flavour is of this experience. When you remember it, you know what it is, and you don't need to focus on where it is located. It is true, that this experience is in the head, and it is experienced in the third eye, which is one and half inches inside the skull. But when this energy is activated, it's like electricity, it sends waves to the whole brain; that's how you can experience it in different areas of the head.

When you are active, when you are busy in life, and you remember the State of Presence, this experience is located more at the back of the skull, because, naturally, attention turns back. When you sit in meditation, it can be experienced in the whole area of the head. This state will teach you itself, you don't need to focus on it too much. Just be with the State of Presence, it will teach you, you will see how it behaves.

Now, when you are standing with open eyes, it is good if you practice a little bit of meditation with open eyes. In Zen, for example, you practice meditation with open eyes. Practice with open eyes has some benefits, it helps you to integrate the State of Meditation with life. Sit sometimes with open eyes; sometimes try to meditate when you are standing, with open eyes, and afterwards slowly walking.

**Q:** When I was practicing absorption in the last few days, being in the State of Presence and relaxing it in the head, I got absorbed into this state for one hour. The memory was not active, like everything became frozen. Can you speak about this?

**Aziz:** The State of Presence itself is beyond the field of personality and personal memory, it doesn't have memory, it simply is. When your psyche is experiencing the State of Presence, it adds to it the personal flavour as well as memory, that's why your memory and the State of Presence are mixed. However, when you relax into the Presence more, this personal part of you also somehow relaxes and becomes suspended. In this way, you experience more the timeless characteristic of the Inner State.

We can say that the State of Presence is relatively separated from the psyche. It's more impersonal, there's "no one" who experiences the state. When Being also is added, the connection to the timeless goes deeper and the feeling of abiding outside of the field of personal memory increases. This is the impersonal characteristic of I Am. That doesn't mean, of course, that we are aiming at this and trying to suspend our personal self-reference. The natural situation is when our personal intelligence is mixed and integrated with the Inner State.

* * *

# Transmission: 3rd January 99

**Q:** Many traditions negate ego and you say that the ego is good, can you explain it please?

**Aziz:** You can say that the psychology, that the past traditions are using, is a bit undeveloped and does not describe precisely what is happening in this process of awakening. The ego is nothing else but the conscious movement of intelligence, the ability for self-referral, without which one is unable not only to meditate but even to walk, eat, talk, live... nothing. So the ego, as such, is the only tool thanks to which you can live, you can make progress on the path, you can understand what is happening. Thanks to the ego, you are, for example, listening to what we are saying, your mind is translating this information.

So there's the ego and there's Me. Me is pure I. The essence of Me is in the Heart, but Me uses as well Awareness in the mind etc... The ego is a shadow of Me or, more positively, an expression of it. What all awakened beings are trying to transmit, is understanding that the ego is not Me, or it is not in the centre. When the centre of Awareness is awakened, the centre of identity shifts from thinking to witnessing or Being; and from that place it seems that there's no ego, there is this feeling, but the ego still continues to exist in its own way.

The ego is not negative, although, for some reason, it has been used in a negative terms, not only by traditions of Enlightenment, but generally in common language. The ego in common language designates an attachment to self-image that someone has. The ego as such is a neutral term. It is how we use it that makes it positive or negative. That's why, we have intelligent egos and unintelligent ones....

**Q:** And this ego, in some way, leads me through my spiritual journey into the understanding that I don't really exist as I, God exists, it leads me to a bigger "I"?!

**Aziz:** Certainly. The ego is a function of intelligence, which enables it to grow into the ultimate transcendence.

**Q:** When we think in a conscious way, where does the thinking take place?

**Aziz:** Everything happens in consciousness, consciousness is like a large space of knowingness. Within this knowingness there are many different expressions. Thoughts are simply expressions of consciousness, expressions of the mind, expressions of Awareness. When you are observing thoughts, or when you are consciously thinking, apart from thoughts, which are expressions, there is a sense of Me behind. In this way you experience two dimensions simultaneously. The thinker and the thought, the observer and the observed, the Me and its psychological environment create one field of knowingness. It is all happening in consciousness, it cannot be located as such, because consciousness cannot be located, consciousness is just consciousness, it is located nowhere, like in a dream. Can you locate a dream?

The experience of thinking is a combination of subconscious mental events and intelligence, which creatively tries to create understanding or the right response. When you are not aware of thinking, the subconscious mind only is in operation. When an element of attention is mixed with the thinking process, and there is a sense of co-operation, it means that conscious intelligence is present as well.

**Q:** It felt to me as if this intuitive intelligence was surrounding my I Am. Does thinking come from I Am or from intuitive intelligence?

**Aziz:** The State of Presence itself is not thinking, it is a centre behind thoughts. Thinking arises...you can have a feeling as if it was arising in the State of Presence, but, in truth, it arises from a deeper level than the conscious. The conscious mind is somehow co-operating in this creation of thoughts, but thoughts themselves arise from the subconscious mind. The subconscious mind is another compartment, a separate dimension in the totality of the mind. Between Me, the conscious Me, and the experience of the world, there is this subconscious mind. Subconscious mind is a very fast computer, which is producing a lot of information that altogether gives rise to the perception; it is extremely fast. You can watch the mind, you can be aware of arising thoughts, but can you be aware from where thoughts are arising from? They arise from a very mysterious place below the conscious mind. It is this universal computer, subconscious mind, which has its own wisdom and its own purpose, and which cannot be understood in truth, it is simply there.

Here, the question "where thoughts arise from" has a different purpose than the Maharishi's question about the source of the "I" thought. For him, this question was a device to bring one to the State of Presence. But thoughts do not arise from the State of Presence. The State of Presence is the centre of intelligence, from which the subconscious mind can receive conscious feedback. This is how intelligence awakens.

**Q:** Is it possible to separate the State of Presence from the intuitive intelligence?

**Aziz:** It is possible, but it is not natural. If you are absorbed in the State of Presence, you can experience it in its purity, as separated from this intuitive intelligence. But this happens only momentarily, unless you are in a trance state. This, which allows you to know that you are in the State of Presence, is the intuitive intelligence. They are one in the natural human mind.

**Q:** What is the difference between an awakened being and the one who is not, in terms of functioning and perceiving reality.

**Aziz:** An enlightened being is like a ship; what you see is above the water, what you don't see is under it. The unawakened person lives only above the water; the awakened one exists in both realities. That is the fundamental difference. But because most people are not aware of the inner dimension, they try to judge an enlightened being according to how he/she appears to be. They project many expectations on the one who is supposed to be Self-realised... and many spiritual teachers try to fit themselves to this model behaving in a holy and moral way. Most often it is artificial.

The basic difference, between an enlightened being and the ignorant one, is not how this person perceives the world, but from which place! The ordinary person is the world, ordinary person is the mind and the body, completely identified with the phenomenal reality. In the case of a person who is awakened, this person perceives the world from that place which is beyond manifestation, from the place of complete stillness and silence, where no movement exists.

Before we understand how a person perceives the world, we have to see who perceives the world... and it is the Soul. The

Soul exists between the inner and the outer. When the Soul is awakened, enlightened, she rests in the unmanifested. However, the Soul, by the very way she has been created, still functions in the manifested. The Soul has a purpose of being here, and it is more than liberation. She has a certain blueprint, a vision of completion which includes the outer as well. Often, in order to be complete, it is not enough to reach Enlightenment in the traditional sense. The Soul must evolve in many areas of life and her completion includes the emotional evolution and fulfilment in life.

Let us answer your question in a simple way. The person who is enlightened perceives reality from the space of Absolute Silence, and when the Heart is awakened, also from the Divine dimension. But how the Inner State affects his/her life and ways of behaviour cannot always be predicted; because it depends on the stage of the psychological evolution of Me and the unique type of Soul that one has.

**Q:** You mentioned that the person who is not awakened "is the world" but unconsciously. Is an awakened person the world consciously?

**Aziz:** This person and the world become one; but that is not all, for such a being is beyond the world. From the viewpoint of the Ultimate, this world is just a tiny expression of the Truth. This particular manifested physical universe is just a speck of dust within the Totality. To say, that an enlightened being and the world are one, does not precisely describe the experience. It is more right to say that in the Enlightened Perception all is included, as such, beyond separation, for even if the separation still exists, it is also embraced in transcendental unity. But the abiding place of Buddha is beyond the perceived and the perception. It is Beyond...

* * *

## Transmission: 5th January 99

**Q:** The experience of the Heart, for me, involves an effort, experience of Being is effortless, letting go. I was wondering, if the Heart is my most intimate identity, why should I use so much effort?

**Aziz:** Similarly, Being is your intimate identity, but you had to work in order to experience it. Isn't it true? So there is a paradox. The Heart is your intimate identity, but this innermost identity is not aware of itself, therefore, it has to be awakened. When the Heart is awakened, when this energy centre is activated, resting in the Heart becomes also effortless. That's simply how it is. Your Heart is asleep so you need to wake it up. When it is awakened, its energy is spontaneously present and merges with Being.

**Q:** You said now in the last part of meditation: try to feel the Heart in the context of Being and fall into your wholeness which cannot be grasped. Can you explain why it cannot be grasped?

**Aziz:** In the growth into the Inner State, we are using our intelligence, we are using our ability to understand. This ability to understand is essential to avoid many different pitfalls on the Path. But there is a point where the mind has to simply give up. It's subtle, sometimes you have to use the mind, you have to use your intelligence, but the time comes when you have to give up. In the case of the holistic experience of the I AM, the mind simply gives up and one allows this experience to be beyond comprehension. That is surrender; you let go of your mind dropping into a state of not knowing. But this Not-knowing is not ignorance, it is an holistic experience of pure Being. The mind has taken you to the Golden Gate of Being, and it is no longer necessary. Of course, it wants to go with you beyond this gate... but it is unable to enter...

**Q:** The mind does understand the experience, doesn't it?

**Aziz:** It does on the intuitive level. The mind knows that the experience is real, it is the right experience. You have to see that it is the mind which gives up. It has reached the right place and in humility surrenders to that which is much bigger, beyond comprehension. Reality is beyond the mind. If you will carry this mind along, it will disturb the experience. It is the Not-knowing which allows you to experience fully the I Am. In this experience you become absent...

**Q:** Does the State of Presence exist prior to manifestation?

**Aziz:** The State of Presence itself, as separated from Being and Heart, can be experienced only in the dimension of limitations, like ours. The State of Presence doesn't exist within the Ultimate in separation from Being and Love. The Divine is beyond any divisions, it is extremely holistic. The State of Presence is fragmented when taken out of the context of Being and Heart. You can experience it separately within you, because you are reaching your wholeness from the point of separation. Separation allows you to experience fragments of reality, but from the Ultimate Perspective, something like a separate State of Presence doesn't exist.

**Q:** You emphasise so much the Heart and the Heart space. Is it wrong that I don't feel it especially, I feel my own three centres, Awareness, Being and Heart more or less on the same level and I don't feel especially the Heart. Is it okay? Is there some transcendental, fundamental importance in the Heart?

**Aziz:** The Heart, in our particular design, is a gateway to the Divine, and it is the seat of the Soul. Your Soul, the essence of your individuality is located in the Heart, it is simply how it is. The Heart is the centre of Feeling. That's why when we touch our Heart, we feel something special and sensitive. Even when the Heart is not awakened, every human being feels something special when touching this area. In the Heart you can meet your divine essence. Go inside it and discover... it is a journey into the Heart of God...

**Q:** But it seems to take me away from this holistic experience of Being and Awareness, from this transcendental absolute presence?

**Aziz:** You see, everything is one, everything is one. Reality is resting upon this ultimate peace, this absolute stillness, it is the foundation. Presence or Awareness is simply a space of knowing and clarity, that which makes you conscious. The Heart is the most precious, the most delicate part of the inner reality. That's why, from this perspective we call it the centre. But, in truth, everything is one holistic experience of the I Am. What you call an holistic experience, does not include the Heart. That's why it is not as holistic as it seems.

**Q:** The teachings of Zen and Dzogchen do not give emphasis to the Heart centre. Are they not complete in your view? Can you speak about this?

**Aziz:** Yes, their teachings are not complete. What they do, they choose one part of the I Am, taking it as the ultimate. In Dzogchen they work mostly with the State of Presence regarding it as the Ultimate. In Zen there is a certain combination of Awareness and Being. According to the teaching which we represent, the Heart has to be absolutely included in order to experience oneself holistically. The presence of the Heart is beyond being emotional or even compassionate. It is the pure presence of the Heart itself that we speak about. It is a profound energy experience which touches the deepest place in our Soul. Without the Heart the Inner State is simply fragmented. But even in their teachings, they also, on the intuitive level, feel the necessity of awakening of the Heart. That's why the ideal of Bodhisattva was created, the idea of saving all beings. In this way they indirectly affect their Hearts...

\* \* \*

## Transmission: 18th January 99

**Q:** Can you talk about relaxation?

**Aziz:** The relaxation, we speak about here, is not relaxation of the body and mind. When we normally speak about relaxation, the emphasis is what we relax, which is usually body and mind. However, this that is important is not what we relax, but into what we relax, what we relax into. In reality, we relax into that which is beyond our personal self, our personal identity. It is a combination of Beingness and Heart into what we relax ultimately. Therefore, if you want to understand the true meaning of relaxation, you need to transcend the one who wishes to relax. You need to learn how to surrender into Being. This surrender is a combination of letting go of the mind and the energy-presence of Being. When these energies are not activated, it is physically impossible to surrender. This process of reaching the ultimate relaxation combines our conscious surrender with deepening of energy in Hara. In this way our surrender is received by the matured energies of Being. Is it clear?

**Q:** Yes.

**Aziz:** You are giving birth to this which can receive you and you are learning how to let go into it. It is a double process, two sides of one thing, and it itself is Trust. The ability to rest in Being is trust. The moment you rest in your Being, it means that this self-protective mechanism, which is fear in your mind, is already relaxed, it already has the courage to trust, to let go. Meditation is an act of courage and it is an expression of trust as well. So the real meaning of trust is to completely let go of yourself. We do not speak about having trust that nothing bad will happen to you. We speak about the real trust, trust to let go of yourself... the real trust. Trust not to be, not to be a fixed person; to completely surrender to your original purity, this is trust.

**Q:** To be awakened to your Soul, is it gradual or is it an event?

**Aziz:** Gradual. There are some events, but this journey is gradual, because the Soul has enormous depth. To be awakened to the Soul is not identical with being awakened to the Heart. This awakening includes the realisation of your blueprint and the vision of completion. The more you are aligned with your Soul, the more you know what you are doing here and what elements you need in order to become fulfilled. The realisation of the Soul unfolds itself. As long as you are alive, this awakening will be presenting itself to you. The awakening of the Soul is not merely a discovery of what is already there. You are creating yourself, you are becoming your Soul.

**Q:** Yes. What is the difference between awakening of the Heart and awakening of the Soul?

**Aziz:** Awakening of the Heart is impersonal, awakening of the Soul is personal. The Soul is present at all times. For example, she brought you here to meditate. You are your Soul! But the complete awakening to the Soul happens in the Heart. In the Heart is the true essence of the Soul. When you discover yourself in the Heart as pure Me, the light merges into light... there is a complete unity with oneself, there is a complete recognition.

Because the energy of the Heart is always a little bit present even in the case of insensitive individuals, one can sometimes have a glimpse of the Soul. Particularly in situations when you fall in love, when you experience something tragic in your life, when you are shaken... the Soul comes to the surface. But the complete awakening to the Soul cannot take place unless the Heart is awakened. The Heart is like a space, environment, in which the Soul can fully recognise itself. The experience of the Heart is energetic. The Heart is made of very sensitive and expansive frequencies of energy. But when you recognise your Me in this Heart, something new is being added. This experience is no longer impersonal, it is deeply personal. In this space the Prayer is born.

Without the foundation of I Am, however, without Awareness and Being, the Heart cannot be experienced in its depth. The Heart, which is disconnected from Being, by nature, is too emotional and fluctuating on the energy level. That's why, only the continuity of Awareness and the ability to rest within, can allow you to enter the Heart fully and to realise the Soul. So there are many different elements. But the Soul one can experience already, even without the complete awakening of the Heart, in certain situations, it is not permanent, but one has some glimpses...

\* \* \*

## Transmission: 21st January 99

**Q:** If you have pain in your Heart and suffering, how can you transform this pain to get out of the suffering?

**Aziz:** Initially, you can use this pain to come closer to your Soul, because this pain is from the Soul. So when you direct your attention fully to your Heart, in a very prayerful way, breathing to your chest, feeling your Heart, you can transform those energies.

You see, there are many reasons we are suffering, but the primal reason of our suffering is that we are separated from the Creator, and this primal feeling of separation can be felt in the Heart, can be found in the Heart. When you go deeper into this feeling, there is, at the same time, all this energy of coming back home, of uniting with the Creator. It is a mystical experience, a religious experience where you transcend your individuality. So from one side, you are an individual and you experience your suffering, and from the other side, you can find this fundamental unity with the Creator; all this happens in the Heart. So you can use this suffering, these feelings, to come closer to your Soul and to really reach the depth of your Soul, and to find that which is unconditional, beyond your personal life, beyond this life.

The transformation of these feelings, however, can happen only when you bring them into your Heart. Breathe to your chest and stay for a while with these feelings. Some time is needed, you need to stay with it. The energy will change, it will be transformed. Heart is the centre of transformation. Anything, which can be transformed, in terms of certain tendencies and negativity, can be done only through the Heart. Awareness/mind cannot transform tendencies and patterns from our past. They cannot be transformed only from the mind. Even observing, even awareness of them doesn't help. They have to be brought into the Heart. The belly, the Hara dissolves those energies, the Heart transforms them.

**Q:** When I focussed in my practice on the Heart without Being, it was a very emotional experience. But now, after I have been practicing a lot with Being, I feel that Being pulls the experience of the Heart and simply dissolves it.

**Aziz:** We know what you mean. It is not that it dissolves, it brings it into its depth. Because when Being dissolves the Heart, it means that you lose the Heart. It means that the energy of the Heart is truly dissolved into the Hara and the Heart is lost.

However, when the Heart is fully activated it is not lost. You can say that Being itself gravitates towards the Heart. So it is not only that the Heart gravitates towards Being and is becoming dissolved, it is Being gravitates towards the Heart and gives it depth. These two centres are united. That's why you experience the depth of the Heart not in an emotional way. It is an energy experience and there is a certain deep feeling but it is not emotional, because the energy goes in not out.

**Q:** Practicing Being one is completely surrendering, letting go of will. Is there an element of will in practicing with the Heart?

**Aziz:** Yes, particularly in this process of awakening of the Heart. Because the Heart is a feeling centre, so you activate it through feeling, through paying attention, through breathing into it. It has to be activated, opened up.

Because the Hara is the centre of gravity, we don't need to do anything in order to cultivate it, because through Non-doing the energy is being pulled there. In this case you rather undo than do; you do Non-doing, that is, you surrender, let go. Heart itself needs to be activated through certain efforts. You have to pay attention to the Heart, you have to breathe to your chest, you have to pray, touch your Heart, you have to listen to music that moves you...

Apart from awakening of the Heart as an energy experience, there is also awakening of the Soul which is very personal. You have to be in a sense very personal in the Heart, simultaneously as you are impersonal, in order to awaken the Soul. So you are using these two energies: personal and impersonal to have this full experience of the Heart, which is energy and the Soul, Energy and Feeling.

When the Heart centre is open and activated, there is less and less effort necessary in order to cultivate it, and ultimately Non-doing also reaches the Heart. Being and Heart become one. But even when all is unified, there is always certain relating to the Heart. You can say a certain personal energy in the way you discover your Heart and you feel it, because you are alive and your Soul is alive.

**Q:** Can you talk about the relationship between Me and the Inner States? Many people, if they are moving away from a more common way of perceiving, from the world of ignorance and separation into the Inner States, it can be quite confusing.

**Aziz:** What is confusing?

**Q:** This re-adjustment/integration process. The past identification changes.

**Aziz:** First of all, Me is not Ego. Ego is a shadow of Me. Ego is, you can say, Me in the mind, Me as thinking. Me itself, the centre of Me is in the Heart: it is the Soul. Me is using the energies of the mind, is using Awareness and so forth, but itself is located in the Heart. So when Me is ignorant, it is identified with the mind and lives in a "shadow reality." It only sees its satisfaction in the outer world: emotional, physical, mental satisfaction. That's how it survives, how it nourishes itself. But when the Me awakens the Inner States, it receives certain reality within. It not only lives in the context of the outer world, it has also a home inside. So it can rest inside... and in this moment Me is in a very interesting situation. It still lives in the world, it still has the emotional body, it still has emotional desires, it still has physical needs — it is still connected with this reality, but at the same time it abides in the internal reality. It can rest within.

This "Me" is in-between. Because it is in-between it cannot exclusively let go into the Inner State. It cannot renounce its connection with the world completely because it lives Here as well. It is in-between. That's why, how to relate to the Inner State, while living in the outer reality as well, is a skill, it demands balance. It relates directly to evolution of the Soul. The Soul has to feel at what stage of evolution she becomes fulfilled in the world, and to what extent she can let go of the world. She still lives here, it means there is still connection, but she can surrender almost completely to the internal reality inside.

So it is a skill and it is a personal question because the answer can be given only to a particular person. Whether this person still has to fulfil himself/herself in the world, which means that the relationship with the Inner State is not one of complete surrender, or whether the Soul is fulfilled already and can afford surrender.

Before we talk about how Me relates to the Inner States, you have to see whether Me is aware of itself. To be aware of Me, to be awakened to Me is to be awakened to the Soul. It means to be awakened to yourself. Who are you? What are you doing here? What are you doing in this world? What do you want from this world? What do you want from the Inner States? The self-knowledge of who you are as a Soul, in combination with your desires, with your blueprint, with your longings, with the vision of your completion, all of this allows you to know how can you relate to the Inner State.

* * *

## Transmission: 28th January 99

**Q:** Other than being in Satsang are there any physical ways or any behavioural patterns in daily life which we should follow?

**Aziz:** First of all, one has to meditate on a regular basis. One needs to do retreats sometimes. But most important is to recognise the centre of Awareness in the mind and to bring it into activity. The centre of Awareness, the State of Presence is cultivated not just in a sitting position but in every situation. You need to remember it in every situation: whether you walk, eat, talk and so forth.

But if one does not recognise the State of Presence, it is a more difficult issue because one doesn't know how to practice. In that case, we would recommend simply connection with the breath as a regular basis; simply Awareness of breathing and mindfulness of environment. These are two basic practices for those who don't recognise the State of Presence.

**Q:** You said that there are two Paths. The Path of Grace and the path of will. Can you speak about the path of Grace?

**Aziz:** The Path of Grace has been created from understanding that the phenomenon of Enlightenment is caused by an energy transmission. There is a certain energy transmission on the esoteric level which changes the state of a disciple. You can say that the Inner State becomes transmitted. This energy transmission happens through the Master, or directly from the Beyond, from the esoteric dimension. Such a phenomenon exists and it is certain.

But what is the relationship between receiving Grace, receiving help from the Beyond and your own effort? The path of will is using only the personal effort and understanding. There are simply certain things to be done: one practices, and one reaches the goal. One relies on oneself, on one's own energy. So what is the connection between the path of Grace and the path of will? They complement each other. You can say that the destiny of a human being is to use one's own effort, one's own striving in order to reach completion and at the same time to receive help from the Beyond. These are two sides of one thing, which is called evolution.

We, our human dimension is completely surrounded by the Other Dimension which is the Divine. We are not aware of the Divine. We think that we are living in the physical dimension on our own. But in truth, these two dimensions are inter-linked. We are surrounded by the realm of spirits, by the reality of the Creator herself and we constantly receive help. There is constant help. These two realities merge. They meet each other. But at the same time we experience our dimension somehow separately for the fun of it.

Grace is not something magical or mysterious. It is simply a law. A law of Universal Consciousness according to which the higher, more evolved energies help the lower evolved energies. They enter into their structure and they chang their vibration, their quality. It is simply a law. Grace exists, but it acts more strongly when one invites it, when the Heart is open. When the Heart is closed, when you have this attitude that "I do everything by myself, I don't need any help," the Grace also comes, but less. It is simply not invited so strongly.

Q: I have been contemplating lately what is this sense of "Me." Many traditions negate the ego, negate the Me. They say: "You should not feel that it is the Me who is doing, it is Me who is speaking," and so forth. But, at the end of the day, I have been wondering, if the source of the sense of Me is God herself which says "I AM"?

**Aziz:** God is the source of all. This that you call "me" is an individual expression of the Source or God. It is how the Creator, which is beyond sense of Me, in truth, experiences herself in manifestation, in an individual manifestation. So Me itself is a reflection of the Universal I AM. A reflection in an individual form.

However, through the contemplation of this Me, through the expansion within this Me, one returns back to the Source. So this Me, which has been given to you, is at the same time the only tool to return home through the expansion within this very Me. This Me grows within itself, reaching deeper and deeper layers of itself, until it melts back to the source, which is beyond Me. The Universal I AM, you can call "pure Me", but this pure Me does not have a sense of Me. The sense of Me exists only in the realm of separation, where you are able to create a self-image.

**Q:** When this merging with the source happens, do you feel simultaneously beyond the sense of Me and the Me?

**Aziz:** Within the human dimension yes.

\* \* \*

## Transmission: 29th January 98

**Q:** You said that recognition of the State of Presence happens in time, from moment to moment. Is it correct also about the Absolute State?

**Aziz:** It is correct but recognition of the Absolute State is more on the side of the Timeless, it is closer to the Timeless. It is a mixture of recognition and non-recognition. It is simply more subtle, closer to the Timeless but there is certainly a touch of time in this experience, otherwise there would not be any recognition of it.

**Q:** So is it correct to say that the Absolute is the Timeless but the recognition of it does happen in time?

**Aziz:** It is, of course, correct.

**Q:** Is there a way to recognise which thoughts arise from the subconscious mind and which belong to the intuitive intelligence? What is the intuitive intelligence?

**Aziz:** Intuitive intelligence is the one who is aware in the mind. Intuitive intelligence is closer to you, it doesn't have a crystallised form yet. Thoughts are already tangible; they can be grasped. Intuitive intelligence cannot be grasped, it is a movement of spirit which is a form of understanding rather than a crystallised thought. Understanding is deeper than thought, it is more on the intuitive level, more immediate, more pure and more formless.

**Q:** But sometimes the intuitive intelligence does formulate itself as words in the mind?

**Aziz:** Certainly, because it is not separated from the mind. It is a deeper part of the mind, which lives within the mind and through the mind. It is able to express itself, to verbalise itself through language and to use past knowledge in order to create understanding.

**Q:** If a person is stabilised in the State of Presence: how does one experience the centre of Presence when there is involvement in life which takes our whole attention?

**Aziz:** There are two levels of recognition of the State of Presence. First is the primal recognition: the energetic vibration of the state itself. When a person is stabilised, the State of Presence becomes automatic on the energy level. At the background of the mind the State spontaneously vibrates. The second level of recognition belongs to the intuitive intelligence. It is simply you who becomes aware of the state. For example, you may say to yourself "oh, I am in the State of Presence, wonderful!" It is important to understand that it is not in the human capacity to become constantly aware of anything. But it is possible to experience a constant Presence on the energy level.

If a person who is stabilised in the State of Presence, is absorbed in some activity, the whole attention of the mind goes to this activity, but the centre of Awareness is vibrating at the background. Simply, the intuitive intelligence does not pay attention to it. There are two extreme situations: one is when the intuitive intelligence is fully focussed on the State of Presence and the second, when it is fully absorbed in something else. Between these two extremes, there are many variations of relating to the State of Presence. The inner attention is simply divided. For example, when you drive a car, you can fully rest in the State of Presence, simultaneously being aware of driving; or, in a different case, you can be actively absorbed in certain activity, but your intelligence is still connected to the State of Presence. Here, we do not need to control the behavior of the State of Presence. There is a natural wisdom of the mind which brings the right balance into the inner economy of Awareness.

**Q:** How can you be sure that the State of Presence is not lost when you are very involved? Let's say, I am not contemplating the State for a few moments and suddenly I remember - how can I be sure that the energy of the Presence was vibrating during the time of not paying attention to it?

**Aziz:** It is a good question. It requires sensitivity, certain observation. You need to observe yourself more, becoming more sensitive to how the Inner State behaves. What does it mean to be in the state without recognition? What does it mean that the State of Presence is there, but you are not recognising it being, for instance, lost in thoughts? By tuning in more to your subtle memory, you become more sensitive to the moments of losing the state and know when it is not lost. When you come back to yourself, after getting out of involvement, you have a way to remember whether the Inner State was there or not. You can feel if there was something which was constant at the background of the mind. You can check if you were not fully lost in the apparent reality. What we would recommend is more introspection and inner observation. This will help you to grow in understanding of who you are and how your Awareness behaves. There is no other way...

**Q:** In the process of merging into Being one lets go of self-referral. In this case, who is the one who experiences Being? The intuitive intelligence is suspended...

**Aziz:** It is a good question and can be answered on many different levels. The deepest answer to this question is: it is the Soul which experiences everything. The Soul is in the Heart but she experiences all. The Soul is using its intuitive intelligence. To whom does the intuitive intelligence belong? It belongs to the Soul. It is the Soul who lets go of the self-reference in the mind and melts with Being. Before merging into Being, the Soul awakens her Awareness and becomes free from the mind. The Soul herself is beyond consciousness - she does not know herself. She becomes aware of herself through consciousness. That's why, if consciousness is undeveloped there is no way the Soul can know herself deeply.

Firstly, the Soul recognises herself as an ego, as the movement of mind. Next, the Soul recognises that there is something more than ego - she awakens to the State of Presence. Afterwards, the Soul recognises the necessity of surrender into Being. All of this is experienced through the Soul only. But still the Soul is not awakened to herself. Therefore, the final awakening is the discovery of the Soul herself, which takes place in the Heart. There is a possibility that one is resting in Being and not knowing Who is resting.

**Q:** Is it possible that you sit in pure meditation and, in one moment, you turn around to check who is resting in Being? I feel this answer is in the Heart.

**Aziz:** Absolutely, you experience yourself in the Heart and when the Heart is awakened, there is no need to ask this question because the energy-presence of the Heart and Being are integrated. So it is one holistic experience where the Soul and I Am become one; the Soul and Being become one. The need for asking this question exists only as a tool of self-discovery in the Heart. Later all questions simply drop off. True Shikan-taza, or the complete state of Being, includes energies of the Heart, includes sensitivity of the Soul.

You must understand that the intuitive intelligence is always a part of any experience. When it surrenders into Being and Heart, it is absorbed, it simply becomes very gentle and sublime. But it remains as long as you are alive - one with I Am and one with the sensitivity of the Heart. That's why even in deep absorption, you can know that you are having this experience - and it gives you joy!

**Q:** Is it as if one feels oneself and the Inner State at the same time?

**Aziz:** The experiencer and the experienced create one field of Experience. The Soul is resting in the Inner, but from time to time feels herself in the Heart or is experiencing herself in the form of intelligence.

Merging with the Inner State one enters the New dimension, beyond unity and separation. The Divine Dimension, the absolute unity of Being and Heart, is no longer you. It is the Divine, the other side of Reality. The Soul exists on two levels: one is, in motion and the second is, in rest. When the Soul is in rest, in complete rest, she experiences purely the Divine. When the Soul is in motion, she retains her individuality and lives through herself. That's why you feel yourself, you can get hurt, you can be happy...all these feelings are registered in the Heart and in the mind as pertaining to your particular story, your particular identity.

**Q:** So this original unique flavour in the Heart, which we call the Soul, is originally unconscious?

**Aziz:** It exists below consciousness, like in a deep sleep state. The Soul expresses itself in this dimension through the physical form and grows within this form. Otherwise your body and your brain would not be necessary. On the earth dimension, which is not the most sophisticated one, the Soul needs a vehicle of physicality in order to become conscious of herself.

\* \* \*

## Transmission: 31st January 99

Q: Is it important to master feelings, in a similar way as we master the mind through the State of Presence?

Aziz: Feelings have two sides, positive and negative. They are a natural part of you, therefore, need to be acknowledged. The mind, in the case of human beings became too important. That's why, humanity is more and more disconnected from feelings and getting lost in the mind. For that reason, we don't emphasise control of feelings, because the majority are already disconnected from feelings. However, there are certain emotions which are unconscious and disturbing. In such a situation, it is not enough to acknowledge them, but one has to transform this negative energy. This is one of the reasons that we insist on breathing into the belly. The centres which are responsible for experiencing emotions are in the belly: second and third chakra. That's why breathing into the belly pacifies them, brings them into their inherent tranquillity, calmness.

From the other side, coming to the Heart we acknowledge our real feelings, feelings which are coming from the Soul, which are related to our evolution and natural response to certain situations. Many feelings in the belly are unconscious, instinctive, conditioned by the past, they don't necessarily have wisdom, but feelings you experience in the Heart relate to you, to your Soul, they usually carry important information and important messages.

The State of Presence is not just mastery of the mind. It is simply a centre in Awareness. This centre is within the mental body but it affects your emotional body as well, for it gives you a stable sense of identity. You are no longer completely identified with the fluctuation of emotions.

The emotional body is unconscious. That's why work with the emotional body is difficult. What changes the emotional body? Firstly, one has to have a foundation of I Am. If you don't have the foundation of I Am, you are too unconscious to change your emotional body. The foundation of I Am is the State of Presence, which is a centre in Awareness, and Being. But this that changes the emotional body is the combination of Presence and Heart. The energies of the Heart bring transforming power into your emotional body. The evolution of the emotional body is quite slow, it takes time. It is very complex. There are many different elements.

When you are rooted in the I Am, you have distance from your emotions. You don't negate them, you are simply rooted deeper in reality; and because of this distance, for the first time, you have a chance to work with your mind and with emotions. You can transform yourself only from the place of freedom. You already have a refuge in the inner realm. You are not the emotions or the mind, something more is added. When the I Am is present, there is this spaciousness in you which allows the re-construction of the emotional and mental body to begin.

Presence of the Heart transforms. When the energies of the Heart are activated they bring miracles into how you experience your emotions. But certain crystallisation of attention is absolutely necessary, otherwise the person doesn't have any continuity of intelligence and is fundamentally unconscious.

**Q:** My experience of Being feels like a gap. Could you speak about that?

**Aziz:** The energy of Being is recognised through consciousness. Consciousness allows you to recognise it; that's why you know that there is a feeling of gap. The energy of Being means rest. It is an energy experience. Being itself is energy. When you are in a deep sleep state, you are in a condition of pure Being, but there is no Awareness and no recognition. In meditation the energy of Being and Awareness are combined, which allows you to recognise the experience. The problem with the way you translate your experience is, that you see this "gap" as something which is "out there." It shows that the way you experience your Being is not mature. What you need to do is to surrender into this gap, to let go of watching this gap, to completely sink into it, drown into it. Drop into this gap, so that you don't even know whether it's a gap, you don't even know if it's emptiness, but you know that you are. There is a clear experience of Being, which cannot be understood by any concept but which is present.

Learn how to be in this gap without checking it and without
watching it, just to be, surrender into it; like falling into it and
in this moment you become absent. You as a mind, you as a
watching intelligence, you become absent, but completely one
with Being, and this is freedom.

* * *

## Transmission: 4th February 99

**Q:** You mentioned that the ego is a passage between the animal
consciousness and the Buddha state. Could you speak about this?

**Aziz:** In order to give rise to the Awakening, there has to be first
the self-referral in consciousness. If consciousness is not able
to create a self-referral, it is completely lost in phenomenal reality.
Animal consciousness is fully identified with the process of living
in this world, and is very much like a dream state. When we
dream, for instance, we have a very similar state of consciousness
to the one of an animal. Animal consciousness is called the
subconscious Me. In the subconscious Me, consciousness is fully
objectified and identified or merged with the movement of perception and experiencing.

When the ego is born, it indicates that the mind, the brain has
evolved enough to be able to create self-referral and self-image.
Self-image is quite an interesting phenomenon. For example, one
creates an image of being beautiful. It is just an image but apart
from this image there is a quick self-referral, which means that
consciousness is able to relate to itself. It knows... one knows
saying "I am beautiful" that it relates to the Me, to the one who
"owns" this quality of being beautiful. You know that the image
you create relates to you, and this is called self-referral. Self-
referral means that the mind is able to create a relative centre in
intelligence.

This self-referral can be used for spiritual purposes as well.
It can bring Awakening. It is ego who asks the question: "who
am I? who am I before the mind?" The ego is able to direct the
energy of consciousness back to itself, to the Source. Without
ego there is no spiritual search and no Enlightenment. You see
how precious the ego is!

The ego is a sign of a highly evolved consciousness but one cannot stop at this stage. The ego is a tool of intelligence which can accelerate its evolution towards reaching complete Self-knowledge. But one can, unfortunately, remain only on the ego level using it only for lower purposes. When one lives only in the ego-world, one lives in the reality of self-images, in the virtual and arrogant reality of the mind. Living in such a reality, one experiences very painfully the fact of being separated and isolated from the rest of Existence. One constantly relates to oneself as something, where the open space of I Am is contracted into an image and information.

The ego is a passage from the subconscious Me to the I Am. It is not a comfortable passage, that's why, even being on the spiritual path we experience so many difficulties. But the ego, the intelligent, sensitive and spiritual ego is the only tool of Awakening. When the ego is living only in the mind, it is a neurotic ego. When the ego is connected with the Heart, it is a sensitive ego. When the centre of Awareness is born and the ability to rest within, the ego transcends itself within the I Am. When the centre of identity is found in the Heart, for the first time Me is awakened. The ego is simply a tool of Me in the mind. But Me itself is much, much deeper and infinitely more meaningful.

**Q:** Can you speak about God?

**Aziz:** God is Mystery... however, we have access to some parts of this Mystery. God is Total Reality which is composed of Absolute Beingness, Absolute Awareness and infinite Intelligence and Love. These are the building blocks of God, so to speak. Apart from these building blocks, there is the Unknown, the Mystery which is beyond our comprehension... and that must be respected with humility.

The reality of God cannot be deciphered but one can have a clear experience of merging with God, of becoming one with her Majestic Presence. We are not speaking about some unclear and hysterical mystical experiences which some imbalance and superficially emotional individuals have. We speak about the

realisation which can be measured with the utmost clarity and
which contains intelligence and dignity of the Soul.

No more questions? In Zen there is a concept about the
importance of combining on the Path the elements of Great Faith
and Great Doubt. Great Faith refers to our trust in the Teaching,
in the practice and in our Buddha nature. When this conviction
is rooted in us, we simply do not have any doubts. But without
Great Doubt we cannot grow either. Without having Great Doubt,
we are not moving forwards; we are neither able to transcend the
past nor reach the future. Great Doubt represents the intensity
of questioning reality and our evolution. Without this element
we cannot really co-create our Awakening.

That's why asking questions is so important. If you don't have
any questions, it means that you don't have doubts; and if you
don't have doubts, it means that you are still in the twilight zone.
When one is in the twilight zone, there is simply no clarity and
the intelligence is not aligned with the awakening process.
Formulating questions is an art. In truth, the kind of questions
you ask always reflects the state you are in and your level of
spiritual evolution.

**Q:** How can we be sure that we have reached the complete Inner
State?

**Aziz:** Yes... You see, there are a few levels of Enlightenment.
What level of Enlightenment the Soul wishes to reach relates to
what we call the "blueprint." When a Soul fulfils its blueprint
and reaches a certain depth of I Am which is sufficient, her
evolution is complete. In such a case, there are no more doubts
and the Soul simply relaxes into the depth of realisation, which
she has attained. In the case where the Soul is "extreme" and
wants to reach the final depth of inner reality, she will not rest
until it is accomplished. Within the final depth of I AM one is
absent, one is completely absorbed into the presence of the
Universal I AM. The one who could doubt is dissolved.

* * *

## Transmission: 17th February 99

**Q:** When I sit, I am able to experience attention in itself, but when I move out, the connection with the inner gets lost. Do you have any comments?

**Aziz:** Because your Awareness is not fully awakened, you experience these difficulties. You are not able to experience two realities simultaneously - the inner and the outer. You are not able to experience attention in and attention out at the same time. Your attention is either in or out. But what you are learning is to experience these two realities simultaneously, which is the function of the economy of attention. The awakened attention is like a double-edged sword: it is aiming out and aiming in simultaneously. We want to develop this ability that part of you is constantly aware of the state of pure "I" or subject, while the other part, is freely participating in life.

But at the beginning, this ability is difficult to be attained and one needs to undergo some training. You grow gradually, like a baby: first you recognise the State of Presence and next you learn slowly how to retain it in activity. You learn to keep it while walking, eating, reading and interacting with others. At all times, you keep attention in, directed to the centre of Awareness. As you grow, the challenge will increase and you will be able to retain the State of Presence in the most disturbing circumstances. A tremendous energy in the mind is required in order to create continuity of self-attention. That's why it is a difficult task. But in time it becomes easier and easier... It is evolution.

**Q:** It takes so much effort. I am afraid it takes too long.

**Aziz:** It takes a long time and it doesn't. We live in a special time. The evolution is truly accelerated, this dimension is cooking up. What took twenty years in the past, can now be done in a few months. We are not saying this just to comfort you — it is reality. That's why, this is the time when it is really worthy investing in one's evolution, because the results will be present quickly. But there are difficulties on the way also — one has to simply make a great effort. That is your responsibility. In

reality, you have no choice. Either you go back to unconsciousness or you grow into the light. You have no choice... it is
wisdom. One has to overcome these difficulties and one will get
support!

Do you recognise the State of Presence? Are you able to feel
it when your eyes are open? What is the experience? Do you
experience it in the head?

**Q:** When I look yes, but when I don't look, it is also in the other
areas.

**Aziz:** No, the experience of the State of Presence is only in the
head. The other experiences you are having relate more to Being.
The experience of the State of Presence is in the third eye; it is
an experience at the back or in the middle of your head, it is an
energy experience. It is as if your eyes are looking in, and you
recognise the centre. You have to learn how to be connected with
it and how to create a continuity of the state. To experience it
is not enough. It is the continuity of Awareness which changes
the structure of the mind. The continuity transforms, an experience is nothing. One can have all kinds of mystical experiences,
but they are worthless. That which has continuity is real only.
First keep continuity in meditation; next slow walking on the
beach, very slow walking. Give yourself a task of creating the
continuity and you will quickly see the results. It is simply a
matter of time.

The awakening and stabilisation in the State of Presence takes
place on the energy level, it is not only a function of will. It is
not that you do not remember. Your energy is not ready to receive
the State of Presence and to retain it constantly. If this is the
case, it would cook itself up. Your energy has to transform, the
whole energy system needs to transform in order to be able to
contain the higher frequency. That's why, breathing into the
belly is essential because it deeply affects your energy system.

In order to succeed, you have to sacrifice that which takes you
away from the inner work. You don't need to sacrifice sex, that
would be stupid. You don't have to sacrifice money, you only
need to sacrifice that which disturbs your growth. You have to

sacrifice everything which takes you away from the State of Presence. In truth, what you need to sacrifice is your own forgetfulness.

There is a point in the practice, like turning over, where you find yourself on the positive side of the effort. You still need to practice but you are on the bright side already. There is more and more happiness and joy in your practice. It is the stage where one cannot go back. The force of the light is too strong. At your present stage, you can still go back. You can easily forget about the importance of the inner work. That's why, be careful! Do not let yourself get discouraged. The power of your past is like a heavy shadow cast upon your Now. Certain tendencies can pull you into negativity and unconsciousness. As you stay with the Inner Light, the past gets more and more erased, and what remains is purity.

**Q:** Is Me different than the I Am?

**Aziz:** The Me is more dynamic. Me is related to the mind, to the mental body and to the emotional body. The mind and the emotional body have been created throughout many lifetimes. They have been conditioned by many past events. That's why, even when you reach a deeper state of consciousness, you might notice that your Me behaves in the same way as it did in the past. You might notice that certain emotional patterns have not actually changed. This is the paradox which many enlightened beings have had to face. They have discovered that even reaching the transcendental state, doesn't eliminate certain neurotic tendencies. Why is it? Because the evolution of Me and the evolution into I Am are not the same. It is a parallel evolution and complementary but, at the same time, taking place in different dimensions of reality.

The question is: how can we transform Me, how can we purify Me or the psyche? This issue is quite complex as it involves many different elements. Sometimes, in order to work with Me, therapy is needed. Other times, different elements are necessary. But fundamentally there are two elements which transform Me: one is Awareness and the second is the Heart. The mind, which doesn't have any centre of attention, is deeply unconscious and there is no real way of healing it and changing its fundamental structure. For that reason, nobody becomes fully transformed by therapy. It can help certainly, but not transform. To transform is to create the New. Otherwise, we are only trying to fix the past.

The centre in the mind brings radically new energy into the mind. The Me for the first time has a real centre of intelligence. But the healing and transformation of Me does not happen through Awareness. One can witness the mind for a hundred years and it will remain the same! Transformation takes place through the Heart. The Heart has transforming power, the power of Grace.

If you wish to transform your Me, you have to become more aware of your mind in the psychological sense and simultaneously crystallise your attention, giving rise to the centre of Awareness. From that place go into your Heart. Bring all your energy into the Heart and pray for healing, pray for help. Transformation of Me is not a sudden event, it is the process of cleansing and healing which takes some time.

Transformation of Me does not mean that Me becomes perfect. It simply leaves the unnecessary burden of past negative experiences and reaches the minimum of neurosis, which is inherent to being Here. You will never be perfect but you are always going into the direction of perfection. You should always accept yourself fully, but, within this acceptance, use your intelligence and your sensitivity to live as close as you can to your higher nature. See what the reasons are that you act in a certain way, bring understanding into your patterns. In your Heart and in your mind ask yourself: "do I want to change this part of myself?" Sometimes, the experience of negativity cannot be avoided for it is difficult to be a human being. Sometimes, to get angry is fine, because it might be the right response at that time. A human being is never perfect for she/he lives in the dimension which is far from perfection. It is not only a fault of humanity; this very need to survive by competing with other beings, which is inseparable from living on earth, is truly a sign of imperfection. The moment you decided to incarnate as a human, you agreed, on the Soul level, to experience this imperfection.

When you evolve into I Am, you evolve into Perfection. When you reach fully the I Am, you reach Perfection itself. But, paradoxically, because your Me continues to exist, the imperfection remains as a part of your reality. To have this body is imperfect, to have this mind is imperfect... your emotions will never be perfect. However, in the process of evolution you are purifying them, you are reaching the optimum. The optimum where you feel okay, you feel it is all right to be a little bit imperfect.

**Q:** So what about these patterns which need to be changed? How can we deal with them if they keep re-occurring?

**Aziz:** Certain teachings assume that observing the mind or witnessing the mind is sufficient to transform it. Behind this concept is an incomplete psychological understanding of who we really are. Observing gives you a certain space of freedom and distance. We may assume that the observed (the psychological self) is not Me, therefore, it has no longer any impact on our wellbeing. But, unfortunately, the situation is a bit more complex. The observed in the mind is also Me. That's why those who exercise observing of the mind, in truth, at all times need to use strong will in order to remain disidentified! Because the observed and the observer are both Me, that's why, more holistic understanding and inner work is required.

This that changes the mind is a combination of understanding, the centre of Awareness, presence of the Heart and a certain cleansing of the subconscious mind. Firstly, you have to understand why you experience these negative patterns and emotions. This understanding is not enough but it is a foundation. If you have no understanding, how could you change? We speak about certain understanding and we suggest not being too analytical, for it involves too much energy from the mind. Next, you must find your real centre in the mind. Where is your position within the movement of the mind? If you don't have any solid location in the mind, it itself is a neurosis.

From the place of understanding and having a clear centre of

Awareness, you go into the Heart. Why is the Heart so important in the transforming process? Because the Soul is in the Heart and the Soul is linked with the power of Grace directly. Here, you express clearly the intention of changing yourself and ask deeply for help from the Divine. The cleansing which follows is a result of the higher technology of transformation. It is beyond human capacity to cleanse the mind, which has been crystallised from the infinite past. But Grace does it. It is not necessarily a sudden event, it is a process, it is evolution. Pray and breathe into your Heart, putting your hands on the Heart. In this way you activate the energies of the Heart, which bring transformation and you invite help from the Beyond. In truth, this help has the biggest role in our transformation.

**Q:** I was wondering about the belief that we are responsible for everything what happens in our life and that we create our reality through our belief system. Do you share this view?

**Aziz:** This is a "New Age" concept. This concept assumes that we create our reality from inside, so to speak. For that reason, by changing our belief system we can create a better reality or a "super reality." This belief is a half-truth. The proper understanding is that we co-create, in truth, our reality. We do not create our reality but we co-create. Did you create your body? Did you create your mind? Did you create your DNA? It has been given to you. You found yourself in particular circumstances of life without your will. Suddenly you found out that you've got particular parents and you live in particular country. You didn't have any choice. Now you are trying to do your best in order to improve your situation.

Before you are really conscious, there is no possibility of co-creation. In such a case, only the subconscious mind operates. Now because you have become conscious you can have some impact on your life. It is not simply a matter of a belief system. This very mind that you have and intelligence only have a limited capacity. You cannot jump above your own head. You co-create within your limitations. You co-create with Existence, but Existence is much bigger than you! You are just a tiny point of reality surrounded by the ocean of Existence, by the ocean of Universal Intelligence. It is this Universal Intelligence that has created you and is creating you in each moment. You create and you are being created, that is the Co-creation. Existence creates you, and you create your life within this Existence. You flow with Existence but within this flow you do your best to be in harmony. You are using all resources that you have been given to you to do your best. At the same time, you should be clear that your capacities are limited.

The concept that by changing your belief system, you can change your reality is arrogant. In the New Age, it has been discovered that we do have power to change our life and it relates directly to our belief and the vision of life we have. But if we take this concept in a too extreme way, we simply lose balance. We should never forget that we are children of God. If you wish to change your reality, pray for it. Of course, some elements of working with your mind must be included. If your mind creates too much negativity and is not able to create a positive vision of your life, you must look deeper into your belief and conditionings. It is very helpful to have a clear and positive vision of your future. In this way it can manifest more easily. You cannot create your future but you can co-create it. Existence will support the realisation of your deepest desires.

**Q:** I am not clear what part of our being is really uncreated?

**Aziz:** The question is: what is Unborn? That which is beyond time, the Unborn, is reached through the expansion within Being. Awareness itself is both, created and un-created. Awareness on some level is eternal and on some level arises in time. That's why, you experience the awakening of Awareness as an event in time. But that which is fundamentally beyond time is called the Absolute. The Absolute is this that you experience in a deep sleep state without dreams. It is the original energy. When the shift to the Absolute takes place, one becomes united on a conscious level with this original energy.

You see, your question cannot be answered in a simple way because it touches the multi-dimensionality of Reality. One part of the Unborn is that which is at complete rest, that which does not move — the bottomless Primal Absence, which IS. But the Ultimate is more than the Absolute. Apart from the presence of the original energy of Pure Rest, there is also the Divine Dimension. The Divine is unborn as well, but it is not the same as the Absolute. Finally, we discover also our Soul. The Soul is neither created nor uncreated. The Soul is eternal but the experience of her arises in time. Reality is quite complex. We cannot simply pinpoint one thing in us which is beyond time. Linear logic will not do.

Let us answer your question in a simple way: that which is impersonal, which is beyond your individual Me, is the field of Beingness. When you simply relax, surrendering into Being, in truth, you relax into that which is eternal. This Me, which is born is time, discovers that which is eternal by the force of its spiritual expansion. In Buddhist language, when they speak about the Unborn, they refer to the Absolute State. The Absolute is at complete rest and beyond Consciousness. That's why, the Buddha himself spoke about that which is beyond Brahman. According to his interpretation, the Brahman was equivalent to pure consciousness. At one stage of his spiritual evolution, which did not necessarily take place under the Bodhi tree, he discovered that there is something beyond consciousness. He shifted to the Absolute State, to the condition of Rest in the unmanifested. An Enlightened being is in a deep sleep state while remaining conscious. That's why, the experience of the Unborn is conscious. It seems paradoxical that one is in a deep sleep state, which is beyond consciousness and one remains conscious of it. This apparent paradox is the reality for the one who is fully Self-realised.

Q: I have one more question. In the tradition of Nisargadatta Maharaj, individuality is denied. If, for example, I would ask a master of this tradition: "is there individuality on the absolute level?" The answer would be: "who is asking this question?"

Aziz: This response: "who is asking this question?" was created a long time ago in the tradition of Non-duality. In this way one points to the subject. The question "who?" turns the mind back to its own centre. It is simply a teaching device. The question is good but not precise. That's why, even though the question is good, the expected answer is not complete. Certain conclusions, which have been created in the philosophy of Non-duality, do not always reflect the whole truth. If the purpose of interrogation "who is asking the question" is realisation of the Absolute, it means that the expected conclusion is certainly wrong. It is not the Absolute which is asking the question. It is you! But what is this you?

The purpose of this question is to bring you to this point beyond ego. When I ask you: who are you? You cannot find anything, isn't it true? But you cannot find anything because you are not sensitive enough, you are not seeing that which is subtle. The right answer to the previous question is: the Soul, or simply Me. When an unawakened person says "me," it means truly nothing. In the mind of such person there is no real centre of identity, just an ignorant chaotic movement of thoughts. However, when an awakened being says "Me," it means something. It is a solid experience of oneself. Me is a state, a wholeness of oneself centralised in the Heart. Me is a unique flavour of oneself in the Heart which is using intelligence. Me itself is a movement of intelligence which is rooted in the Heart.

Let's draw a conclusion: the question is good but the expected answer is incomplete. That's why, in the teaching which we represent, the Final Enlightenment is not to the Absolute but to Me. Enlightenment to Me is much more subtle than Enlightenment to the Absolute State. Why? Because Me is the closest to you, it is so near that you cannot catch it. You can capture, in a sense, the experience of the Absolute State because you rest in it. But who is resting? It is easy to say "no one" but it is not true. Me is resting and this Me is very precious, very special. Me dwells in the Heart but it uses intelligence, uses Awareness, rests in Being. The centre of Me is in the Heart, it is the Soul. For that reason, we differentiate between the awakening to the Self and to the awakening to the Soul.

**Q:** Ramesh Balsekar, has this concept of awakening as liberation from the thought of being a doer....

**Aziz:** The psychology, which Ramesh Balsekar uses is quite linear...and that is alright. If his intelligence is satisfied with such a vision of reality, that is alright. But it does not mean that this vision is complete. The psychological language and understanding which he represents is not incorrect, it is simply incomplete. The psychology which was created two thousand years ago, in order to reflect the complexity of Enlightenment, does not any longer satisfy our needs for clarity. It is much too simplistic. The past psychology has not grasped the complexity of various inner processes and the co-existence of Me with the Inner State. A new psychology is necessary to bring clarity into the paradoxical nature of awakening. A new multidimensional understanding is required to allow us to see that Non-doing and being a doer — co-exist.

For example, you are sitting and meditating. You are trying to reach your I Am. Aren't you? Who is doing it? Who is trying to reach it? You can say "nobody is trying" but it is false, it is hypocrisy! It is you, your intelligence, whatever this you is. Your Me uses its intuitive intelligence, it uses sensitivity, uses knowledge and memory, in order to reach Peace. You will simplify your life a lot by accepting this basic truth. It is common sense. You don't need to become confused by all these concepts. They do not help you at all. You simply get more stuck in the mind. Whether you are a doer or a non-doer, still, you must do something! This doing is a part of life. The danger of certain spiritual concepts is that they sometimes lose touch with reality.

**Q:** Yes, I am a little confused whether I should do something or just realise "what is" by letting go of everything.

**Aziz:** The problem with you is that you encounter many teachings. All these teachings offer different concepts and you keep on comparing them trying to get to some conclusion. Because, some traditions have contradictory concepts in comparison to the other ones, you feel insecure not knowing which path you should commit yourself to. But at one point, you have to find what is right for yourself. Your intelligence must mature! There is no one Teaching, there are many teachings and not all bring you to the same place. The teaching, which is presented here, is beyond traditions. You cannot compare it with other teachings, for it is multidimensional. It is a New Teaching, a revelation to humanity. This teaching includes the presence of Me, which has been denied all along. It includes the dynamics of being Me, the dynamics of psyche and the presence of the Soul. It includes many different elements. The Goal of this teaching is not liberation but Transcendence, reaching the Wholeness within which the Me is contained and fulfilled. The traditional teachings negate the Soul. According to these concepts the Soul is an illusion; according to the teachings which we represent, the concept that there is no Soul is an illusion.

**Q:** What about the Buddha's concept of "no-self"?

**Aziz:** When the Buddha realised emptiness and concluded that there is no-self, it was his Soul who realised it. It was his Soul who expressed this understanding. It was a wonderful discovery but it does not take away from the truth that the Soul does exist! He was awakened to the Heart but his conceptual tools, his understanding did not reflect the subtle presence of the Soul. Buddha was awakened to the Heart but the way he translated it was impersonal. The personal was lacking. So even though his experience was complete, still, the way he translated this experience for others, was not.

Relax and start the practice from the foundation. Crystallise the State of Presence and practice self-remembrance. We assure you that it is You who is practicing self-remembrance! It is not just an impersonal Consciousness. This practice is your responsibility, you cannot just wait for a miracle. Your own suffering and feeling of incompleteness will not allow you be passive. You have to meditate with the clear intention of meeting yourself. Not to reach Enlightenment, which is just an idea in the mind, but to meet Yourself. Connect to your Being, bringing more and more the holistic experience of I Am, and finally go into your Heart and merge with your Soul. The one who is sitting here is you! The one who wants to experience peace and escape from suffering is YOU. Know who you are....

* * * * *

# Spontaneous Talks

The awakening of the Heart is much more complex than the awakening of consciousness. The awakening of consciousness is comparatively simple. There are certain states you shift to, then you stabilise and the state is permanently there. In the case of working with the Heart there are many, many layers because evolution into the Heart doesn't have an end. But there is something like Enlightenment of the Heart and stabilisation in the Heart. You can say, we reach the optimum of the Heart, it opens fully and this experience is stabilised. One cannot lose it, but even though one still evolves into the Heart, it is never-ending. This is not a contradiction. There is Enlightenment to the Heart, stabilisation of the Heart but the never-ending journey into the Heart continues. What you are aiming at, is to reach this optimum where the energy centralises in the Heart, where it vibrates in an optimum way and the Heart opens fully.

**Q:** Is stabilisation in the Heart similar to the one in Presence?

**Aziz:** It is a little bit different because the energy of the Heart, when it's fully open, merges with your Being. So it's not necessary that for twenty four hours you experience it in the chest. It becomes one with your whole energy system. However, most of the time certainly you experience it in the chest. But the Heart is sensitive, it has wisdom and there are certain situations in life where it closes. For example when you are in a situation that is insensitive, where the energies are of ignorance and darkness, the Heart closes as a self-protective mechanism.

The experience of the Heart, stabilisation in the Heart is a little bit different than stabilisation in the State of Presence. What you are aiming at now, from your perspective, is to feel it as much as you can, to experience energy in the Heart centre almost at all times, and this energy deepens. It deepens and when you sit in meditation later on you will experience that Heart and Being are together. Like you rest and, at the same time, this energy is resting in the Heart, abiding in the Beloved. Being and Heart become one and there is a certain letting go. You have pure experience of the Soul. That's what the Soul is. Although the Soul is located in the Heart centre, she is more. The Soul encompasses all those other centres, all other aspects. Being, Heart and Awareness plus a certain letting go give rise to the complete experience of the Soul, which embraces all of you. It is not only in the chest.

The moment you surrender to the Heart, Being is always included. Through feeling your Heart you are awakening it, but when the Heart is clearly felt you surrender. Surrender means Being in the Heart. Surrender means Non-doing in the Heart, dropping into the Heart. But you are unable to drop into the Heart, you cannot surrender to it unless it vibrates enough. Therefore, first one must awaken the Heart centre on the energy level.

If the Heart is not awakened when one surrenders, the energy drops into Being bypassing the Heart. It goes too low. Surrender means that one lets the energy gravitate downwards. When the Heart is included the energy is distributed equally to Being and the Heart.

**Q:** Is there a stabilisation in the Soul?

**Aziz:** When the Heart is stabilised, you experience the Soul all the time, but how you are aware of your own Soul is more complex. It relates, for example, to your intelligence and intuitive connection to the totality of your Me. The Soul is Me in the Heart. The Soul is your personal unique flavour in the Heart, in connection with your intelligence and the vision of evolution or blueprint. Certainly, if your Heart is fully awakened then the experience of the Soul is stabilised. You are not losing it, but your relationship with your Soul, which means how the Soul relates to herself, still evolves.

**Q:** If the Soul is stabilised in the Heart, are there still some moments of separation in the human condition or there is a constant unity with God?

**Aziz:** You know that the Soul is experiencing simultaneously oneness and separation with the Creator. When you know it, you know that separation is a part of this experience. It is only because you are separated, that you can experience unity with the Creator. The separation itself is positive, paradoxically.

As long as you have personal desires, as long as you evolve in this dimension, you will experience a certain amount of separation. Yes, the separation is transcended only when you completely give up the connection with this particular dimension and with your individuality. This is not necessary for it doesn't have to be the choice from your Soul. It is an option. The Soul can choose, she can give up. But even when you give up your human part, a slight separation, a slight experience of the painfulness of being a human always remains, as long as you are alive, because you are Here. You are in this physical form. You experience a relatively separated emotional body, physical body and mental body and because of this relative separation, you cannot avoid a certain amount of suffering. Even the most realised beings, those who have renounced completely, they have moments of sadness when they simply cry. We call it Pure Suffering, for it doesn't relate to anything but just to the fact of being human and being Here.

**Q:** How is it possible that the Soul has personal characteristics?

**Aziz:** The I AM itself is a dimension of pure knowingness without any personal characteristics, but when it manifests itself into this reality, into another reality, differentiation is created. It becomes something, differentiation is created, multi-varsity is created. Different elements of which the reality is composed, are experiencing themselves from their own perspective. You experience yourself differently. This tree experiences itself differently. It is how this manifestation has happened. Many different flavours which give rise to the One universal flavour of this universe. This universe is composed of many different flavours, different elements, different points of view. For example, how you see reality and how someone else sees reality is different. Even though, everything is one, there are differences. You are evolving from your own perspective, other beings evolve from their perspective, and these realities meet, penetrate each other and give rise to a bigger structure.

The Soul is simply an angle of perception and because it is an angle of perception, that's why she is unique. What is the Soul really? It is nothing else but how the Creator perceives herself from the viewpoint of separation. A blueprint is superimposed upon this particular Me and the unique viewpoint comes into existence.

The moment you are awakened fully to yourself in the Heart, it is how the Creator perceives herself through you. But when you are not awakened, it is how you experience yourself.

**Q:** Is the Soul personal or impersonal?

**Aziz:** She is both. The personal means that the Soul is intimate with herself and it is you. The impersonal means that she dissolves into the higher knowingness, which is not you. It is you, it is not you. Both. Yes? In our human dimension awakening is possible only within this polarity of separation and unity. If you were not one with the universe, if you were not one with the Creator, you could not become one! You can only realise the oneness which is always there, but you can realise this oneness only because you are separated. That's why this meeting is possible. This meeting... there is no accident in this meeting. It is not just an illusion. The separation is a part of this plan. The Creator discovers herself within the relative separation. This is Lila, divine play.

Manifestation as such is not only this particular universe. Manifestation is everything. There are dimensions of reality which are formless. The physical universe is just a part of Creation which is not the most sophisticated one. For any knowing, for any recognition to take place, a Creation has to take place. In the Original State there is not knowing. That's how the Creator is experiencing herself is Not-knowing. The Creator knows herself through Creation, through Me. But the universal Me, the Me which is the closest to the Beloved, is like an ocean of knowingness without any separation and where the information is not translated by any particular Me.

Evolution means nothing else but feedback. From its original state, Original Energy manifests itself and expands outwardly. Through evolution, it comes back to itself and recognises its own everlasting light. This circle is called spiritual evolution, coming back to the zero point, returning home. To be awakened means to be at the meeting point between Creation and the Creator. It is still not the Creator, for one exists as Me, but the unity is already there! It is not the dissolution as such which is the purpose of Creation, but this exact sublime space that exists just before being dissolved, where a slight separation is still present.

**Q:** I experience this longing for Being, to dissolve into it. It feels like to die... I almost pray for it.

**Aziz:** Death means change of identification. Death means change. It is not that you die. It means that your past identification, your past Me dies and the new Me is born. Many, many me's die but they die in the real Me. It is a paradox that in order to go beyond the Me you have to find your real Me. Your real Me is the Soul! By finding yourself, by becoming one with yourself, a certain merging happens, certain transcendence takes place. The moment you merge with yourself, you become part of the bigger Me, bigger whole. So you cannot go beyond your Me just by negating it. You can go beyond your Me only by realising it fully, this is a law. Accept your Me as it is and go deep into its reality. In this way, suddenly you will see that it is no longer this little separate me, it is the Great ME, Me which is experiencing unity with Creation, with the Creator.

* * *

**Q:** I have a question about the eternal nature of the Atman. According to Buddhism it is a false belief in "eternalism." Is it eternal?

**Aziz:** It is a subtle issue and linear logic will not do. It can be seen from several perspectives. Firstly, the Self is the whole experience of the I Am. The no-self is the Absolute, which is beyond Consciousness; but the Absolute is not merely nothing. It is the Primal energy on which everything else is resting. So the Self and the no-self are seen here from our perspective of human Enlightenment. But the Universal I AM or the Divine, the Universal Intelligence exists independently from our limited point of view. The Divine is not merely the Absolute. It is a Mystery and the simplistic logic of Buddhist philosophy sounds rather like a joke.

Next, the Soul herself is neither the Absolute, nor the Divine, nor the I Am. Maybe you have noticed the distinction between the I AM and the I Am? The I AM is universal. The I Am is the universal experienced within the individual. The Soul is certainly not eternally conscious as Me, but she exists timelessly within the Divine and becomes manifested according to her blueprint. She is neither created nor uncreated.

You see Buddhist logic here does not apply. How to measure the depth of Reality depends on the tools we are using. One cannot understand Rainbow by mathematics equations for example. Reality is Subtle and cannot be deciphered. The Soul exists and has to be realised. The I Am exists and has to be realised. The experience of Atman is only the State of Presence. It is not a question of whether it is permanent. When it is realised it is relatively permanent. For example, in a sleep state it goes to sleep as well. But it represents that which is Universal at the same time.

The Experience of the Absolute is called the Absolute State. When it is realised, it is permanent. But in deep sleep there is no recognition of it. The Absolute is permanent but the recognition of it is not. Because it is the Me which is recognising All! Me is simply a relative angle of perception — an expression of the Universal I AM. Our problem is that the only channel to experience this reality is our very Me. This Me has not been understood at all and, on the contrary, it was negated. Without Me, from

our point of view, there is no experience. The Buddha realised
the Absolute, that's why he negated the permanent Brahman (the
I Am). He found that any experience can vanish, but the Unborn
remains. But he forgot that it was only from his Me point of
view. We cannot pinpoint the Reality for it exists independently
from our point of View. It is God!

Any recognition is not permanent, or rather not constant. The
Ultimate is beyond experience, which means there is no Me in
it to which the information of existence returns. However, the
purpose of being here is to experience this reality as deep as
possible... and precisely this impermanence gives depth to the
experience. In Vipassana the concept of impermanence neither
allows them to stabilise in the State of Presence nor to discover
the Soul. They close themselves in the coffin of Buddhist
philosophy waiting for death.

To understand these matters non-linear transcendental logic is
necessary. Do not forget that there are mysteries! When human
destiny is exhausted it is not always the end of evolution. Evolution
into the Universal Me has no end. And there are secrets of which
the human consciousness with all its great traditions, is unable
to conceive. With this understanding we reach Humility and
openness to the Unknown. That's why there is a place for Prayer,
this is a part of the creative limitation of being human.

* * *

Q: I have a question about the experience of concentration rising
from different meditation paths. One can have a deeper experience, reach jnana, go beyond the mind from practicing the
mindfulness of breathing, just sitting, metta bhavana, Satori experience... or Absolute Meditation - a fuller, deeper more positive
experience of the Self. Yet there is a different flavour arising
out of each path. Being a Buddhist, of course, I had in mind the
list of jnana factors: one-pointedness, concentration of mind, bliss,
rapture, equanimity. Each level of jnana refining and deepening
the preceding ones, yet my experience of Absolute Meditation
doesn't fit the model, not surprisingly. I would appreciate your
perspective.

**Aziz:** I understand that you wish to translate the approach of Absolute Meditation into the traditional model. It is possible but can be dangerous, for the energy behind the traditional model is not always the same. Concentration or one-pointedness refers to the presence of attention. One-pointedness based on following the breath is designed for those who are not awakened to the State of Presence! Of course, following the breath can induce a deep absorption, but it is artificial. It is like taking a drug or going to a techno-party. The essence of one-pointedness is the State of Presence, for it is the essence of Awareness. When the State of Presence is recognised, one cultivates the stabilisation of its constant presence. The level of absorption does not always relate to the depth of I Am. When Awareness is active one naturally cannot reach the trance-like Samadhi. Pure Meditation is Shikan-taza, just being. Just Being is a very subtle and profound state. Just Being can be present both in deep absorption as well as when one is aware of the fact of sitting or of the environment.

First, we have the evolution of Awareness, which is not directly related to Samadhi or absorption. Next, once the centre of Awareness is more and more established, we surrender into Being. In Being the self-referral mechanism is transcended. In the case of Awareness, Me is always mixed in; in the case of Being, Me becomes released from itself. Evolution into Being is not about reaching temporary Samadhi, but about being more and more grounded in the dimension of Beingness.

The highest experience of Being is the Absolute State, which is beyond movement. Before being in the Absolute State, there is a movement within Being. That's why, there are different states of absorption. In the case of the Absolute State, the movement of Being is transcended, one dwells permanently in the deep sleep state, in the State which is motionless, beyond manifested reality. In India they call it: Sahaja-Nirvikalpa-Samadhi: Natural, permanent unity with the Source. That's why, Hui-Neng, Zen master said: "as far as the essence is concerned, it does not decrease in disturbance nor does it increase in Samadhi." The more Being deepens, the more comfortable it is to dwell within, the easier it is to be Received by the dimension of Beingness. It is evolution in the direction of the Source which is the center of Gravity. Breathing into belly helps to transmute the energy system. It is not to get into a trance or absorption, but to reach the natural groundedness within Being.

In truth, there is only one Real experience of the Self. How can you know if it is the real one? By Non-doing. Meditation is Non-doing. You should contemplate the meaning of Shikan-taza more, just being. It is only when You are absent that the real Meditation State can be present! But as you know, you should also be present within your absence. These matters are subtle and only those who seek truth and clarity will understand fully the Inner Realm.

True Bliss comes from the Heart. Samadhi, where the Heart is not included, is more Peace. Bliss is a particular frequency of energy which is generated in the Heart. The Presence of the Heart and the experience of one's particular Me which is the Soul, cannot be comprehended using the traditional model. The conceptual tools, which the past traditions use, are not subtle enough. Seek for Truth, and not to fit yourself into any model. Awareness is the essence of the mind. When the State of Presence is recognised, to practice any kind of one-pointedness, apart from abiding in I AM, is simply unintelligent! Next, one learns how to surrender into Non-doing. Non-doing is the key of the true experience of meditation... and after the meditation is over, what happens to the I Am? These are important questions.

Apart from the experience of rest, in the State of Meditation, there is the whole journey into the Divine. When the Heart is activated and one with Being, a new evolution begins, the evolution of dropping deeper and deeper into the depth of the Heart Dimension. One merges more and more with the Heart of the Creator.

* * *

Q: Can you describe the state of total dissolution?

Aziz: There is no one to describe it (laughter). Total dissolution can be experienced on two levels: one is called a deep sleep state without dreams. The second is Universal Consciousness. Dissolution into the Universal Consciousness contains the element of knowing, but does not have a sense of Me. One can have an experience of it either in Samadhi, where Me is completely absorbed, or after the death of the physical body. If that is the destiny of the Soul to return back to this state. Otherwise the Soul remains below the conscious level, in a deep sleep, and afterwards incarnates again.

Q: When the state of dissolution is experienced within life, not after death, is it an altered state of consciousness or can it be experienced even now while I am speaking? Can the speaking be functional while my Being is absolutely dissolved and one with the Beloved?

Aziz: Certainly it can be experienced when you are alive, which means that the Me is present. In this case, there is a co-existence of Me and the I AM. There are levels of how Me dissolves into the I AM. The different levels of dissolution relate to the depth of Being and also certain emotional surrender, where Me doesn't hang emotionally on itself, but it lets go into the I AM. When the depth of Being is present, it happens naturally. In such a case, the Me on the energy level is dissolved, but still can know this experience; still can use its intelligence to verify the experience.

There is a possibility of dissolution into the Absolute State, and there is a possibility of dissolution into the unity of the Absolute and Heart. In this way the experience is different, the dissolution is more complete and holistic. As you can see, the dissolution varies depending on the level of surrender and the kind of dimension we dissolve into.

Q: This feeling of dissolution, do you feel it with great joy and happiness or is it more neutral?

Aziz: There are two kinds of joy and happiness within the inner experience. Firstly, there is the experience itself and secondly, there is how you interpret it. Because when you dissolve and you remain conscious, your Me still exists within the experience and, therefore, the Soul can rejoice. Apart from the joy which comes from Me, the state itself is one of happiness on the energy level. This is the primal happiness which is the energetic experience of the state, of the Universal I AM. The appreciation from the Soul comes on top of this experience which is already present.

**Q:** I really felt bliss in the meditation....

**Aziz:** Of course. It is always a combination of the state itself, how deep the state is, and the intelligence plus the sensitivity of the Soul. When the Heart is included, the bliss is stronger because the bliss comes from the particular frequency of energy within the Heart. It is this frequency which we later translate as being in bliss. On top of the Inner State, is the Me who gives evaluation to the experience it is having. This Me can, for example, sit in the Inner State in a very dull and unappreciative way. So it is not only how deep the Inner State is, but also how deep and mature the intelligence is of the one who is in the state.

For example, how you translate the fact of sitting in this room depends on how deeply you see reality. You can, for example, think that you are simply sitting on the floor and there is nothing special about it; or you are able to truly see that where you are sitting upon is the Universal I AM, God herself! It is a religious experience. It is the space in which prayer is born, true prayer. True prayer means that between the Soul and her Creator there is a connection, communication. The space between the Soul and the Beloved is prayer. In this space one is completely silent. One experiences the presence of the Divine and from the other side, the absence of oneself. As a drop falling into the ocean; the drop and the ocean are one, but still there is the drop...

**Q:** Can you speak about the Soul as a child of the Beloved?

**Aziz:** But you already answered your question (laughter). Before the Soul becomes Me, a conscious individual being, she exists in her pure form. It is the original flavour of the Soul, the original point. When the Soul is in her original form, she is one with the Creator, which means that she does not know that she exists. There is no experience. When the Soul manifests herself in time, in physicality, she becomes aware of herself as an ego, as a body. Next through evolution, the Soul discovers deeper parts of herself, awakening Awareness, Being and Heart. Through her expansion within herself, she discovers that which contains all, the Universal I AM.

Initially, the Soul evolves not being conscious of herself and gradually she awakens to herself, giving rise at one stage to the experience of Pure Me. The Soul is all the time the child of the Beloved, but she needs to mature in order to know it. When the Soul begins her conscious evolution, she, in truth, begins to co-create with the Beloved.

The understanding that the Soul is the child of the Beloved cannot be explained. It is simply reality. This is the mystical and religious experience which one has when getting in touch with this purity and utmost sensitivity in the Heart. For the first time one knows who one truly is. The child of the Beloved...

**Q:** When the Soul realises that she is separated from the Creator, does she start the journey of spiritual evolution?

**Aziz:** Certainly, but the Soul does not consciously know it, she doesn't say "oh, I am separated from the Creator, so now I will start my spiritual journey." The Soul knows the truth of separation indirectly through the experience of suffering. This means that the Soul recognises her own suffering and that something is fundamentally wrong. The fact that something is wrong makes the Soul look for a remedy, for the medicine. This medicine is called the "spiritual path." It is not a conscious process. The Soul is forced to evolve by the suffering she experiences. Through this suffering the intelligence of the Soul grows, and gradually she is able to formulate the right questions. However, in the beginning it is an unconscious process. Most, who are pulled into the spiritual path, do not know, at all, what they are doing...

**Q:** What is the meaning of appreciation of the Inner State?

**Aziz:** The meaning is the attitude of love. It is like being in love with the Inner State. You are in love with I Am! This love includes different elements: amazement, prayer-like feeling, humility... many different elements which create the rainbow of this love. It cannot be said clearly, for it depends on the sensitivity and quality of a particular Soul; each one has a different capacity and intelligence. This appreciation is directly connected to intelligence. Through this intuitive and sensitive understanding you are able to recognise what it is that you experience, for the experience is extraordinarily subtle...

When there is not enough intelligence and sensitivity, one is unable to give real appreciation to the inner experience. One knows neither who is sitting nor in what one is sitting. Through the growth of your sensitivity and understanding, you start to see the subtle colours, feel the subtle energies and feelings, and the experience is more and more comprehended. Of course, the depth of the experience is primarily on the energy level.

**Q:** Who is the one who is appreciating the Inner State?

**Aziz:** That should be already known...(laughter). It is your Soul which appreciate all states using her intuitive intelligence.

**Q:** The state of being rooted deeply in the Inner State. How does it reflect on the outer?

**Aziz:** First of all, when you have a proper relationship with your Inner State, your attitude towards the outer changes; because how you relate to yourself always reflects on how you relate to the outer. When you have a proper connection with your Inner State, you simply relax inside, you are at home, you have a foundation, you have roots... Because of the Inner Space there is more trust and certain psychological openness and comfort. You are no longer so contracted, so agitated...

As long as you are alive, however, and you are young, there are still many experiences for you in the outer reality, different challenges. You continue to evolve in the outer as well. But when the Inner State is present your perception of life is simply more holistic. It is not that you will not have problems with living this life, but something more has been added to you, and this "something more," ultimately is your only freedom. In this way, as you go on, you realise more and more this happiness inside, this basic contentment that does not need anything from the outside.

In the process of returning home, our sense of identity gradually becomes transformed. We are less and less Here and more and more Now. The external reality matters less and less and is less and less a part of our conscious experience. This reality can be experienced in many different ways depending on the evolutionary level. We think that we are sitting here, in one room and everybody has the same experience. But it is not true. All of you are living in different realities. This that allows us to meet here is the fact that our realities are similar, in some respects. There are many, numberless realities which are inter-connected; they create the totality of Lila.

If you met a fully Self-realised person, you could have an impression of being in the same earthly reality. But Buddha is not on the earth. The Buddha is beyond the Here, dwelling in the Heart of Reality, one with the Absolute Subjectivity.

You may think that an awakened being is still functioning Here, being consciously connected to this reality. In your body there are so many processes happening which keep you alive, of which you are not conscious. Are you conscious of the blood flowing through you body? If you were, you would become insane! Similarly, someone who is absorbed in the Self, is able to perform many activities in the outer world without being aware of them. All is simply happening. The body and mind are Here, but the Soul herself has merged already with the Divine...

So, as you can see, the final step is not to be aware of anything... (laughter). In the beginning, as in Zen, one tries to be aware of everything and at the end of Nothing. There is a Zen story about a monk who entered the Master's room and was asked "in which direction did you put your shoes behind the door?" The Master was checking how mindful the monk was. If the monk was one with the Divine, he would have answered "what shoes???" (laughter)..." did I have any shoes?"

Q: Can someone be deeply absorbed in the I AM and still have a contraction of personality?

Aziz: The evolution of Me, the evolution of psyche, and the evolution into the I AM, are not the same but parallel. In our journey into wholeness we are not only awakening the I Am, but purifying our Me too. Me, in order to be purified needs to cleanse the subconscious mind. Certain important cleansing of negative energies and tendencies has to take place. These tendencies are already programmed in our subconscious mind; that's why they need to be either erased or transformed by the power of evolution. In this process Me becomes re-aligned with the I Am. The purity of I Am is reflected in the purity of Me. This Me is never perfect, because it lives in imperfect reality. It means that the minimum of negative experiences will be always there. But it will reach the optimum of sanity. It takes some time...

For the moment, it is not the wish from your Soul to have a purified Me. The wish of your particular Soul is to transcend Me and to reach fully the I Am. When you are comfortable enough with the Inner State, then you will be at ease with your inner evolution, you will begin the work with the Me. You will start to pay more attention to your personality, to your psychology. It is not your personal work only. When the Soul wishes to purify the Me, she naturally attracts the power of Grace who enters and does the final work. In that way, your subconscious mind becomes cleansed and purified. For that reason, it is so important to pray for help to the Other Dimension! Your own efforts to reach purity and the presence of Grace, bring about total transformation.

There are two ways. The Soul has a choice either to completely negate the personality, the Me, or to accept it as a part of her multidimensional wholeness. In the first case, one, being rooted in the I Am, denies the reality of Me. This approach is popular in the Advaita path, for example. In the second case, the Soul takes the responsibility for her Me. In order to transform Me, one has to become responsible for it! You need to take responsibility for your Me. You need to acknowledge that all feelings, responses, desires and fears which you experience are part of You.

**Q:** Which of these two ways is the valid one?

**Aziz:** They are both valid, but from the perspective of a complete human being, the second is more holistic. That is the difference between liberation and Transcendence. In order to become liberated, it is enough to reach the Inner State and to negate Me. But transcendence takes place when the presence of the Inner State embraces the wholeness of Me. Here, one truly transcends.

If one wishes to awaken the Soul, the Me must be accepted. If one wishes to negate Me completely, the Soul cannot become awakened. It is through Me that the Soul recognises its own light. Otherwise, she simply dissolves into the I AM. In the first approach, only this into what we dissolve is recognised. The one who dissolves is not seen. Traditionally, the question "who is experiencing the I AM?" was designed to negate the Me. The expected conclusion was that there is nobody experiencing anything. There is nobody in terms of being a specific entity, or a solid ego. However, when we use more subtle tools, sensitive tools in this inquiry, we will find that there is someone there, and this someone is our Soul.

When an ordinary person is asked "who are you behind the self-image," this person either is not able to give a clear answer or discovers that there is nobody behind. It is all coming from the lack of inner experience, understanding and sensitivity. The One behind the personal self is our intimate identity. Behind the illusion of ego, the movement of the mind, which creates an illusion of being some kind of "me," there is the real Me. This needs to be discovered.

Q: Can you speak about the Over-soul?

Aziz: The Over-soul is simply the higher structure of reality than the Soul. The Soul is like a dew drop and the Universal I AM is like the infinite space containing this dew drop. The Over-soul is in-between. The Over-Soul is the spirit of Guidance linking the Soul with the Beloved. The Beloved represents pure transcendental impersonality, but through the power of Grace she is also personal in her relation to the Soul. The personal aspect of the Beloved is called the Over-soul. Praying to the Over-soul and receiving Guidance, know that it is the way you are being taken care of by your eternal Parent, your divine Mother, the infinite ocean of Love: the Beloved.

**Q:** Does the Soul need the outer in order to purify her Me?

**Aziz:** Absolutely, because without the outer, Me does not exist! It means that your mind, your emotions need the outer in order to become manifested. If there is no outer reality, consciousness dissolves into the Soul and only the Soul remains. In such a situation there is no mind, no feelings, only the Soul in her original state. In the case of the Universal Intelligence, the outer does not exist, but there is no individual sense of Me, only a vast space of Being and Knowing, which is Love.

\* \* \* \* \*

# Spontaneous Thoughts

● There is a negative evolution and a positive evolution. Negative evolution is getting out of misery, suffering. When you are awakened to your own light, the evolution becomes positive, it doesn't stop, it is the expansion into wholeness that cannot have an end, it is bottomless, infinite.

● Heart is the beginning and the end. It is the Heart that seeks, and it is the Heart that has to be found at the end.

● The State of Presence is the pure I of Awareness, pure subject because attention becomes aware of itself without any object. It is the centre of the mind, the centre of intelligence, the essence of consciousness, it is the point where consciousness recognises itself, frees itself from the realm of objects, from the perception, from perceiving the outer. It recognises itself as the only reality, that which does not change, that which is always at the background of the flow of becoming. The awakening to the State of Presence takes place in the mind.

● In the awakening to the I Am, the goal and the seeker meet, it does not mean that the Path is over but it is no longer dualistic. The goal is no longer in the future. It unfolds continuously as a part of your Now. The Great Way is a continuous awakening within the Now until your path is complete. Now is multidimensional. It is not a point between future and past. Now has a depth, the depth of reality, and we go deeper and deeper into the Now, until we reach a point where our individuality merges with the Wholeness. Here human evolution ends and the universal evolution continues in a mysterious way beyond comprehension.

● Have the courage to let go. To let go you have to have courage, courage that comes from trust and understanding. You are not

alone, the wisdom of Existence sees your life, sees your destiny.
The less you worry about yourself, the more you are protected
for you trust. You have matured to trust.

● It is important to understand that the term no-mind can refer
to many areas of the I Am. In the case of Zen, for example, they
try to base their vision of the enlightened state on the attitude
of non-conceptualisation. It is called suchness. The ideal is not
to fabricate any concepts but to see reality from the place of not
thinking. But the I Am is much more rich. What about the
vertical evolution into Being? What about the Heart? The
difference between the no-mind in Awareness and the no-mind
in the Absolute State is enormous. Therefore, we have to use
more precise conceptual tools in order to reflect the reality of the
Inner State.

● Vipassana is not Meditation but a meditation technique.
Therefore, if one chooses to use it, one should consider it only
as a temporary device. Vipassana taken as a life path can be very
damaging. The method which is based on observation and
disidentification, at one stage, must turn against itself, preventing
one from reaching the Natural State. Observing the body and
mind can be an important step in the evolution of consciousness,
but should not become an addiction. In such a case, this method
would cripple one's spontaneity and block the natural evolution
of feelings.

It is not only Awareness of the mind and body which creates
a conscious human being, but participation in them too! Spiritual
realisation takes us not merely to liberation from the psychological
dimension. The final goal is the Transcendental State where the
depth of I Am and the presence of our physical, mental and
emotional bodies are experienced as one unified organism of ME.
Here, one is not observing anything, what remains is the natural
awakened human being. The addiction to the attitude of observation
and disidentification from natural feelings and desires keeps one
glued to the mind and closes the Heart deeply!

● It is not enough to be enlightened in order to teach. The
dimension of practice, the complexity of Spiritual Path must be

studied deeply. Most teachers giving Satsang don't have the basic knowledge of the awakening process. Mostly they are using Advaita slogans, which confuse students who usually have, at most, only a partial inner experience. Such teachers are only able to describe their own state in a poetic way and to express surprise that not all are sharing the same experience. There is Enlightenment to the Self and there is enlightenment to Ignorance. To be enlightened to ignorance means that one understands the laws of Spiritual Path and the lower states of consciousness. Unfortunately, most teachers do not even understand their own Inner State neither the further evolution into the deeper experience of I AM.

● The Spiritual Path is noble and should not be taken lightly. There are many seekers who play the game of spirituality. They take a new name, call themselves Sanyasins or followers of some kind, creating an illusion of being on the Path. It is very sad. What do they do to reach I Am? Nothing! Pseudo-spiritual path is full of mediocrity.

● The dangerous phenomenon of the spiritual path is the strong ego-image which many masters project into the collective consciousness of seekers. In this way most seekers do not look anymore for the Natural awakened state, but for the fulfillment of their projections about Enlightenment. Those pseudo-masters who call themselves Avatars or Bhagwans and place themselves in an unattainable position, bring a bad name to the spiritual dimension. The way, the mind of an average seeker functions, is already deeply confused. Why bring more confusion into it by projecting the unreachable vision of Enlightenment? Humility for an enlightened being is not a religious pose but a sign of true intelligence...

● This must be clear, for all spiritual teachers, that few seek Truth! It is not that most seekers cannot attain Self-realisation — they do not want it! Even if the enlightened state was given to them they would not give it any appreciation, they would not be able to Live it! With this understanding one transcends the "messiah" complex. The true Teaching can be heard by so few that, indeed, it can be expressed without raising the voice...

● It is truly interesting to see how the force of authority operates which some spiritual traditions project. For example, in Zen environment everyone accepts unquestionably the absolute validity of the koan system. Instead of reaching the Inner State directly, thousands of Zen adepts try to solve obscure riddles according to the set Zen convention. Why not look directly into the Heart of I Am?

● One of the most profound and skillful teachings about the State of Presence has been developed in the tradition of Dzogchen. The misconception of this tradition is the belief that rigpa or pure Awareness is the Ultimate. Unfortunately this teaching does not differentiate between Awareness and Being. For this reason, we cannot find the important differentiation between awakening to the State of Presence and to the Absolute State. On the other hand, this tradition is not aware of the presence of the Divine Dimension and the importance of the Heart. The Buddist ideal of compassion and saving other beings, which is a part of Dzogchen teaching, can be seen more on the moralistic level than pointing the realisation of the Heart itself. Because only the crystal clear original mirror like mind is emphasised, there is no place for the awakening of the Soul.

As far as the relationship of the State of Presence with the arising of thoughts is concerned, the teaching of Dzogchen is higher than other traditions that negate and suppress thinking activity of the mind. In the vision of Dzogchen, the presence or absence of thinking has no real impact on the state of Awareness itself. One allows thoughts to manifest and in this acknowledgement, they return to their original condition. This model, however, lacks the concept of the intuitive intelligence or "conscious thinking" where one not only liberates oneself from arising mental formations, but actually participates creatively in the thinking process. We can say that the relation between the naked awareness and the intuitive intelligence has not been fully comprehended.

● No-mind state can be seen on several levels. There is No-mind as pure Awareness, the State of Presence or consciousness beyond thinking. Next level of No-mind is the Absolute State, beyond consciousness. Further, we discover No-mind as the complete presence of the I Am, including the awakened Heart and sensitivity of the Soul. Finally, we awaken the Complete No-mind as Pure Me, full realisation of the Soul in the context of the Universal I AM.

We must be aware of the possibility of being in a state of "negative" no-mind too, which designates different states of being "spaced out." The spaced out state, even though the movement of thoughts and self-referral are suspended, only represents the subconscious Me. This state is not grounded in the Self.

● How arrogant is the mind which equates Enlightenment with reaching psychic powers! How arrogant is the mind which is looking for confirmation of Self-realisation in performing "miraculous" actions! How ignorant is the mind which cannot recognise the simplicity and the profound ordinariness of the Awakened State! This mind does not know humility and severely lacks intelligence...

# The Last Blessing

*May the Infinite Love and all-pervading Grace coming from
the Heart of the Beloved assist unconditionally our journey in
time, from the darkness of ignorance to the Eternal Light of I
AM.*
*May we transcend the sorrow of separation and reach the
joy of Re-union with our Divine Mother.*

# Explanation of Terms

**Absolute:** The original energy, the Unmanifested, the Unborn. The Centre of Gravity. The Source of manifestation.

**Absolute Meditation:** A system of meditation aiming at the awakening of the complete I Am. It is based on the understanding that the I Am, the Inner State of wholeness, is composed of three aspects: Awareness, Being and Heart.

**Absolute State:** The condition of Pure Rest. The dimension where the Soul becomes one with the Absolute, remaining conscious.

**Advaita Vedanta:** The Path of "Non-duality." Mystical-philosophical assumption that Self-knowledge annihilates the "illusory" in its essence presence of Me. Philosophical interpretation of the enlightened state which denies the presence of Me as being a part of the experience of Self-realisation.

**Awareness:** The ability to know. The light of Clarity and the essence of Intelligence.

**Being:** One of three aspects of the I Am. The ability to rest within. The energy link of an individual being with the Absolute.

**Beloved:** The Heart of Creation. The power of Love and Intelligence inherent in Creation and beyond. Divine Mother. The Soul's eternal Parent.

**Buddha Mind:** Equivalent to the Absolute State. Complete unity with the Original State.

**Christ Consciousness:** Complete realisation of the Soul. Oneness with the Divine. Enlightenment to the Heart.

**Conscious Me:** The intuitive intelligence. A state where Me can partially sense itself apart from the movement of subconsciousness. The ability to give conscious feedback to the experience. As in the case of the subconscious Me, the experience refers to the sense of Me, so in the case of the conscious Me, the sense of Me refers to the experience.

**Consciousness:** The ability to be "conscious of." A unity of intelligence and Presence. Equivalent to Awareness.

**Divine:** The Beloved. Universal I AM. Universal ME.

**Ego:** Self-conscious movement of intelligence based on the inherent sense of Me. The ability of self-referral.

**Eighth State:** Beyond Polarities. Me becomes one with the Beloved.

**Emptiness:** Equivalent of the Absolute. The original state prior to Consciousness. Also Pure Awareness without content: the manifested aspect of Emptiness.

**Enlightenment:** Awakening to the deeper sense of identity than the personal self. Many levels of Enlightenment: Enlightenment to the State of Presence, pure Awareness; Enlightenment to the Absolute State, beyond Awareness; Enlightenment to the Heart; Enlightenment to the Soul. Re-union with the Universal I AM. Oneness with the Beloved.

**Fourth State:** The State of Presence.

**Fifth State:** The Absolute State.

**Guidance:** Conscious presence of the Over-soul. The dimension of Universal Intelligence guiding lovingly the evolution of the Soul.

**Heart:** The centre of the Soul. The energy centre responsible for the experience of the Divine. The centre of sensitivity and love.

**I AM:** Absolute Subjectivity. The Beloved. The Divine. Universal Intelligence and Love. A transcendental unity of Being, Love and Intelligence.

**I Am:** The experience of the Universal I AM within the energy system of an individual being. A reflection of Wholeness in the individual Soul. A meeting point of the Soul with the Universal I AM.

**Intuitive Intelligence:** The faculty to co-create with the thinking process. A meeting point of Me with the subconscious mind. The ego. Conscious feedback from Me to the subconscious mind.

**Liberation:** Becoming one with the I AM.

**Lila:** Play of God. The mystery of Creation. The illusion and adventurous character of time-space reality.

**Maya:** Manifested reality. Play of phenomena. The Here, the environment of the universal subconsciousness. Creation perceived as if in separation from the Creator.

**Me:** The Soul. The expression of the Soul. Complete Me: unity of Awareness, Being and Heart. The centre of Me: Heart. The mind: consciousness of Me.

**Meditation:** Conscious effort to reach the I Am. Pure meditation: just being, Non-doing, resting within the I Am.

**Mind:** Movement of thoughts. The centre of the mind: pure Awareness. Intuitive Intelligence: self-consciousness of the mind. Subconscious mind: impersonal arising of thoughts.

**Mystical State:** An experience beyond the mind but not centred in the I Am.

**Non-abidance:** To rest upon "nothing." State of pure Being without referral neither to objective nor to the subjective reality. Partial Non-abidance: rest in the Absolute, to abide in the Unmanifested. Complete Non-abidance: pure rest in the Beloved, where the Absolute and the Divine are one. The highest meaning: Pure Me, beyond the Inner (the Absolute) and the outer (the Creation), rests in the Universal I AM, meets the Beloved.

**Non-doing:** Pure rest in Being. State of ultimate surrender into the Now.

**No-mind:** State of consciousness beyond thinking. The State of Presence. Absolute State: deeper dimension of the no-mind. Unity of Awareness, the Absolute and the Heart: complete No-mind.

**Over-Soul:** The loving expression of the Beloved, controlling compassionately the evolution of the number of Souls which are linked by the similar vision of completion. The link between the Soul and the Universal Intelligence. The power of Guidance and Grace.

**Prayer:** Conscious connection with the Beloved. A deep feeling of unity with the Heart of the Creator.

**Pure Me:** Fully awakened Me experiencing itself beyond the subconscious mind. A unity of thought-less Awareness, pure rest in Being and the awakened Heart. The Soul in her purity experiencing herself beyond the inner and the outer states.

**Pure Suffering:** Suffering which is not cause by negativity or ignorance but by the fact of being human and being Here.

**Samadhi:** Pure rest in the I AM.

**Sat-chit-ananda:** The Ultimate Reality. Sat: Being. Chit: Awareness. **Ananda:** Heart.

**Satsang:** Sitting in the presence of a Self-realised being. Higher meaning: abiding in the I AM.

**Self:** The I AM. The dimension of Pure Subjectivity. Self-knowingness. The direct experience of Reality without the medium of thought or perception. Pure Consciousness.

**Self-conscious Me:** The State of Presence. Me fully conscious of itself apart from subconsciousness. Self-awareness. Attention aware of attention. Witnessing consciousness. Centre in the mind.

**Seventh State:** Enlightenment to Me.

**Shikan-taza:** Pure meditation. Just sitting. Non-abidance. Non-doing state beyond the personal will.

**Sixth State:** Enlightenment of the Heart.

**Soul:** A unique taste of the I AM, being experienced in its individual manifestation. Pure sense of Me being centralised in the Heart.

**State of Presence:** Pure Awareness. The centre of the mind.

Attention aware of attention, free from object. The centre of Me in intelligence.

**Subconscious Me:** A state where the sense of Me is fully merged with the Here or impersonal subconsciousness. The impersonal movement of subconsciousness referring to the apparent Me (through the physical, mental and emotional bodies), which is devoid of any centralised quality. Dream state or day-dreaming. Spontaneous activity of the mind not being interrupted by the feedback coming from the Conscious Me.

**Subconsciousness:** The impersonal movement of intelligence and life, which occurs bellow the conscious level.

**Transcendence:** Beyond Liberation. The state which, apart from the presence of the complete Inner State, encompasses completion in the dimension of Me. The state when the Soul is fulfilled both, in the Inner and in the Outer.

**Transmission:** Satsang. An event taking place in the presence of a Master, who transmits the experience of Enlightenment through his/her own energy and understanding. A power of Grace coming from the Beyond through a Master in order to bring transformation.

**Turija:** The fourth State. The State of Presence.

**Turijatitta:** Beyond the Fourth State. Various levels of merging into Being from the place of awakened Awareness.

**Unconsciousness:** An astral plane. The bridge between the Universal I AM and the Universal Subconsciousness.